CINEMA JOURNAL

54, No. 4, Summer 2015

On the Web | www.cmstudies.org
Archival News
Professional Notes
In Focus
Conference Reports
Author Postscripts

Cinema Journal is published for the Society for Cinema and Media Studies by the University of Texas Press.

Cinema Journal (ISSN 0009-7101) is published quarterly in Fall (November), Winter (February), Spring (May), and Summer (August) by the University of Texas Press, Journals Division, 2100 Comal St., Austin, TX 78722-2550. Subscription rates are $200/year for institutions and $55/year for individuals. PERIODICALS POSTAGE PAID at Austin, Texas, and additional mailing offices. POSTMASTER: Send address changes to Cinema Journal, University of Texas Press, PO Box 7819, Austin, TX 78713-7819.

Cinema Journal is published in cooperation with the Society for Cinema and Media Studies; members of the society receive the journal as one of the benefits of membership. For further information on membership, see inside back cover of this issue. All business inquiries (subscriptions, advertisements, and change-of-address notices) and requests for back issues should be addressed to the Journals Division, University of Texas Press, PO Box 7819, Austin, TX 78713-7819, or visit our website at http://www.utexaspress.com. All views or conclusions are those of the authors of the articles and not necessarily those of the editorial staff, the University of Texas Press, the University of Texas at Austin, or the Society for Cinema and Media Studies. Subscription rates: $200/year for institutions, $55/year for individuals. Canada subscriptions add $30 to each order. For international subscriptions add $44 to each order. Single issues are $56 for institutions, $22 for individuals. All prices are subject to change on September 1 of each year. Domestic and non-US claims for missing issues must be received within 90 days of the publication date. Issues returned "undeliverable" are available for reshipment at cost of new shipment. To process a claim please see our claims form at the UT Press website.

This journal is a member of CELJ, the Conference of Editors of Learned Journals. It is indexed in *Academic Search Premier*, *Arts and Humanities Citation Index*, *Film Literature Index*, *IBR (International Bibliography of Book Reviews)*, *IBZ (International Bibliography of Periodical Literature)*, *International Index to Film Periodicals*, and *MLA Bibliography* and abstracted in *Academic Search Premier* and *Extended Academic Abstracts*.

Cinema Journal is available electronically: current content through Project Muse, a full archive through JSTOR, and back issues through ProQuest, Ebsco, and Gale/Cengage Inc. The journal is also available in microform and can be purchased from NA Publishing.

© 2015 by the University of Texas Press.

∞ The paper used in this publication meets the minimum requirements of American National Standards for Information Sciences—Permanence of Paper for Printed Library Materials. ANSI Z39.48-1984.

Animating the *Cinéfils*: Alain Resnais and the Cinema of Discovery

by Karen Beckman

Abstract: This article examines the relationship between animation and an idea of cinema as it has evolved in the postwar period, particularly under the influence of the writing of André Bazin. Through close readings of Alain Resnais's films, as well as their critical reception, the article highlights the great importance of animation, comics, and other ephemeral graphic images to an earlier generation of French critics and filmmakers. Recovering this importance will help us navigate the confusing media landscape we inhabit today and build continuities across apparently distinct aesthetic and historical practices.

> It is clear that *Last Year at Marienbad* . . . is a ritzed-up live-action no-violence child of the Road Runner series; and that the same key unlocks them both if you like that kind of workout.
>
> —Richard Thompson, "Meep Meep!"[1]

Animation and the Cinéfils. A few years ago I was surprised to encounter not one but two animated adaptations of Alain Resnais's 1961 film *Last Year at Marienbad*, both from 2008: *You, Starbucks!* (Jennifer Levonian, 2006, revised 2008) (Figure 1) and *Last Year at Marienbad 3D* (Kota Ezawa, 2008) (Figure 2).

Although both participate in a more widespread contemporary practice of animating sequences from European art cinema, this doubling provoked me to think specifically about Resnais's films through animated and graphic lenses. The encounter of Resnais and animation is particularly important because these two unlikely bedfellows have begun to haunt—together—contemporary discussions of what cinema was and is becoming through the process of digitization, particularly in

---

1   Richard Thompson, "Meep Meep!," in *The American Animated Cartoon: A Critical Anthology*, ed. Gerald Peary and Danny Peary (New York: Dutton, 1980), 223. First published in *BBM December* 13, no. 2 (1971): 216–222. Thanks to Oliver Gaycken for drawing my attention to this essay.

Karen Beckman is Elliot and Roslyn Jaffe Professor of Cinema and Modern Media at the University of Pennsylvania. She is most recently author of Crash: Cinema and the Politics of Speed and Stasis *(Duke University Press, 2010), coeditor of* On Writing with Photography *(with Liliane Weissberg; University of Minnesota Press, 2013), and editor of* Animating Film Theory *(Duke University Press, 2014).*

© 2015 by the University of Texas Press

Figure 1. *You, Starbucks!* (Jennifer Levonian, 2006, revised 2008). Courtesy of Jennifer Levonian.

Figure 2. *Last Year at Marienbad 3D* (Kota Ezawa, 2008). Courtesy of Kota Ezawa.

contrast with postwar art cinema.

In contemplating the strange coupling of Resnais and animation that Levonian and Ezawa perform, I hope to make a few useful interventions. First, I suggest that the polarization of animation and a Bazinian "cinema of discovery" that Dudley Andrew posits in *What Cinema Is!* and that he aligns with *Cahiers du cinéma* does not adequately reflect the intense interest in animation and affiliated image forms such as the comic strip and the cartoon demonstrated by many of the critics and filmmakers involved with that journal.[2] This applies to Resnais in particular, whose films come to exemplify what Donald Crafton describes as Andrew's "more heavenly 'aesthetic of discovery.'"[3] *Cahiers du cinéma*, Serge Daney, and the critical discussions of Resnais's films in the late 1950s and early 1960s all inform Andrew's position. He states, "[Daney] took over *Cahiers* and formulated the dictum that Resnais provoked and I repeat: '[T]he cinema is tied to reality and reality has nothing to do with representation.'"[4] For Andrew, the problem is not that he longs for a naïve representation of reality that puts its faith in the truth of the indexical image; for he, like the *Cahiers* circle, most values the tension that

2 For Andrew, animation is separated from a certain idea of cinema by what he calls "the *Cahiers* line": "Let's draw the line at camera-less animation. Indeed, let's draw the line that separates one conception of cinema from another. What I call 'the *Cahiers* line' amounts to the genealogy of an 'idea of cinema' that preceded and now coexists with this 'cinema as animated storyboard,' which is how I would characterize much of today's audiovisual entertainment." Dudley Andrew, *What Cinema Is! Bazin's Quest and Its Charge* (Malden, MA: Wiley-Blackwell, 2010), 4.

3 Donald Crafton, "The Veiled Genealogies of Animation and Cinema," *Animation: An Interdisciplinary Journal* 6, no. 2 (2011): 94.

4 Andrew, *What Cinema Is!*, 45.

exists in Resnais's cinema between images and facts, reality and imagination, showing and creating, in frame and out of sight. Rather, the problem mainstream cinema now faces is that, from Andrew's perspective, it has lost its relation to reality altogether, with images being so "densely composited" that they "deserve to be classified as 'animated films.'"[5] The importance of the *caméra-stylo* and of cinema as *écriture* persists throughout *What Cinema Is!*, and for Andrew, the qualities of the "aesthetic of discovery" stand "at the antipodes of a cinema of manipulation, including most animation and pure digital creation."[6] When he does allow a place for animation, he suggests that it must always be "in the service of cinema."[7] Yet the subordinate position prescribed for animation here loses sight of the great importance of animation as well as of ephemeral graphic images such as comic strips to this earlier generation of critics and filmmakers. Recovering this importance will help us navigate the confusing media landscape we inhabit today and build continuities across apparently distinct aesthetic and historical practices that will in turn serve as a useful foundation for the field's intense focus on the topic of animation.

If Andrew represents one side of this conversation, on the other side we find media scholars like Lev Manovich, for whom cinema is instead only a subset of animation, and whose alternative swings too far in the other direction, repressing some of the complexity of how these image forms or terms have interacted historically.[8] Manovich writes, "Born from animation, cinema pushed animation to its periphery, only in the end to become one particular case of animation."[9] But does film history really support either this narrative of animation's vanishing and reappearance in cinema or these swinging paradigms of dominance and submission? Crafton rightly suggests that the construction of "animation" and "cinema" as a hierarchically organized pair results in reductive and "disingenuous" definitions of both terms.[10] Hoping to move past these alternatives, this article attempts to think differently about the complex mutual investments and tensions between "cinema" and "animation," as well as between photographic and graphic images, and it attempts to do so by looking more closely at Alain Resnais.

Although Resnais, as a member of the Left Bank group, does not belong to *Cahiers*'s inner circle, he, and particularly his contemporaries' critical discussion of his 1955 film *Nuit et brouillard* (*Night and Fog*) is central to the twentieth-century film debates that inform the "*Cahiers* line" that Andrew describes regarding the morality of style,

5 Ibid., 51.

6 Ibid., 42.

7 Ibid., 59. Even as Andrew subordinates animation, he still recognizes the importance of engaging it when he notes, "[A]nimation is one ascendant category, promoted by some to the top of the hierarchy of film styles today. As it was put to me not long ago: '[A]nimation is cinema in its purest form'" (ibid., 30).

8 Rodowick also notes that "Manovich's understanding of [cinema's] history and theory lacks depth and complexity." D. N. Rodowick, *The Virtual Life of Film* (Cambridge, MA: Harvard University Press, 2007), 95. Tom Gunning makes a similar point in "Moving away from the Index: Cinema and the Impression of Reality," *differences: A Journal of Feminist Cultural Studies* 18, no. 1 (2007): 38.

9 Lev Manovich, *The Language of New Media* (Cambridge, MA: MIT Press, 2001), 302.

10 Crafton, "Veiled Genealogies," 94.

the "ethos" of the cinema he values, and the place of animation within this discussion.[11] Jacques Rivette's 1961 *Cahiers* essay "On Abjection," for example, illustrates the difference between moral and immoral uses of the tracking shot by comparing the depiction of the camps in *Nuit et brouillard*, which offers "the brute, *real* facts" to the spectator's gaze in a form to which "you cannot accustom yourself," with a shot in *Kapo* (Gillo Pontecorvo, 1960) that employs a forward tracking shot to reframe Emmanuelle Riva's body just after her character has committed suicide, thereby earning Rivette's contempt.[12] Invoking both Luc Moullet's and Jean-Luc Godard's insistence that the tracking shot is a "matter of morality," Rivette outlines through the example of *Kapo* the reasons why their claims about the imbrication of style and morality cannot simply be dismissed as "the height of formalism" and illustrates through this example what cinema is for him in 1961: "To make a film is to show certain things, that is *at the same time*, and by the same mechanism, to show them with a certain bias; these two acts being thoroughly bound together."[13]

What Cinema Is! embraces Rivette's sense of cinema, updating it for a new generation of readers as well as a new moment in cinema's history, but it simultaneously reproduces Daney's later juxtaposition of animation with the type of cinema that Rivette affirms in his review of *Kapo*, and Daney rejects animation outright:

> Captivated by cinema, I didn't need—as well—to be seduced. No need either for baby talk. As a child I had never seen *any* Disney movies. . . . Worse: for me, animated movies would always be something other than cinema. Even worse: animated movies would always be a bit the enemy. No "beautiful image," especially drawn, would match the emotion—fear and trembling—in front of *recorded* things. And all this, which is so simple and took me years to formulate in a simple way, began to come out in front of Resnais's images and Rivette's text.[14]

Unlike Andrew, Daney explicitly aligns himself only with Resnais's earlier works, those that depict the "damaged and disfigured human species right after the Nazi camps and the atomic trauma."[15] He describes himself as "the rather bored spectator of Resnais's 'other' films," and he declares, "It is therefore not with Resnais that I will make the journey of 'modern' cinema but with Rossellini. It is not with Resnais that the moral lessons will be learnt by heart and conjugated but always with Godard."[16] Daney's double dismissal of animation and Resnais's modernist work might beg the question of whether, and how, these two modes of filmmaking are related, and whether the continuities that exist between Resnais's earlier work and a more modernist work like

---

11 Andrew, *What Cinema Is!*, 4.

12 See Jacques Rivette, "On Abjection," in *Order of the Exile*, trans. David Phelps with Jeremi Szaniawski, www.dvdbeaver .com/rivette/ok/abjection.html; first published in *Cahiers du cinéma* 120 (1961): 54–55.

13 Ibid.

14 Serge Daney, "The Tracking Shot in *Kapo*," trans. Laurent Kretzschmar, *Senses of Cinema* 30 (2004), n.p.; first published in *Trafic* (1992) just before Daney's death.

15 Ibid.

16 Ibid.

Last Year at Marienbad could dislodge some of the entrenched positions outlined earlier about what, today, should count as cinema.

Yet the importance of Resnais as a figure who disrupts an idea of cinema that we might too easily associate with him does not stop here. Andrew aligns himself with a cinematic tradition in which both the *cinéfils* (the son or lover of cinema) and the auteur play a central role. Now, some versions of the *cinéfils*, including those we find in the writing of Roland Barthes or Daney, have a distinctly queer potential, often troubling normative models of relationality: homosocial communities meeting in the dark for pleasure, men who identify the same object as both parent and lover, and so on.[17] But the *cinéfils'* view of the screen can also be rather exclusive (even the queerest of *cinéfils* tend to erase female filmmakers, spectators, and critics, if not female performers). Consequently, the traditions and paradigms that inform Andrew's delimitation of "cinema" predetermine that few female filmmakers will be relevant to the argument about or illustration of "what cinema is" (Maya Deren, Marguerite Duras, Agnès Varda, and Nicole Védrès), and, although occasionally a female scholar, such as Marie-José Mondzain, is written into the history of ideas that grounds this book, major blind spots occur when this particular history becomes the foundation for a manifesto about what cinema was, is, and should be. As Geneviève Sellier argues in *Masculine Singular: French New Wave Cinema*, it is impossible not to associate *Cahiers du cinéma* with the formation of "masculine sociability," "a band of boys," the establishment of film criticism as "an almost exclusively masculine activity," and the positing of a "cinephilic gaze" that is "necessarily male, heterosexual, and directed toward icons, fetishes, and female sexual objects."[18]

While Andrew's approach suggests an authoritative grasp of what cinema is and is not in a time of media transition—most visibly performed by his transformation of André Bazin's "?" to a "!"—this authority derives from a somewhat mystical "cinematic ethos" that is attributed to both Bazin's thinking (in spite of the major difference Bazin's question mark makes) and the work of three key auteurs: Roberto Rossellini, Robert Bresson, and Alain Resnais. I concentrate here on Resnais because, of those invoked, he offers most resistance to this version of cinema. As Sellier argues convincingly toward the end of her feminist critique of the *Cahiers* group:

> Despite the enthusiastic reception that Alain Resnais's first feature-length film, *Hiroshima mon amour* [1959], received from the *Cahiers* group . . . , the film breaks with dominant New Wave representations. This is the case not only because the political and professional itinerary of the left-wing filmmaker is fundamentally different from that of the *Cahiers* group, but above all because his films evince a different logic than the one I've tried to define in this volume. . . . There is no trace in his work of the romantic posture dear to the New Wave. . . . For Alain Resnais, creativity is not associated with the expression of his own subjectivity. Throughout his career, he never varied on this point:

---

17 On Barthes's queering of the movie spectator, see Jean Ma, *Melancholy Drift: Marking Time in Chinese Cinema* (Hong Kong: Hong Kong University Press, 2010), 108–111.

18 Geneviève Sellier, *Masculine Singular: French New Wave Cinema*, trans. Kristin Ross (Durham, NC: Duke University Press, 2008), 28–29.

his visual and aural inventiveness is expressed on the basis of material written by someone else, someone he usually chose and always considered his full partner.[19]

In their recent study, Suzanne Liandrat-Guigues and Jean-Louis Leutrat similarly highlight Resnais's resistance to the notion of a singular auteur, his advocacy for collaborative practice, and his ambivalence about becoming a filmmaker—and all of this in direct contrast with other filmmakers of his generation.[20] Furthermore, Resnais's alternative model of authorship and filmmaking frequently intertwines with his interest in ephemeral, low, perhaps "juvenile," and composited forms of image-making practices.

Resnais's short essay film from 1956, *Toute la mémoire du monde* (*All the Memory in the World*), exemplifies for Andrew the Bazinian "cinema of discovery" that differs in fundamental ways from animation and digital cinema.[21] Challenging this polarization is my main purpose here, and I do it by looking closely at (1) the critical landscape of *Cahiers du cinéma*, which offers a nuanced and complex sense of cinema's relationship to animation in the postwar French context that is often overlooked; (2) the morphing critical reception of Resnais over the course of time within cinema and media studies; and (3) two films by Resnais: *Toute la mémoire du monde* and his feature-length film *Last Year at Marienbad*.

Mobilizing Resnais as a counterpoint to the graphically composited image, the digital, and animation underestimates the resonance of his work with line-based images such as drawing, lithography, engraving, drawn animation, graphs, maps, charts, and the lowly comic strip, as well as with a variety of other forms of animation like pixilation—the frame-by-frame shooting of live-action figures—and puppet animation.[22] The filmmaker's demonstrated interest in the high and low graphic arts and animation both within and outside of his films challenges us to contemplate what it means for the graphic to inhabit the photographic and the cinematic and resists the separation of these terms. Yet my argument goes beyond this. For this Daney-inspired version of Resnais is symptomatic of an official film historical narrative that has repressed the great significance of several forms of animation to postwar French filmmakers—that is, to the *cinéfils* themselves—throughout the 1950s and 1960s. Ignoring the importance of animation to this generation of filmmakers potentially forecloses useful lines of thinking about cinematic time and image composition that underscore continuities from the past to the contemporary moment.

Hervé Joubert-Laurencin has done and continues to do pioneering work in this arena, first by highlighting in *La lettre volante* (1997) the significance of Bazin's writing on animation, which has largely remained untranslated, unanthologized, and underread, in spite of the Bazin renaissance we are currently enjoying, and second, more

19 Sellier, *Masculine Singular*, 211–212.

20 Suzanne Liandrat-Guigues and Jean-Louis Leutrat, *Alain Resnais: Liaisons secrètes, accords vagabonds* (Paris: Cahiers du Cinéma, 2006), 32–37, 42–46.

21 Andrew, *What Cinema Is!*, 42.

22 Liandrat-Guigues and Leutrat also briefly comment on Resnais's interest in graphic literature in *Alain Resnais*, 37–40.

recently, by highlighting the importance of Bazin's contemporary, the largely forgotten critic André Martin.[23] Martin played a key role in introducing a special animation section to the Cannes Film Festival in 1953 and was a founding figure of JICA, or International Days of Animation, which in 1960 was institutionalized as the Annecy Animation Film Festival. Louis Marcorelles declared in *Cahiers* that "for the first time in history, animation had the right to a festival of its own" and celebrated his discovery at Annecy of "authentic auteurs."[24] Contrary to the impression we get from English-language film theory anthologies and anthologies of *Cahiers* essays in translation, a wide variety of critics, scholars, and filmmakers wrote at length in *Cahiers* and elsewhere on the topic of animation during this period—not only Bazin and Martin but also Georges Sadoul, Chris Marker, Louis Marcorelles, John Hubley, Francis Lacassin, Gilles Deleuze, and Marie-Thérèse Poncet, a medievalist who was part of the filmology movement and who wrote the first dissertation on animation in 1951, along with several other publications on the topic.[25]

Cahiers authors' engagement with animation during this period generates, among other things, an expanded vocabulary for moving images that challenges the singularity of Alexandre Astruc's 1948 conception of the *caméra-stylo* (camera–fountain pen), a term that was clearly central for the French new wave filmmakers but that has now become completely synonymous with them as if there were no other possible narratives. In one of four 1958 special issues of *Cahiers du cinéma* dedicated to the animator Norman McLaren, Martin published an image of McLaren drawing directly on celluloid alongside this comment: "After the 'camera-stylo,' which, without a fountain pen, revolutionized the cinema, here's the stylo-camera, which, without a camera, reinvents it."[26] Soon afterward, in 1962, Sadoul dedicated an entire *Cahiers* article to

23 Hervé Joubert-Laurencin, *La lettre volante: Quatre essais sur le cinema d'animation* (Paris: Presses de la Sorbonne Nouvelle, 1997). For examples of the renewed interest in Bazin, see Dudley Andrew with Hervé Joubert-Laurencin, eds., *Opening Bazin: Postwar Film Theory and Its Afterlife* (New York: Oxford University Press, 2011); Dudley Andrew, ed., *André Bazin's New Media* (Berkeley: University of California Press, 2014).

24 Louis Marcorelles, "Annecy an un," *Cahiers du cinéma* 109 (1960): 34–35.

25 See, for example, Hervé Joubert-Laurencin, "André Martin: Inventor of the 'Cinema of Animation': Towards a History of Statements," in *Animating Film Theory*, ed. Karen Beckman (Durham, NC: Duke University Press, 2014), 85–97. Martin's essays on animation include "Mystère d'un cinema instrumental," *Cahiers du cinéma* 81 (1958): 41–46; "Une occasion manquée," *Cahiers du cinéma* 110 (1960): 59–60; "Pour qui sont ces Trnka? I," *Cahiers du cinéma* 104 (1960): 31–44; "Pour qui sont ces Trnka? II," *Cahiers du cinéma* 105 (1960): 22–34; and "Pour qui sont ces Trnka? III," *Cahiers du cinéma* 106 (1960): 28–43. Marker's early writing on animation includes "L'esthétique du déssin animé," *Esprit* 182 (1951): 368–369, in which he reviews a doctoral thesis by Marie-Thérèse Poncet at the Sorbonne on the aesthetics of animated cartoons; "*Prince Bayaya* de Jiri Trnka, une forme d'ornement," *Cahiers du cinéma* 8 (1952); and "Cinéma d'animation: U.P.A." in André Bazin et al., *Cinema 53 à travers le monde* (Paris: Cerf, 1954), 136–143. Poncet's work is currently being explored by Vinzenz Hediger and is also discussed in Edward Lowry, *The Filmology Movement and Film Study in France*, Studies in Cinema 33 (Ann Arbor, MI: UMI Research Press, 1985). Poncet's publications include *L'esthéthique du dessin animé* (Paris: Nizet, 1952); *Étude comparative des illustrations du Moyen Âge et des dessins animés* (Paris: A.-G. Nizet, 1952); *Dessin animé art mondial* (Paris: Le Cercle du Livre, 1956); "Le dessin animé," *Diagrammes du monde* 138 (1968); and more recently, *La genie de Walt Disney: Un Walt Disney vivant* (self-published, 1995). It is worth noting that Poncet, a female animation scholar, was also the very first recipient of a film doctorate at the Sorbonne (Lowry, *Filmology Movement*, 55).

26 Bernard Clarens [and André Martin], *André Martin: Écrits sur l'animation*, vol. 1, *Pour lire entre les images: Textes rassemblés par Bernard Clarens* (Paris: Dreamland, 2000), 189. First published as André Martin, "Question: Attentats? Poèmes? Attentats et Poèmes?" [Question: Attacks? Poems? Attacks and Poems], in *Cahiers du cinema* 77 (1957): 7–10, 10.

animation.[27] It begins by contemplating the possibility that animation might constitute an "eighth art."[28] Although this separation of animation as a distinct art initially seems to reinforce the line that Andrew (following Daney) draws between cinema and animation, Sadoul gradually expands into a more hybrid sense of cinema through the term *cinéplastique*, borrowed from Elie Faure's 1920 essay "The Art of Cineplastics."[29] He then ends his short article with a discussion of Czech animator Jiri Trnka, a figure also of intense interest to both Martin and Marker, describing him as "the auteur of animated sculptures."[30] But Sadoul does not always categorize manually constructed moving images as animated but not necessarily cinematic forms of another art (in this case, sculpture), for he also celebrates multiple alternatives to the *caméra-stylo*, all of which still appear to be designated as a form of cinema. He notes the "endless possibilities of the camera-paintbrush or a painterly cinema (*la caméra-pinceau ou ciné-peinture*); of the camera-chisel or sculptural cinema (*la caméra-ciseau ou ciné-sculpture*); of the camera-pencil or cinema of drawing (*la caméra-crayon ou ciné-dessin*), and the camera-burin or cinema of engraving (*la caméra-burin ou ciné-gravure*)."[31] Perhaps surprisingly, one of Sadoul's privileged examples of this eighth art is Resnais and Robert Hessens's 1950 collaborative film *Guernica*.

And Sadoul is not alone. Thinking about animation often makes film theorists think about Resnais's films, and vice versa, as my opening quotation from Richard Thompson's 1976 essay on the Road Runner illustrates.[32] Bazin is no different, and it is worth taking a moment to explore both Bazin's writing on Resnais's painting films as well as Andrew's responses to it. Also referencing *Guernica*, Bazin insists that cinema's role in films about painting must be neither "that of a servant" nor "to betray the painting," but rather "to provide it with a new form of existence." This symbiosis between cinema and painting does not compromise or destroy painting; on the contrary, it "is in the process of saving it."[33] Resnais is also close at hand for Bazin both in his discussion of "free adaptation," where he mentions Resnais's 1948 film *Van Gogh*, a film on which Bazin advised Resnais, and in his discussion of "aesthetic symbiosis," where he discusses *Van Gogh* and *Guernica*.[34] Animation haunts Bazin's discussions of cinema's

27 Georges Sadoul, "Divagations sur le 'Huitième art,'" *Cahiers du cinéma* 132 (1962): 8–13.

28 Sadoul, "Divagations sur le 'Huitième art,'" 9.

29 Sadoul gave the following footnote for this source: "Texte recueilli en 1922 dans *L'Arbre d'Eden* pp. 277–304 et repris en 1953 dans *Fonction du Cinéma: De la Cinéplastique à son destin social* (1921–1937), préface de Charles Chapin (Librairie Plon, Paris)." Sadoul, "Divagations sur le 'Huitième art,'" 9n1. "Cineplastics" includes filmmakers like Eggeling, Richter, Ruttmann, Fischinger, and Léger; works produced frame by frame or with a montage of up to twenty or thirty continuously shot frames at a time (e.g., films of the Polish filmmaker Walerian Borowczyck), some trick films, and some films about art. Do we really want to exclude all of this from our idea of cinema?

30 Sadoul, "Divagations sur le 'Huitième art,'" 13.

31 Ibid., 12.

32 Thompson, "Meep Meep!," 223.

33 André Bazin, "Painting and Cinema," in *What Is Cinema?*, trans. Hugh Gray (Berkeley: University of California Press, 2005), 1:168.

34 On "free adaptation," see Bazin, "*Le journal d'un cure de campagne* and the Stylistics of Robert Bresson," in *What Is Cinema?*, 142; Bazin, "Painting and Cinema," 168. For Andrew's discussion of Bazin, Resnais, painting, and cinema, see Andrew, "Malraux, Bazin, and the Gesture of Picasso," in *Opening Bazin* (New York: Oxford University Press, 2011), ed. Andrew and Joubert-Laurencin, 155–160.

relation to the other arts, and eventually Bazin actively, and somewhat suddenly, re-presses this specter, asserting, "Films of paintings are not animation films."[35] But of course, *Guernica* might very well be described an animated film. While superimpositions and dissolves create the illusion that the various paintings and drawings on screen metamorphose before the eye, Henry Ferrand's special effects do seem to animate specific drawings throughout the film, magically revealing aspects of them in sequence, punctuating each revelation with synchronized sound effects. The animated text also would have to have been shot on an animation stand.[36] These animated effects are not childish; they are inseparable from the violence of total war that the film's voice-over describes.[37]

Elsewhere, Andrew engages and refines Bazin's own denial of animation as it appears in his discussion of *Van Gogh* and goes some way to acknowledging the "animatedness" of Resnais's cinema, but even here, he remains anxious to hold at bay the encroaching specter of the cartoon:

> [Resnais] has made a sort of animated film about Van Gogh's travails, using him as a cartoonist, except that, unlike animation cells, each painting exists beyond the film, carefully guarded in a museum. "What may seem symbolic and abstract takes on the solid reality of a piece of ore," Bazin says, whereas the drawings that go into cartoons are used up by the film for which they are designed. We call them "transparencies." Van Gogh's paintings are anything but transparent.[38]

This reading of Bazin elevates painting as a physical presence above the ephemeral and culturally worthless object of the single cel drawing that is fabricated for a film but apparently holds no cultural value and does not seem to exist as an object in its own right. The painting's value derives from its imposing physical presence and its acceptance into a cultural institution, the museum, and for Andrew, cel drawing clearly fails to offer viewers painting's quality of solid reality.

Philip Rosen, discussing Bazin and "impure cinema," is helpful here. He writes:

> But for Bazin, the cinematic apparatus is inseparable from a relation to something *exterior* to its technology. In the "Ontology" essay, this exteriority amounts to the worldly entities registered by the camera. The very nature of cinema, then, is precisely *not* to be something in and for itself, but to be constituted in relation to something outside itself. This would mean that cinema history and even cinematic specificity *necessarily include the non-cinematic*. This definitional inclusion of the non-cinematic within the cinematic also pervades Bazin's account of adaptation.[39]

---

35   Bazin, "Painting and Cinema," 169.

36   Thanks to Alison Loader for pointing this out.

37   Philip Rosen, "Belief in Bazin," in *Opening Bazin* (New York: Oxford University Press, 2011), ed. Andrew and Joubert-Laurencin, 111.

38   Andrew, "Malraux, Bazin, and the Gesture of Picasso," 159.

39   Rosen, "Belief in Bazin," 111.

The animation cel becomes caught in an impossible place: neither cinema nor its outside. Perhaps, though, it marks a line that helps us understand the various ways in which cinema and concern about the world might be related. Resnais's *Toute la mémoire du monde*, to which I turn shortly, focuses our attention on these issues through its elevation of ephemeral graphic images, its playful mobilization of those images in a form of proto-animation, and its ambivalence about the process through which an object is sanctioned by admission to cultural institutions (in this case, a library rather than a museum).

A Cartoon-Friendly Resnais. Film scholarship used to more readily acknowledge a cartoon-friendly Resnais than it now does. But as an academic discipline was born in the 1960s and 1970s, scholars worked hard to transcend the realms of biography and criticism, as well as the specter of silliness. Unfortunately, this is exactly the moment when some critical interest is paid to what I will call "the graphic Resnais," and I think it is useful to recover some of this unfashionable scholarship. In 1966, Francis Lacassin published an important article on Resnais's love of comics, first in French under the title "Alain Resnais et les bandes dessinées," and a year later as "Dick Tracy Meets Muriel."[40] He begins, "Any amount of critical analysis has been devoted to Resnais the film-maker. Not much has been written about the founder and vice-president of the Centre for the Study of the Literature of Graphic Expression and member of the editorial board of *Giff-Wiff*, the first magazine in the world devoted to the history and documentation of the comic strip" (Figure 3).

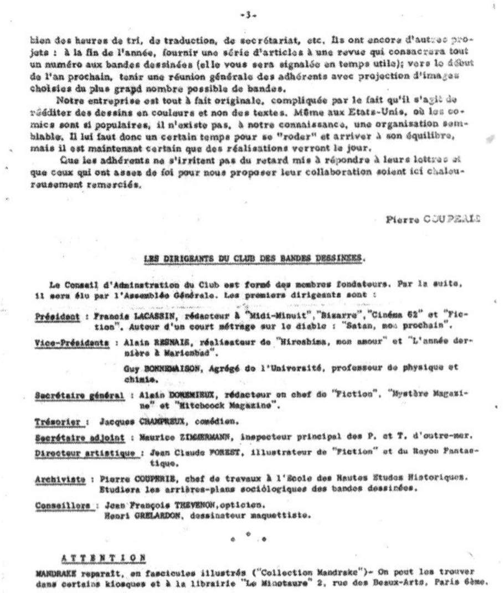

-3-

bien des heures de tri, de traduction, de secrétariat, etc. Ils ont encore d'autres projets : à la fin de l'année, fournir une série d'articles à une revue qui consacrera tout un numéro aux bandes dessinées (elle vous sera signalée en temps utile); vers le début de l'an prochain, tenir une réunion générale des adhérents avec projection d'images choisies du plus grand nombre possible de bandes.

Notre entreprise est tout à fait originale, compliquée par le fait qu'il s'agit de rééditer des dessins en couleurs et non des textes. Même aux Etats-Unis, où les comics sont si populaires, il n'existe pas, à notre connaissance, une organisation semblable. Il lui faut donc un certain temps pour se "roder" et arriver à son équilibre, mais il est maintenant certain que des réalisations verront le jour.

Que les adhérents ne s'irritent pas du retard mis à répondre à leurs lettres et que ceux qui ont assez de foi pour nous proposer leur collaboration soient ici chaleureusement remerciés.

Pierre COUPERIE

LES DIRIGEANTS DU CLUB DES BANDES DESSINEES.

Le Conseil d'Administration du Club est formé des membres fondateurs. Par la suite, il sera élu par l'Assemblée Générale. Les premiers dirigeants sont :

Président : Francis LACASSIN, rédacteur à "Midi-Minuit", "Bizarre", "Cinéma 62" et "Fiction". Auteur d'un court métrage sur le diable : "Satan, mon prochain".

Vice-Présidents : Alain RESNAIS, réalisateur de "Hiroshima, mon amour" et "L'année dernière à Marienbad".
Guy BONNEMAISON, Agrégé de l'Université, professeur de physique et chimie.

Secrétaire général : Alain DOREMIEUX, rédacteur en chef de "Fiction", "Mystère Magazine" et "Hitchcock Magazine".

Trésorier : Jacques CHAMPREUX, comédien.

Secrétaire adjoint : Maurice ZIMMERMANN, inspecteur principal des P. et T. d'outre-mer.

Directeur artistique : Jean Claude FOREST, illustrateur de "Fiction" et du Rayon Fantastique.

Archiviste : Pierre COUPERIE, chef de travaux à l'Ecole des Hautes Etudes Historiques. Etudiera les arrières-plans sociólogiques des bandes dessinées.

Conseillers : Jean François THEVENON, opticien.
Henri GRELARDON, dessinateur maquettiste.

ATTENTION

MANDRAKE reparaît, en fascicules illustrés ("Collection Mandrake")- On peut les trouver dans certains kiosques et à la librairie "Le Minotaure" 2, rue des Beaux-Arts, Paris 6ème.

Figure 3. Alain Resnais appears as vice president of *Giff-Wiff*. Image courtesy of La revue Giff Wiff, http://anafbd.free.fr/giff.htm.

Lacassin continues, "All the same, it was the comic strip enthusiast in Resnais who preceded, awakened, and nourished the film director."[41] Furthermore, he notes that Resnais's delight in comics was shared with Marker, adding that *Toute la mémoire du monde* features a shot of piles of comics in the Bibliothèque Nationale.

According to Lacassin, Resnais was most interested in the possibility of "reciprocal borrowings" between the two media, and he felt that comic strips "preceded the

40 Francis Lacassin, "Alain Resnais et les bandes dessinées," *L'avant-scène du cinéma* 61–62, "Spécial Resnais" (July–September 1966); translated as "Dick Tracy Meets Muriel," *Sight and Sound* 36, no. 2 (1967): 101–103.

41 Lacassin, "Dick Tracy Meets Muriel," 101.

cinema in discovering and using the close-up, the CinemaScope image and the tracking shot," one of the signature shots of the cinema of discovery.[42] Although comic strips are not equivalent to animation, many animated cartoons derive from comics, and both forms inhabit a cultural space that is often deemed to be juvenile.[43] Andrew's version of film history compares a "very juvenile cinema" that was engaged with "the adult arts of fiction, theater, and painting" with today's mature cinema, which gets its "vitality, its necessary impurity" through contact with "comic books, television, popular music, video games, and computer culture."[44] This paradigm underestimates not only the ways in which fiction, theater, and painting continue to inspire a mature cinema but also the long history of filmmakers' interest in comics. Roy Armes's (1968) *The Cinema of Alain Resnais* cites Lacassin but also expands Lacassin's claims, noting the comic strip's provision of a "non-realistic method of narrative," its use of a verbal commentary that is separate from the visual image to advance the narrative, and its creation of an "illusion of movement, flow and action through the linking of static pictures."[45] James Monaco's *Alain Resnais* (1978–1979) further reinforces this graphic Resnais by highlighting the filmmaker's unrealized projects, including a collaboration titled "The Monster Maker" with Stan Lee of Marvel Comics and a planned film about the popular serial detective of the 1920s, Harry Dickson.[46]

Resnais has never hidden his love of comics and animation; indeed, he often celebrates it, most explicitly in his 1989 film *I Want To Go Home*, a story about an elderly and generally forgotten American comic-strip artist in Paris. While in this late film drawn characters interact with live-action figures, in Resnais's earlier work his engagement with both the comic strip and animation is more subtle and less oriented toward comedy, although a gentle humor often accompanies the appearance of drawn images. The early awareness of this frame for understanding Resnais has gradually been erased, in contrast to the critical treatment of Resnais's longtime collaborator, the late Chris Marker. With Marker, scholars have had no trouble acknowledging comic book and cartoon aesthetics as being both serious in nature and of primary importance. Fortunately, because it is hard to keep these two filmmakers apart, their mutual imbrication can help render visible a different view of Resnais, and this in turn complicates how our own moment articulates its relationship to a particular aspect of postwar French cinema.[47]

---

42   Ibid., 102, 103.

43   In *The Poetics of Slumberland: Animated Spirits and the Animating Spirit* (Berkeley: University of California Press, 2012), Scott Bukatman links animation's association with childishness to the American dream and rebellious, playful, transformative energy.

44   Andrew, *What Cinema Is!*, 94.

45   Roy Armes, *The Cinema of Alain Resnais* (New York: A. S. Barnes, 1968), 23.

46   James Monaco, *Alain Resnais* (New York: Oxford University Press, 1979), 159–166, 145, 148. Resnais had discovered these serials in the 1930s, collected all 178 issues, spent years planning a film version of them, and pursued the identity of the series' author, not known at that point, finally meeting him in 1959. For more on Resnais's Harry Dickson project, see Emmanuel Burdeau, Jean-Louis Leutrat, Suzanne Liandrat-Guigues, and Philippe Met, eds., *Les aventures de Harry Dickson: Scénario de Frédéric de Towarnicki pour un film (non réalisé) par Alain Resnais* (Nantes, France: Capricci, 2007).

47   Resnais declares his debt to Zig and Puce in Serge Daney and Danièle Dubroux, "Entretiens avec Alain Resnais," *Cahiers du cinéma* (1983): 35. For musical serialism and *Marienbad*, see David Bordwell, *Narration in the Fiction*

***Toute la mémoire du monde* (1956).** *Toute la mémoire du monde* was one of Resnais's many collaborations with Marker, who is credited in the titles as "Chris and Magic Marker" (Figure 4).

Other scholars, like Raymond Bellour and Nora Alter, have previously noted this credit line, but I add that this bold instrument contrasts in important ways with the elegant, intellectual, and writerly fountain pen evoked by the *caméra-stylo*.[48] Discussing the film, Catherine Lupton mentions in passing that the Left Bank group "slipped friendly allusions to each other into their works," noting that "Gatti and Varda feature as extras and Marker surfaces in the proxy guise of a book." Lupton also points out that the book featured throughout the film is "actually a fake volume about the planet Mars from the Petite Planète series."[49]

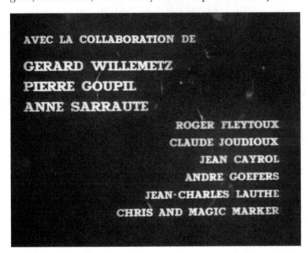

Figure 4. "Chris and Magic Marker," in *Toute la mémoire du monde*.

But both this fictional book and the "Magic Marker" are worth a closer look.

Toute la mémoire du monde tracks the book *Mars* from its arrival at the Bibliothèque Nationale's mail room through to its final shelving. Although there's nothing particularly remarkable about the early footage depicting a day in the life of the library, the cutout newspaper image of three kittens peeking out from under a pile of papers might make us pause—is this a group of three feline filmmakers (Figure 5)?

As is well known, Marker often represented himself as a cat; indeed, just a couple of years earlier in January 1952, the same year as his directorial debut, *Olympia 52*, he had published a short essay in *Esprit* magazine titled "Le chat aussi est une personne" (The cat is also a person) in which he claims that "cats are the most widespread and accessible form of God."[50] Although they have gone unremarked to date, cats

Film (Madison: University of Wisconsin Press, 1985), 277–279. In his recent BFI guide to *Marienbad*, Leutrat mentions an animated cartoon viewed in Resnais's childhood, as well as the strong impression made by Karel Zeman's animation film *The Fabulous World of Jules Verne* (1958). See Jean-Louis Leutrat, *L'année dernière à Marienbad*, trans. Paul Hammond (London: BFI, 2000), 14–15.

48 Raymond Bellour has also noted this nomenclature. See Raymond Bellour, "The Book Back and Forth," in *Qu'est-ce qu'une Madeleine? A propos du CD-ROM Immemory de Chris Marker*, ed. Yves Gevaert (Paris: Centre Georges Pompidou, 1997), 108. Bellour describes Marker as "one of those who have most contributed to dissolving the gap between the recorded image and the drawn or constructed one" (ibid., 137). Nora M. Alter, *Chris Marker* (Urbana: University of Illinois Press, 2006), 124.

49 Catherine Lupton, *Chris Marker: Memories of the Future* (London: Reaktion Books, 2005), 43, 61.

50 Chris Marker, "Le chat est aussi une personne," *Esprit* 186 (1952): 78.

prowl throughout *Toute la mémoire du monde* as a sign of Marker's presence as much as they do in Marker's own work. They do so in graphic as well as photographic form; and they both signal and resist the individual consciousness of the auteur as they hover between human and animal, human and divine, singularity and clowder.

Guy Gauthier has also commented on the way Resnais winks at his col-

Figure 5. "Three Feline Filmmakers," in *Toute la mémoire du monde*.

laborators: "This work, from the *Petite Planète* series, which Marker effectively directed, had the title *Mars*. One can glimpse the name of the author of this fictional book: Chris Marker."[51] Gauthier here is both right and wrong in ways that are interesting. The card catalog documents the book in question, *Mars*, as a work of astrophysics in the Petite Planète series that was indeed founded by Marker in 1954; the listed author, however, is not actually Marker, but rather a woman, Jeannine Garane.

Struck by how rare it must have been for a woman to publish in the field of astrophysics in the 1950s, and initially unaware of the book's fabricated nature, I discovered that Garane had worked a few years earlier as assistant director for Marker's debut film, *Olympia 52*.[52] Like Petite Planète books, a woman's face appears on the cover, in this case, the Italian actress Lucia Bosé.[53] Although the image does not feature the face of the author, it does reinforce the film's attention to the role of women in the filmmaking process.

But Garane is not the only complicating sign of authorship, for as we watch the book being labeled—with a magic "marker," of course—two different abstract images of a black cat stare out at us from the early pages of the book. For a very brief instant, we might also snatch a glimpse of a photograph of Marker himself printed alongside one of these cats before the librarian nudges the book aside, placing Marker's face where it often was: just beyond the limits of our vision. It is not that the auteur is absent—after all, another shot reveals that the index of the book contains a series of auteur in-jokes with chapter headings such as "X-Ray," "De Wells [*sic*] à Domenach,"

---

51 "Cet ouvrage, de la collection *Petite Planète*, alors effectivement dirigée par Marker, avait pour titre: "Mars". On peut entrevoir le nom de l'auteur de ce livre fictive: Chris Marker." In Guy Gauthier, *Chris Marker, écrivain multimedia au Voyage à travers les medias* (Paris: Harmattan, 2001), 203. My translation.

52 See "Olympia 52," Swedish Film Database, http://www.sfi.se/en-gb/Swedish-film-database/Item/?itemid=36684&type=MOVIE&iv=PdfGen.

53 Stephen Ungar identifies Bosé in "Scenes in a Library: Alain Resnais and *Toute la mémoire du monde*," *SubStance* 41, no. 2 (2012): 58–78, 72.

and "Agnès de . . ." But even these cameo appearances of Nicholas Ray and Orson Welles reframe the role of such film directors in *Cahiers*, for here they appear with "Agnès" in a book apparently authored by Jeannine Garane (with some help from Marker and his two-dimensional feline accomplices).[54] Before *Mars* is temporarily shelved, we get a brief flash of the adjacent books, the first of which is a children's book of songs, *La route aux oiseaux*, by Francine Cockenpot (1952), also unremarked to date in the writing on this film.[55] When I tracked down this book (like *Mars*, it too is no longer available in the Bibliothèque Nationale, but unlike *Mars*, it is a real book), I discovered that Chris Marker illustrated it with fifty-eight cartoon drawings, mainly of birds (with one signature cat) (Figure 6).

These books appear alongside others that are actually part of the Petite Planète series: *Autriche* (Austria), *Allemagne* (Germany), and *Suisse* (Switzerland).[56] But what are we to make of this close-up filming of *Mars* (supposedly volume 25, although in the series volume 25 is actually a volume about Yugoslavia) amid cartoon cats and birds and travel books featuring key countries from World War II? By foregrounding, through the reference to Garane, Marker's debut film about the Helsinki Olympics of 1952, Resnais highlights and shares in what Alter has described as Marker's own "vehemently antiproprietary stance regarding his intellectual output"—his nod to Garane can also be read as a pro-feminist gesture.[57] This gendered reading is supported by the Left Bank's habit of including female filmmakers; by Resnais's own active collaboration with female authors throughout his career—Sellier describes his "creative posture" as "a sort of alternative in its entirety to that of the *Cahiers* group;" and by the presence on the bookshelf of Henri Georges's *Sans tricher: Information sexuelle*

Figure 6. "Title page of Francine Cockenpot's children's songbook, highlighting Chris Marker as the illustrator," in *La route aux oiseaux* (Paris: Éditions du Seuil, 1952).

54 The spelling of the name *Wells* without an *e* first suggests H. G. Wells and reinforces the film's investment in science fiction, but given the index's other auteur references, I would argue that Welles is also invoked. I'm grateful to Martin Lefebvre for highlighting both the index and the photograph of Marker. Stephen Ungar also discusses the index in Ungar, "Scenes in a Library," 67–68.

55 Francine Cockenpot, *La route aux oiseaux* (Paris: Éditions du Seuil, 1952).

56 Claude Vausson, *Autriche*, Petite Planète 1 (Paris: Éditions de Seuil, 1954); Joseph Rovan, *Allemagne*, Petite Planète 7 (Paris: Éditions de Seuil, 1957); and Dominique Fabre, *Suisse*, Petite Planète 9 (Paris: Éditions de Seuil, 1955).

57 Alter, *Chris Marker*, 4.

des garçons de 15 à 18 ans (1953), a sexual handbook for adolescent boys that promises to offer the complete truth.[58] Here, the film seems to raise the question of what truth is for the (male) adolescent postwar cinema of the *cinéfils* and which alternatives to that approach might be available. However, Garane's presence, as well as Marker's addition of the year 1952 to the title *Olympia*, raises the specter of yet another female film-maker, Leni Riefenstahl, and the other *Olympia* of 1936. Repeatedly, it is as if Resnais, through a network of authorial references and images, were posing the question of how to create cinematic truth in 1956 in the wake of the fascist use of documentary film. Along with collaborative authorship, ephemeral and simple graphic images—the kind that would never be catalogued in this library—seem to participate in his answer to this implied question, not least because the film constantly and explicitly bemoans the imprisonment and domestication of cultural artifacts. There is something special about those objects that manage to escape and that are suspended between cultural permanence and cinematic ephemerality.

Once permanently shelved, the book looks like the interloper it is, and the deep voice-over seems to address this concern when it asks, "Who is to say what is the noblest, the finest, the rarest?" The structure of this question, a question about taste as well as about the inherent value of cultural objects, recalls an earlier moment in the film when the same voice-over had asked in the periodicals room, "Who knows what else may come to light among these pages? Who knows what will be the most reliable testament to our civilization?" Although we may now be convinced of the historical and ethical value of the films of Resnais, it is worth noting that one of the values his film encourages us to adopt here is an openness to the as-yet-unrecognized potential of seemingly worthless image forms, a commitment to the position "Who knows?" While the latter question is accompanied by the camera moving over a whole range of printed graphic images or texts, including a stack of Resnais's beloved *Harry Dickson* serials, in the former example, the camera crawls up a tower of papers until it alights on the front covers of *Mandrake the Magician* and *Dick Tracy* comics. (Resnais smuggled all the comics into the library because it did not hold them, as he did Gabane's fictional book and Cockenpot's songbook. They are all examples of books that did not and still do not reside in the library, so this whole film might be read as a fantasy about a different type of cultural memory or storehouse, one made up of culturally unsanctioned objects that perhaps offer a counterhistory.)

The front cover of *Mandrake* reads in giant letters, "World War in Ten (or X) Dimensions!," a headline that foregrounds a key aspect of Resnais's work. In both *Toute la mémoire du monde* and later in *Marienbad*, Resnais, like many of the animators of the 1950s, including Trnka, Zeman, and McLaren, all under discussion in *Cahiers du cinéma* during this period, explores how cinema shuttles between two- and three-dimensional spaces, among printed graphic, photographic, and projected cinematic spaces. These various types of images do not all lead to the same destination and they cannot be conflated with one another. Rather, they offer a variety of possible trajectories that could be taken as we think about cinema's relation to the world through the images

58 Sellier, *Masculine Singular*, 212.

presented on screen. But the *Mandrake* headline, like Garane's *Mars*, also reminds us of both Resnais's and Marker's interest in science fiction, and in cinema as a vehicle for impossible journeys in time as well as space, in leaving the historical and physical present to understand it better.[59] In 1962, Marker would use photographs to transport us backward and forward in *La jetée*, just as he had turned to drawn animation in *Letter from Siberia* (1957) to move viewers back to the time of the mammoths. Although Resnais visually gestures to the possibility of cinematic time travel in 1956 through a comic book's cover, it is in *Last Year at Marienbad* that we see him most ambitiously activate and complicate, or resist the boundaries of graphic, photographic, and cinematic images as he works to find a form to convey the simultaneous experience of personal and historic time, both of which are depicted as traumatic.

Last Century at Marienbad: Toward a Cartographic Resnais. In his discussion of *Last Year at Marienbad*, Gilles Deleuze links Resnais in two different ways to animation and graphic forms of representation—and here it is worth noting that animation is neither always graphic in nature nor essentially opposed to the photographic. First, he switches without explanation from Resnais's film to Piotr Kamler's animated film *Chronopolis* (1982), which was showing outside the festival at Cannes while Deleuze was writing his cinema books. And second, he notes that while Alain Robbe-Grillet, supposedly the film's screenplay writer, used what Deleuze calls a "photographic method," Resnais, he claims, prepared the film using cartography and diagrams of layers of time, which, Deleuze points out, "survive . . . as integral parts of the film."[60] But what Deleuze means by these references to maps and diagrams in Resnais's process has been largely ignored, even in Tom Conley's book on Deleuze's "cartographic cinema."[61] In September 1961, *Cahiers du cinéma* published a diagram, a graphic time organizer, designed to give the actors in *Marienbad* a sense of order to "their game," a sense that, as Robbe-Grillet wryly observed, they might otherwise have lacked (Figure 7).[62] Robbe-Grillet had explicitly warned readers *against* viewing the diagram as a "key" to the film, so he may have been surprised to see it published in *Cahiers* a second time only two months later under the title "The Last Key of Marienbad" (Figure 8).[63] After "a month of research," *Cahiers* editors discovered that they had initially published the diagram upside down. Footnotes attempted to explain the way time had been spatialized in the film: "each large, clear, horizontal rectangle indicates a day of the week, beginning

---

59 Ungar describes how Resnais and Remo Forlani "planned sequences to be shot in the style of a futuristic 'science fiction' film" in the first synopsis of the film. See Ungar, "Scenes in a Library," 65.

60 Gilles Deleuze, *Cinema 2: The Time Image*, trans. Hugh Tomlinson and Robert Galeta (Minneapolis: University of Minnesota Press, 1989), 121.

61 Richard M. Blumenberg may gesture to these diagrams in 1971 when he opens his discussion of *Marienbad* thus: "Conjectures about 'meaning' in *Last Year at Marienbad* seem as redundant as the graphs and charts people have designed to 'explain' the film. Having made such graphs and charts myself, I do not wish to burden the field with further graphic explanation." Richard M. Blumenberg, "Ten Years after Marienbad," *Cinema Journal* 10, no. 2 (1971): 40.

62 Marienbad diagram, *Cahiers du cinéma* 123 (1961): 9.

63 "The Last Key of Marienbad," *Cahiers du cinéma* 125 (1961): 48.

on Sunday," and so on.[64] We find an interesting bridge between this odd form of scoring the live-action film *Marienbad* and animation or frame-by-frame practices that involve the use of a dope sheet, such as the one recently discovered in the Russian film archives by Mihaela Mihailova and John MacKay that shows how Dziga Vertov used an animator's method to plan each individual photographic frame within one of the montage sequences of his 1929 film *Man with a Movie Camera*.[65] Such documents suggest that throughout the history of film, many filmmakers, including those not particularly labeled "animators," have crafted cinematic time and space using a graphic and frame-by-frame planning method, and it is in such cases that we see the usefulness of a more fluid understanding of the relationships among terms like cinema, photography, and animation.

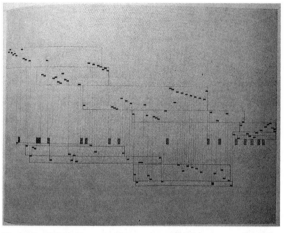

Figure 7. First graphic organizer for *Last Year at Marienbad*, printed upside down in *Cahiers du cinéma*, September 1961.

Marienbad's time map is only one of many elements in the film that evoke graphic and animated visual practices.[66] Yet as I demonstrated earlier, for Daney, the very idea of thinking about cinema, and especially Resnais's cinema, together with—instead of in opposition to—animation and the drawn image, was practically impossible.[67] It is precisely this association of Resnais with a cinema that opposes the drawn

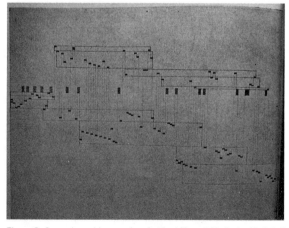

Figure 8. Second graphic organizer for *Last Year at Marienbad* (printed correctly), in *Cahiers du cinéma*, November 1961.

64 Ibid.

65 See Mihaela Mihailova and John MacKay, "Frame-Shot: Vertov's Ideologies of Animation," in *Animating Film Theory*, ed. Karen Beckman (Durham, NC: Duke University Press, 2014), 145–166, especially 158.

66 See Tom Conley, *Cartographic Cinema* (Minneapolis: University of Minnesota Press, 2007).

67 Daney, "The Tracking Shot in *Kapo*," n.p.

image and the animated image that I want to decouple while simultaneously disrupting the belief that Daney's position is representative of an entire generation of French filmmakers and critics.

Most critical discussions of *Marienbad* see Resnais's and Robbe-Grillet's formal experiments as a sign of the film's indifference to the "real world," especially when compared with other, more explicitly political films like *Night and Fog* (1955), *Hiroshima, mon amour* (1959), and *Muriel* (1963), which Resnais in a 1983 interview groups together, somewhat ironically, as his "virtuous projects, with grand, noble ideas . . . [,] subjects that treat the great dramas of our époque—unemployment, social subjects, pacifism, films against torture."[68] Indeed, when writing about Resnais, critics tend to avoid *Marienbad*—it simply doesn't line up with his other work of the period, and its languid and anxious aestheticism has always been a little embarrassing. Rosalind Galt and Karl Schoonover deem it to be possibly "the most difficult major art film of the period to redeem today."[69] Naomi Greene, like Andrew, approaches Resnais through Daney. She writes, "In the postwar period, says Daney, Resnais was the only one to understand that cinema 'had to deal with an extra person: the human species. And that person had just been denied (in the concentration camps), blown up (by the bomb) and diminished (by torture). Traditional cinema was incapable of "portraying" that. A way had to be found. And thus Resnais.'"[70] On the next page, Greene notes, without further comment, that *Marienbad* seemed simply "to turn [its] back on history."[71] But it strikes me as puzzling that a filmmaker who apparently understood in so singular a way the new challenges for cinema in dealing with the postwar human would or could simply turn his back on history. By understanding better the continuities between the graphic and proto-animated elements in *Marienbad* and Resnais's earlier and supposedly more "virtuous" and historically engaged work, we can not only begin to revise *this* narrative but also start to think about how to understand the ways in which contemporary digital cinema engages the world and history.

Several of *Marienbad*'s characters have trouble recalling whether or not they have met, where and when they are, and what has actually happened. This never-ending confusion instantly became the butt of critical jokes. In a 1963 review, for example, Norman N. Holland tells of one Harvard undergraduate asking, "Have you seen *Last Year at Marienbad?*" His interlocutor responds, "slowly, thoughtfully," "I—don't know."[72] But when read in their geographical, historical, and cartographic specificity, neither the film's spatiotemporal experiments nor the characters' confusion can be read as pure formalism and absurd affectation.

68 Serge Daney and Danièle Dubroux, "Entretien avec Alain Resnais," *Cahiers du cinéma* (1983): 27.

69 Rosalind Galt and Karl Schoonover, *Global Art Cinema: New Theories and Histories* (Oxford: Oxford University Press, 2010), 16.

70 Naomi Greene, *Landscapes of Loss: The National Past in Postwar French Cinema* (Princeton, NJ: Princeton University Press, 1999), 31.

71 Ibid., 32.

72 Norman N. Holland, "Metafilm, and Un-Film," *Hudson Review* 15, no. 3 (1962): 406–412, 407.

Without completely allegorizing the film or offering yet another "key" to unlock this cryptic work, I think it matters that Resnais and Robbe-Grillet set the film in a specific place between two unspecified years in the 1930s. Yet the extensive criticism on the film barely mentions either the decade or the location.[73] The spa town of Marienbad, or Mariánské Lázně, is located in what is now the "Western Bohemian" region of the Czech Republic. A 1929 Baedeker guide describes it as "thronged with patients of every nationality."[74] In the early twentieth century, it was well known as a thriving destination for middle- and upper-class Jews, as Sholom Aleichem's 1911 epistolary Yiddish novel *Marienbad* makes clear, and late nineteenth- and early twentieth-century postcards show that it was frequently the target of anti-Semitic and xenophobic caricatures.[75] On September 23, 1938, the town's German-speaking citizens burned down the town's synagogue while British and French leaders across the border negotiated the Munich Agreement with Hitler that would sanction Germany's possession of the Sudetenland on September 30. By October 1, German troops had occupied the region, and twenty thousand Jews subsequently fled.[76]

In *Last Year at Marienbad*, we find, I suggest, a cinema that conveys as much a sense of "incommensurable regions" as Deleuze locates in Resnais's more obviously political films *Hiroshima, mon amour* and *Muriel*, which shuttle spectators between Hiroshima and Nevers, or Boulogne and Algeria.[77] In *Marienbad*, these incommensurables seem to be marked only by movements through time rather than across space, because the space of Marienbad seems to remain selfsame, although I will complicate this idea somewhat. For the inhabitants of Marienbad in the 1930s, lines on paper are redrawn in ways that determine the basic rights of physical existence in real space. This cartographic trauma provides one context in which to understand Resnais's interest in drawn space and the political energy of the line in 1961, but the aesthetic to which he turns at this moment is not unprecedented, for it recalls his earlier interest in what graphic images offer to cinema, and their potential to open alternative pathways of memory and history, as we saw in *Toute la mémoire du monde*.[78]

Yet *Marienbad* may, after all, be more like Resnais's other split-location films than it first appears, for he shot the film neither in Mariánské Lázně nor in Robbe-Grillet's suggested location, a French casino, but rather in a series of palaces around Munich,

---

73 Lynn A. Higgins's reading of *Marienbad* represents a significant exception here. See Higgins, *New Novel, New Wave, New Politics: Fiction and the Representation of History in Postwar France* (Lincoln: University of Nebraska Press, 1996): 303–322.

74 Karl Baedeker, *Austria, Together with Budapest, Prague, Karlsbad, Marienbad: Handbook for Travellers*, 12th rev. ed. (Leipzig: K. Baedeker; New York: C. Scribner's Sons, 1929), xix.

75 Sholom Aleichem, *Marienbad*, trans. Aliza Shevrin (New York: Perigee, 1984).

76 Mirjam Zadoff, *Next Year in Marienbad: The Lost Worlds of Jewish Spa Culture*, trans. William Templer (Philadelphia: University of Pennsylvania Press, 2012), documents how "Marienbad" signified a well-recognized Jewish space and a center of Zionist activism in the late nineteenth century through the 1930s and the extent to which that identity was repressed after the war.

77 Deleuze, *Cinema 2*, 118.

78 Ungar argues for the importance of reading *Toute la mémoire du monde* in the context of the aftermath of the concentration camps and the history of decolonization. See Ungar, "Scenes in a Library."

which played such an important role in the town's fate in the 1930s. Although Resnais suggests in a 2008 audio interview that the location of Munich was chosen only for "financial reasons" and insists that neither he nor Robbe-Grillet had any intention of invoking either Bavaria or Germany, the incommensurability and dislocation characteristic of Resnais's politically "virtuous" films here persist as we shuttle between Munich and Marienbad, recorded place and narrative location.

Many have interpreted the film's use of graphic ornamentation and illusion as signaling Resnais's turn away from history and politics toward mere formalist games, but at precisely the moment Resnais was shooting *Marienbad*—a film whose title invokes a Czech town, in Czechoslovakia, socialist realist cinema was being cracked open not by the *camera-stylo* or direct cinema but by animated puppets that make way for what Peter Hames calls "Czech and Slovak cinema's golden age."[79] Furthermore, *Marienbad* was shot in the same year as the first Annecy animated film festival, which put animation firmly in the center of the French film scene and which receives close attention from the *Cahiers* critics, causing Martin to dream in the pages of *Arts* magazine of a cinema "that dares to employ a supple visual language . . . passing naturally from reportage to the animation of graphic elements" and that "would not condemn us any more to choose between René Clair and Tex Avery, Alain Resnais and Trnka, Renoir and John Hubley, Rossellini and Émile Cohl."[80]

Although the comic book is not visually indexed in *Marienbad* as it is in *Toute la mémoire du monde*, it nevertheless resonates temporally with the later film, particularly in the way Resnais adapts, as Lacassin pointed out in 1966, the comic strip's noncontinuous temporal blocks.[81] In an interview, Resnais even states explicitly: "*Marienbad* is composed of a series of self-sufficient images. The proof came when, at some festival or other, the film was projected with the spools in the wrong order. Everyone applauded."[82] In a more recent interview from 2008, Resnais goes farther, claiming that Lee Falk and Phil Davis's comic *Mandrake the Magician* had served in *Marienbad* as a "medium of communication" between the actors Delphine Seyrig, Giorgio Albertazzi, Sacha Pitoëff, and Resnais; it was, he declares, their lingua franca. He also claims that Lee Falk saw and loved the film and that one image from the comic was the inspiration for the now-iconic sculpted Marienbad trees.[83]

But this anecdotal role of graphic, composited, and fantastical images extends into the film's structure and aesthetic and to the unusual sense of cinematic time and place that *Marienbad* conveys. We might consider more carefully, for example, the function of the artificiality of this garden scene in which frozen actors cast shadows on the ground while the neighboring bushes do not. It is well established that the shadows

---

79 Peter Hames, *Czech and Slovak Cinema: Theme and Tradition* (Edinburgh: Edinburgh University Press, 2009), 11.

80 André Martin, "80 films au premier Festival du cinéma d'animation," in *Arts*, no. 778 (1960): n.p., cited in Clarens [and Martin], *André Martin: Écrits sur l'animation*, 1: 133–137, 135.

81 Lacassin, "Dick Tracy Meets Muriel," 103.

82 Alain Resnais and Adrian Maben, "Alain Resnais: The War Is Over," *Films and Filming* 13 (1966): 42.

83 Resnais discusses the role of *Mandrake the Magician* in a 2008 interview: "Audio Interview with Alain Resnais," *Last Year at Marienbad*, director-approved special ed. DVD, directed by Alain Resnais, Criterion Collection, 2009.

were painted on the ground, but this observation has not been linked to other visual or conceptual elements of the film. The inconsistency of the shadow patterns here troubles our tendency to trust the "recording," to use Daney's term. Of course, photographic, graphic, and fabricated elements are combined in any shot filmed on a set, but here, "incommensurable" temporal moments are composited seamlessly in a way that prefigures some of the problems digital cinema poses for Andrew, namely the difficulty of distinguishing between shots of "reality" and special effects or authorial interventions into the photographic, and the problems posed by an image in which every element of the picture has been "controlled."[84] Yet this coexistence within the frame of multiple temporal moments, common in both animation and the comic strip, is how Resnais cinematically evokes the experience of trauma's double time in *Marienbad*.

Many other moments seem self-consciously to gesture toward alternatives to an idea of cinema as an automatic registration of the world, even when these moments are filmed continuously rather than made frame by frame. Toward the end of the film, for example, the camera focuses on a drawer filled with piles of almost-identical photographs, as if a sequence of the film had literally fallen apart into individual frames and could now be re-combined in any order. The film is also filled with dramatic cuts between graphic prints, trompe l'oeils, printed and painted illusions of receding space (some of which look uncannily like Ezawa's digital redrawings of *Marienbad* scenes), and live-action shots of outdoor spaces that are elsewhere depicted in graphic forms. In the shooting gallery, Resnais foregrounds the film's proximity to animation and the graphic arts in a couple of ways. As the camera cuts between rows of live men and two-dimensional humanoid targets, it underscores both the extent to which *Marienbad*, like Zeman's contemporaneous mixed-media animation, shuttles the viewer between two- and three-dimensional, graphic and live-action worlds, and how the film's protagonists seem to be played by strange hybrid creatures or actor-puppets.[85]

Repeatedly, the frozen living bodies of actors seem like statues, just as statues and other objects are brought alive through the animating force of close ups, zooms, and camera movements. The film invites us to consider what difference, if any, a live body on film makes if it is treated like an object, to ask how the distinct meanings of animation—to give life to, and to endow with movement—interact. In the script, Robbe-Grillet explicitly describes the setting as having "a motionless, frozen servant in elaborate livery, or else a statue."[86] It is not so much that the difference doesn't matter, as that the film is interested in making us think about when and why this would

<hr>

84 Andrew, *What Cinema Is!*, 20.

85 This tension between two and three dimensions is prefigured in Adolfo Bioy Cesares's novel *The Invention of Morel* (1940), to which, Thomas Beltzer argues, *Marienbad* "secretly allude[s]." Beltzer writes, "The Argentinean masterpiece is about a fugitive, Morel, hiding out alone on a deserted island who one day awakens to discover that the island is miraculously filled with anachronistically dressed people 'who dance, stroll up and down, and swim in the pool, as if this were a summer resort like Los Teques or Marienbad." These Marienbad-esque types turn out to be holograms. See Beltzer, "*Last Year at Marienbad*: An Intertextual Meditation," *senses of cinema* 10 (2000), http://sensesofcinema.com/2000/10/marienbad/.

86 *Last Year at Marienbad*, text by Alain Robbe-Grillet for the film by Alain Resnais, trans. Richard Howard (New York: Grove, 1962), 20.

matter in a very particular time and place. Monaco almost seems to be describing a weird form of puppet animation when he writes of *Marienbad* that "the people are sculptural volumes, masses, to be manipulated like the statues which populate the endless gardens."[87] This description evokes not just any "animation" but another film set in a different garden, McLaren's Oscar-winning antiwar animation short, *Neighbours*, from 1952. In this pixilated experiment with live actors, McLaren replaced the initial actors with animators to close the distance between drawing and acting; only animators, he explains, "knew exactly how to move themselves, for instead of making a series of drawings they made a series of postures."[88] Drawing and acting, it seems, may be closer to each other than we might imagine.

This is not the only way in which McLaren, like Resnais, can help us understand the relation between "cinema" and "animation" in less polarized ways. First, also in *Neighbours*, he confounds one of the distinctions often used to uphold a barrier between animation and cinema by evolving from a single-frame pixilation of live actors to a variable-speed cinematography that demands a more nuanced theorization of cinema and animation's relationships with time and automaticity.[89] Second, as Resnais did in both *Toute la mémoire du monde* and *Marienbad* in various ways, including the tracking shot's penetration of deep spaces, McLaren actively explored the relationship between two- and three-dimensional images, specifically in two three-dimensional animated films that were commissioned in 1951 by the British Film Institute for the Festival of Britain: *Around Is Around* (1951, ten minutes) and *Now Is the Time*, (1951, three minutes). These films were of extreme interest to *Cahiers*' "*cinéfils*," and Ezawa, the artist I mentioned in my introduction, may well build an explicit bridge between *Marienbad* and McLaren in the opening of his sound version of *Marienbad 3D* when he cues us with an intertitle, as McClaren also did in *Now Is the Time* to "put on our glasses." Grant Wiedenfeld has recently noted Bazin's 1956 discussion of these 3-D animations, as well as the critic's comparison of McLaren's with Marker's animation. In 1956, Bazin commented that both filmmakers were able "to say the most serious things in the most silly manner."[90] Marcorelles echoed this sense of McLaren's seriousness a few years later in 1960, when he wrote in *Cahiers du cinéma* of McLaren's films that "maximum special effects [*truquage*] coincides with maximum truth."[91] These "serious things" for both Marker and McLaren included war, and their practice provides a context in which we might frame Resnais's own graphic experiments, forcing us to consider how

87 Monaco, *Alain Resnais*, 64.

88 Norman McLaren, "Further Notes on the Shooting of 'Neighbours,'" (unpublished, National Film Board of Canada, 1973), n.p., quoted in Maureen Furniss, *The Animation Bible: A Practical Guide to the Art of Animating, from Flipbooks to Flash* (New York: Abrams, 2008), 269–270. Furniss also explains in detail McLaren's shift from a frame-by-frame process to variable-speed cinematography.

89 Ibid.

90 Bazin, "*Lettre de Sibérie*," in *Le cinéma français de la liberation à la nouvelle vague (1945–1958)*, ed. Jean Narboni (Paris: Cahiers du Cinéma, 1983), 180, quoted in Wiedenfeld, "Bazin on the Margins of the Seventh Art," in *Opening Bazin: Postwar Film Theory and Its Afterlife*, ed. Dudley Andrew, with Hervé Joubert-Laurencin (New York: Oxford University Press, 2011), 262–267, 265.

91 Marcorelles, "Annecy an un," 35.

graphic images, animated images, and now digital photography and cinema enable us to respond to historical trauma in different ways, as well as how these visual and audiovisual responses affect our understanding of history and memory.

As with today's composited digital images, *Marienbad*'s images at times gave rise to a sense that something was missing, and discussions about cinematic lack often took an affective turn. Today, it is important that we historicize our sense of longing for cinematic plentitude rather than imagining that cinema is only now failing to fulfill our desires. In a *Cahiers* roundtable from December 1961, Rivette claims that films like *Hiroshima, mon amour* and *Marienbad* are "missing a dimension" ("il leur manque une dimension") if they don't touch the public, and for him, *Marienbad* didn't.[92] In the United States, William S. Pechter in the *Kenyon Review* described his response thus: "Neither bored nor interested, neither in comprehension nor confusion, neither liking nor disliking, I sat before the film in what can perhaps best be understood as a kind of impassive, numb neutrality."[93] Norman N. Holland also found the film "cold," but in contrast with other critics, he did not see this as "bad," instead highlighting the affinity between the film's "frozen" quality and two-dimensional print culture, especially rotogravure.[94] Like Leo Bersani and Ulysse Dutoit, who wrote about the film later, Holland is interested in the film precisely because of, not in spite of, its affectless quality.[95] But many seemed not to know what to do with their awareness of what Erwin Panofsky had earlier described as an image's "full mathematical consciousness."[96]

Marienbad exhibits not just a mathematical but also more specifically a binary consciousness, and this enters the film both through the recurrence of black-and-white tiles and through the characters' obsessive engagement in the game of Nim. A version of Nim had been featured in *Scientific American* in February 1958, and as Alex Galloway has pointed out, the game was an object of interest for mathematicians and cybernetic pioneers who "helped invent the field of artificial life."[97] By the time Robbe-Grillet

92 Morvan Lebesque, Pierre Marcabru, Jacques Rivette, Eric Rohmer, and Georges Sadoul, "Débat," *Cahiers du cinéma* 125 (1961): 12.

93 Dwight Macdonald judged that the film had "no affective life," in "Mystification at Marienbad," *Esquire*, June 1962, 49, 54, 56, quoted in Holland, "Metafilm, and Un-Film," 407. See also William S. Pechter, "Last Night at Marienbad," *Kenyon Review* 25, no. 2 (1963): 338.

94 Holland, "Metafilm, and Un-Film," 408. Holland's psychoanalytical approach to Resnais resonates in important ways with Bersani and Dutoit's later comparison of Resnais with the work of Beckett and Rothko in *Arts of Impoverishment*. Noting that *Marienbad* goes in search of an "*affektlos*, sensuous-intellectual response," Holland asks, "Is such a demand bad?" and answers, "Not to me—and I will stick out my cerebrum and call *Marienbad* a metamasterpiece" (ibid., 411). In 1971, Richard M. Blumenberg suggests that the film's form staves off empathy, accident, emotion, meaning, and spectatorial response, and again, this resistance to feeling becomes linked to the way Resnais treats the depiction of space. For Blumenberg, the film uses technology to "dimensionalize" aspects of life that have been reduced from "actions" to "objects"; he writes of "rectangles dimensionalizing into trompe-l'oeil frames" and suggests that the many traveling shots attempt to dimensionalize the environment in order to make the rendition as objective as possible." Blumenberg, "Ten Years after Marienbad," 41.

95 Leo Bersani and Ulysse Dutoit, "Stalled Movement," in *Arts of Impoverishment: Beckett, Rothko, Resnais* (Cambridge, MA: Harvard University Press, 1993), 147–208.

96 Erwin Panofsky, *Perspective as Symbolic Form* (New York: Zone Books, 1991), 57.

97 Alexander R. Galloway, "The Computational Image of Organization: Nis Aall Barricelli," *Grey Room* 46 (2012): 28. Galloway mentions Nim, and another version of it, "Tac Tix," on page 42; he also references *Scientific American*'s publication on the game in February 1958 on this page.

and Resnais were making the film, they may well have been aware of the emerging discourse of cybernetics, which was infiltrating French culture in part through Lévi-Strauss's engagement with it from at least 1958—Robbe-Grillet also later spoke about cybernetics at a Milwaukee film conference in the 1970s.[98] In his 1963 review, Holland, having consulted with mathematician friends, explains the game to readers thus: "The first step is to write (or imagine) the number of matches in each pile in numbers to the base two, arranging those binary numbers in a column for addition; thus,

been kind enough to explain to me. **The first step is to write (or imag-ine) the number of matches in each pile in numbers to the base two, arranging those binary numbers in a column for addition; thus, the** *Marienbad* **version,**

•		1
•••		11
•••••	becomes	101
•••••••		111

Figure 9: Binary numbers and the "Marienbad Game." Norman N. Holland, "Metafilm, and Un-Film," *Hudson Review* 15, no. 3 (1962): 409.

the *Marienbad* version" (Figure 9).[99] So important was Nim to the marketing of the film that William S. Pechter tells readers in his 1963 review that "they were—truly—selling a 'pocket edition of 192 "Marienbad" games' for $1.00 in the lobby."[100] Pechter may have been right in ways he did not yet understand when he commented, "The future with a vengeance, one might say; only it is the present."[101]

In our present, film and media scholars are still bound to consider Bazin's question of what cinema is. And as Andrew himself points out, a Bazinian response must allow for the process of evolution: "Cinema, essentially nothing in itself, is all about adaptation, all about what it has been led to become and may, in the years to come, still become."[102] I am convinced, like Andrew, that until recently cinema's specificity, as well as its political and emotional force, has been rooted in its unique technical capacity to register indexical traces of the world and by the existence of an isomorphic relationship between an event and its cinematic record, as David Rodowick would say.[103] But as film theorists, if we are to follow in the steps of those who precede us, our job is also to make space for the cinemas we don't yet understand. Contemporary cinephilic discussions of the changing media landscape run the risk of foreclosing the possibility of recognizing digital cinema's specific values through the structure of their critical paradigms. But the antidote to this blinkered view of cinema can be found, at least in part, in the values of filmmakers like Resnais and Marker, who persistently declare an openness to cinema's becoming and participate in the creation of cinemas that use new technologies, dispose of or retool old ones, and are permeated and transformed

---

98 Conversation with Philip Rosen, April 2012. I am grateful to Phil Rosen for pointing out Lévi-Strauss's interest in cybernetics and the likelihood that Robbe-Grillet and Resnais would have known of it. For a discussion of Lévi-Strauss's engagement with cybernetics, as well as with mathematics more generally, see Mauro W. Barbosa de Almeida, "Symmetry and Entropy: Mathematical Metaphors in the Work of Lévi-Strauss," *Current Anthropology* 31, no. 4 (1990): 367–385.

99 Holland, "Metafilm, and Un-Film," 409.

100 Pechter, "Last Night at Marienbad," 337.

101 Ibid., 338.

102 Andrew, *What Cinema Is!*, 140–141.

103 Rodowick, *Virtual Life of Film*, 49.

by neighboring arts, including animation and the comic strip. In so doing, they articulate, reveal, and explore emerging relationships to a changing world that we might not even recognize as what Cavell describes as the world "we" share. This, for me, is the risk, the challenge, and the pleasure of cinema.   ✱

Thanks to Dudley Andrew, Lacey Baradel, Eugenie Brinkema, Erna Fiorentini, Vinzenz Hediger, Marc Siegel, Oliver Gaycken, Charles Acland, Martin Lefebvre, Marc Steinberg, Yuriko Furuhata, Thomas Lamarre, Michael Leja, Philip Rosen, Rick Warner, the History of Art Colloquium and the Penn Humanities Forum at the University of Pennsylvania; the ARTHEMIS research group at Concordia University; the participants of the Enchanted Drawing Conference I (Berlin); the Department of Modern Culture and Media at Brown; the Newhouse Center for the Humanities at Wellesley College; the Department of Visual and Environmental Studies at Harvard; and the two anonymous Cinema Journal *reviewers.*

Prometheus in Chicago: Film Portrayals of the Chaining and Gagging of Bobby Seale and the "Real-ization" of Resistance

by GREG BURRIS

Abstract: At the 1969 Chicago Conspiracy Trial, Black Panther Party cofounder Bobby Seale was ordered chained and gagged after asserting the right to represent himself. This article examines film portrayals of this event to trace a lineage of resistance—its conception, its universalization, and its perpetuation across time. By melding together political and psychoanalytic approaches to cinema, I argue that film can serve to imbue Seale's struggle with lasting relevance, bringing attention to the holes perforating power's foundations and connecting the oppressions of the past with the oppressions of the present.

> My day will come: though this
> Commander of the Fortunate
> tortures me, chains me up,
> yet still my day will come.
>
> —Prometheus in *Prometheus Bound*[1]

"Chicago," Norman Mailer observed in 1968, "is the great American city."[2] He meant it ironically. In August of that year, thousands converged at the Democratic National Convention in Chicago. They went to protest racism, poverty, and the war in Vietnam—a "Festival of Life" against the Democrats' "Convention of Death." In return, they were met by an armed National Guard and the Chicago police. As is often the case, the voice of resistance was stifled with tear gas, clubs, and mass arrests.

Ignoring a government-commissioned report that characterized the violence as a "police riot," the incoming Nixon administration brought charges against eight

---

1 Aeschylus, *Prometheus Bound*, ed. and trans. James Scully and C. J. Herington (New York: Oxford University Press, 1975), 37–38.

2 Norman Mailer, *Miami and the Siege of Chicago: An Informal History of the Republican and Democratic Conventions of 1968* (New York: World, 1968), 86.

Greg Burris is an assistant professor of media studies at the American University of Beirut and a recent graduate of the department of film and media studies at the University of California, Santa Barbara. He has previously contributed essays to such publications as CineAction, Guardian, Jadaliyya, *and* Quarterly Review of Film and Video.

© 2015 by the University of Texas Press

of the protesters: Rennie Davis and David Dellinger of the National Mobilization Committee to End the War in Vietnam (MOBE); Tom Hayden, cofounder of Students for a Democratic Society (SDS); Abbie Hoffman and Jerry Rubin of the Yippies; academics John Froines and Lee Weiner; and Bobby Seale, cofounder and national chair of the Black Panther Party (BPP). Together, they stood accused of conspiring to incite a riot.[3]

Forced to divert their attention away from organizational activities, many of the defendants decided to bring the revolution into the judiciary by turning the trial into political theater. They openly mocked the decorum of the court, called for testimonies by countercultural icons, and dressed themselves in judicial robes. But perhaps no event embodied this theatricality more than the confrontation that ensued when Seale, the sole black defendant, attempted to speak.

Before the trial began in September 1969, Seale asked for a delay so that his attorney, Charles Garry, could recover from surgery. The presiding judge Julius Hoffman rejected Seale's request and instructed him to accept representation by the two other defense attorneys, William Kunstler and Leonard Weinglass. Seale chose instead to represent himself. As the trial proceeded, Seale periodically rose to his feet to address the court or cross-examine a witness. Each time, he was admonished and told he was not permitted to act as his own counsel.

Seale's actions cannot be understood without placing them in a broader context—what George Lipsitz calls "the long fetch of history."[4] By demanding a fair application of the law, Seale was assuming his role in the Black Freedom Movement, and he was thereby demonstrating an equality that cut through the court's hierarchical divisions—an equality that, as Jacques Rancière argues, "is not a goal to be reached but a supposition to be posited from the outset and endlessly reposited."[5]

To be sure, Seale was not the only defendant whose courtroom strategy turned on equality. Dellinger, for one, refused to refer to the judge by any honorable title.[6] But whereas his approach was fundamentally deconstructive—*"you are not any better than us"*—Seale's was scandalously affirmative—*"we are equal to you."* By refusing to stay put in his place, Seale was not *appealing for* equality; he was *presupposing* it. This dimension of the conflict was made explicit when Seale compared himself to prosecuting attorney Thomas Foran: "I get up to argue, and he gets up to argue, too, and that is where the disrupting was."[7] Seale saw no difference in their actions, and what Judge Hoffman deemed a disruption was, for Seale, simply an assumption of equality. "You think black

---

3 The Chicago Conspiracy Trial was an all-male cast of characters. Just as the contributions of women to the protest movements of that era were often overlooked by their male counterparts, so too were they ignored by a sexist federal government, and women activists who were in Chicago like Kathy Boudin, Judy "Gumbo" Clavir, and Anita Hoffman escaped indictment. For additional background on the trial, see Jason Epstein, *The Great Conspiracy Trial: An Essay on Law, Liberty and the Constitution* (New York: Random House, 1970); John Schultz, *The Chicago Conspiracy Trial*, 2nd ed. (Chicago: University of Chicago Press, 2009).

4 George Lipsitz, *Footsteps in the Dark: The Hidden Histories of Popular Music* (Minneapolis: University of Minnesota Press, 2007), vii–viii.

5 Jacques Rancière, *On the Shores of Politics*, trans. Liz Heron (New York: Verso, 2007), 84.

6 Judy Clavir and John Spitzer, eds., *The Conspiracy Trial* (New York: Bobbs-Merrill, 1970), 92.

7 Ibid., 180.

people don't have a mind," Seale declared. "Well, we got big minds, good minds, and we know how to come forth with constitutional rights."[8]

In the face of Judge Hoffman's admonitions, Seale eventually resorted to open defiance, calling the judge a racist, a fascist, and a bigot. After a month of battling Seale, the judge had had enough. On October 29, he ordered the jury out of the courtroom and commanded the federal marshals to "take that defendant into the room in there and deal with him as he should be dealt with."[9] Seale later described the ordeal:

> They took me back to the lock-up right outside the courtroom. They got some tape and put it across my mouth. They handcuffed my hands down close to the legs of a metal folding chair and put the irons on my legs. They looped the chain through one of the rods running across the front of the folding part of the chair and brought it out and clasped it to my right leg.[10]

Seale was then carried into the courtroom where he continued to speak through his gags and rattle against his chains. He remained in this state for three days of proceedings until the judge separated his case from the others'. Seale was given four years in contempt charges and removed from the courtroom, the Chicago Eight thereby becoming the Chicago Seven.

As grisly as Seale's shackles might have been, few people actually witnessed them. No cameras were allowed in the courtroom, and the incident was not captured on film. Even in its absence, however, the missing image of Seale's gagged face cast a rather long shadow. Journalistic accounts were widely published, courtroom sketches were broadcast on television, and political cartoons were printed in newspapers. Allusions to the event also appeared in the arts and in popular culture—in artist David Hammons's 1970 body print *Injustice Case*, in songs by Graham Nash and Gil Scott-Heron, and even in motion pictures.[11]

From the outset, the Chicago Conspiracy Trial was accompanied by a flurry of filmmaking activity. Nicholas Ray, director of *Rebel without a Cause* (1955), went to Chicago with plans to make a film version of the trial. Although Ray's project never saw the light of day, several other films about the trial did: *On Trial: The Chicago Conspiracy Trial* (Christopher Burstall, 1970), a BBC-produced dramatization of the proceedings; *The Great Chicago Conspiracy Circus* (Kerry Feltham, 1970), an absurdist blending of dialogue from Judge Hoffman's court with scenes from Lewis Carroll's *Alice in Wonderland*; and *Punishment Park* (Peter Watkins, 1971) and Jean-Luc Godard and Jean-Pierre Gorin's *Vladimir et Rosa* (Groupe Dziga Vertov, 1971), two fictional documentaries that

8   Ibid., 143.

9   In ibid., 162.

10   Bobby Seale, *Seize the Time: The Story of the Black Panther Party and Huey P. Newton* (New York: Random House, 1970), 337.

11   Graham Nash's song "Chicago" begins with the lyrics "So your brother's bound and gagged, and they've chained him to a chair, won't you please come to Chicago just to sing?" Gil Scott-Heron mentions the affair in his song "H2O Gate Blues." Graham Nash, "Chicago," *Songs for Beginners*, 1971, 2011 by Atlantic; Gil Scott-Heron, "H2O Gate Blues," *The Mind of Gil Scott-Heron: A Collection of Poetry and Music*, 1978 by Arista, 2001 by TVT.

situated the trial within the context of a dystopian police state.[12] Even Woody Allen could not resist the trial's allure, parodying it by donning a gag in *Bananas* (1971).

As the decades passed, the memory of Seale's struggle began receding from public consciousness. Even some of the most widely read histories of that era—books like Todd Gitlin's *The Sixties*—neglected to mention the affair.[13] This historical amnesia also extended to film and television, and with the exception of *Conspiracy: The Trial of the Chicago 8* (Jeremy Kagan), an HBO-produced reenactment of the trial first broadcast in 1987, it seemed as if the screen life of the trial were over.

But that is not the end of the story. Like the Freudian return of the repressed, the saga of Seale's chains refuses to remain dead and buried. In recent years, it has been revived, appearing in *Steal This Movie* (Robert Greenwald, 2000), *Chicago 10* (Brett Morgen, 2007), *William Kunstler: Disturbing the Universe* (Emily Kunstler and Sarah Kunstler, 2009), and *The Chicago 8* (Pinchas Perry, 2011).[14] Even Steven Spielberg has reportedly considered bringing the trial to the screen.[15] Filmmakers thus seem to have discovered in Seale a story that continues to resonate. While a judge had attempted to silence Seale, the tale of his plight has proved harder to stifle. As another black dissident from that era once declared, "You can jail a revolutionary, but you can't jail the revolution."[16]

To be sure, no two film portrayals of the event treat it in the exact same fashion. For some, it is a tale of oppression; for others, a tale of resistance. For some, it is a story caged within specific historical confines; for others, its implications are more expansive. This discrepancy also applies to the figure of Seale, and he can be cast as a revolutionary firebrand in one film and transformed into a tame integrationist in the next. One should neither see these contradictions solely as a measure of the films' historical objectivity nor adopt a relativist view in which all are deemed equally valid. Instead, one should locate the source of the variations. As Slavoj Žižek has argued in a different context, this hidden constant is nothing less than a disavowed antagonism, an ever-present trauma that stains all attempts at representation: the Lacanian Real.[17]

The Real is, along with the Symbolic and the Imaginary, one of Lacan's three registers of experience. For Lacan, what is commonly understood as reality is a contingent and socially constructed edifice, a field organized by invisible codes and regulations (the Symbolic). This order can never fully constitute itself as a cohesive, seamless totality, and it depends on fantasy (the Imaginary) to cover up its holes and gaps. These

12 Lewis Carroll, *Alice's Adventures in Wonderland*, 2nd ed., ed. Richard Kelly (Peterborough, ON: Broadview, 2011).

13 Todd Gitlin, *The Sixties: Years of Hope, Days of Rage* (New York: Bantam, 1987).

14 Notably, the filmmakers behind *William Kunstler: Disturbing the Universe*—Emily Kunstler and Sarah Kunstler—are that radical attorney's own daughters.

15 Adam Liptak, "Recapturing the '60s, in DayGlo Colors," *New York Times*, February 24, 2008, AR32, http://www .nytimes.com/2008/02/24/movies/24lipt.html?pagewanted=all&_r=0.

16 Fred Hampton, "The People Have to Have the Power," in *Let Nobody Turn Us Around: Voices of Resistance, Reform, and Renewal; An African American Anthology*, ed. Manning Marable and Leith Mullings (Lanham, MD: Rowman and Littlefield, 2000), 481.

17 See Žižek's remarkable reading of Claude Lévi-Strauss's *Structural Anthropology* in which the latter analyses the spatial arrangements of a Winnebago village. Slavoj Žižek, *The Parallax View* (Cambridge, MA: MIT Press, 2006), 25–26.

fissures within the Symbolic constitute the Real, the traumatic point at which the Symbolic fails.[18]

By taking into account the Real, one arrives at a view of the Symbolic that allows for a radical conception of resistance. This interplay between the Real and the Symbolic operates even at the level of the psychoanalytic subject. In contrast to a structuralist approach in which the subject is understood as a byproduct of successful subjectivization, theorists working out of a Lacanian framework argue that the subject is synonymous with *failure*, that the subject is precisely that which is not subjectivized. At the heart of the subject is a negative void or gap, a piece of the Real that eludes symbolization. As Mladen Dolar puts it, "The subject emerges where ideology fails."[19]

It is this negative kernel that prevents totalitarian projects of social engineering from being complete. As Cedric Robinson writes apropos the resilience of the African slaves, "Slavery altered the conditions of their being, but it could not negate their being."[20] Tales of African docility were betrayed by a continuous history of rebellion. In C. L. R. James's words, "The only place where Negroes did not revolt is in the pages of capitalist historians."[21] There remained in them something that escaped subjectivization, a source of resistance that could not be squelched. In psychoanalytic terms, this something is actually *nothing*; or rather, it is the Real, the constitutive negativity of the Lacanian split subject. Ironically, then, Stuart Hall's critique of Foucauldian resistance as being "summoned up from no-where" turns out to be exactly right.[22] Resistance *does* come from nowhere. It emanates from a nonplace, from the zone of nonsubjectivized negativity that remains beyond power's reach.

Contrary to Foucault's claim that resistance is not "doomed to perpetual defeat," any resistance not located along the fault line of the Real exists in a parasitic relationship with oppression, thriving upon the very power structures that it contests.[23] Hence, it is by orienting oneself around the Real, that part of reality that is more real than reality itself, that resistance has the potential to radically reconfigure the social order, making visible the invisible and possible the impossible. Indeed, it is precisely when the Real begins seeping through the cracks that existing power structures lose their hegemony. What had appeared solid begins to crumble, and what had seemed immutable

---

18 While Lacan developed all three of these registers throughout his career, he gradually oriented his focus around the Real. See, for instance, his discussion of the Real and trauma in Jacques Lacan, *The Seminar of Jacques Lacan*, book 11, *The Four Fundamental Concepts of Psychoanalysis*, ed. Jacques-Alain Miller, trans. Alan Sheridan (New York: Norton, 1998), 53–60. See also Slavoj Žižek, *The Sublime Object of Ideology* (New York: Verso, 1989); Joan Copjec, *Read My Desire: Lacan against the Historicists* (Cambridge, MA: MIT Press, 1994); Bruce Fink, *The Lacanian Subject: Between Language and Jouissance* (Princeton, NJ: Princeton University Press, 1995); Tom Eyers, *Lacan and the Concept of the "Real"* (New York: Palgrave Macmillan, 2012).

19 Mladen Dolar, "Beyond Interpellation," *Qui Parle* 6, no. 2 (1993): 78.

20 Cedric J. Robinson, *Black Marxism: The Making of the Black Radical Tradition* (Chapel Hill: University of North Carolina Press, 2000), 125.

21 C. L. R. James, "Revolution and the Negro," in *C.L.R. James and Revolutionary Marxism: Selected Writings of C.L.R. James, 1939–1949*, ed. Scott McLemee and Paul le Blanc (Atlantic Highlands, NJ: Humanities, 1994), 77.

22 In Lawrence Grossberg, "On Postmodernism and Articulation: An Interview with Stuart Hall," *Journal of Communication Inquiry* 10, no. 2 (1986): 48.

23 Michel Foucault, *The History of Sexuality*, vol. 1, *An Introduction*, trans. Robert Hurley (New York: Vintage, 1990), 96.

starts to disintegrate. It is a vision of destruction not unlike the imagery evoked in the poetry of Aimé Césaire:

I say right on! The old negritude
progressively cadavers itself
the horizon breaks, recoils and expands
and through the shredding of clouds the flashing of a sign *the slave ship cracks*.[24]

In this sense, Seale's resistance was not just real; it was *Real*. Like Marx's proletariat, Seale had *nothing* to lose but his chains. In partaking in that era's collective emancipatory revolt, Seale came to occupy the place of the void—the *hole* in the *whole*—and his disruptive performance in the courtroom threatened to disrupt the social order's smooth functioning. For this, he was gagged. In the view of legal scholar Pnina Lahav, "[The] binding and gagging was designed to silence Seale in order to keep the voice of the old authoritative narrative of the American story intact."[25]

This article is not an attempt to document Seale's personal biography, the political platform of the BPP, or the history of US political trials. Rather, I am concerned with the ways in which the film portrayals of Seale's struggle are organized around a disavowed trauma, a void that is present even in its absence: the appearance of equality amid inequality. By linking resistance to this underlying antagonism, we can trace its lineage—its conception, its universalization, and its perpetuation across time. This article thus weaves together a number of theoretical approaches, finding points of overlap and intersection between the Lacanian Real, Alain Badiou's philosophy of truth, George Lipsitz's notion of counter-memory, and Jacques Rancière's writings on politics and equality. Although this article is primarily a work of cultural theory and psychoanalytic film analysis, it also draws upon the discourse of black radicalism, philosophy, and politics. By putting this diverse ensemble into conversation, I attempt to approximate what Dick Hebdige has called a "do-it-yourself bricolaged theory for do-it-yourself bricolaged culture."[26] I hope such an approach may contribute to the larger project of restoring emancipatory politics to the lexicon of cultural theory. The post-1968 disavowal of liberation has run its course. It's time for talk of revolution to come in from the cold.

Nothing to Lose but a Black Panther's Chains: *Punishment Park* and *Vladimir et Rosa*.

Perhaps the greatest danger for totalitarianism is people who take its ideology literally.   —Slavoj Žižek[27]

---

24 Aimé Césaire, *Notebook of a Return to the Native Land*, ed. and trans. Clayton Eshleman and Annette Smith (Middletown, CT: Wesleyan University Press, 2001), 47. Emphasis mine.

25 Pnina Lahav, "The Chicago Conspiracy Trial: Character and Judicial Discretion," *University of Colorado Law Review* 70, no. 5 (2000): 1358.

26 Dick Hebdige, "Contemporizing 'Subculture': 30 Years to Life," *European Journal of Cultural Studies* 15, no. 3 (2012): 403.

27 Žižek, *Sublime Object of Ideology*, 28.

I wasn't placed in my chair. I was shoved in my chair.   —Bobby Seale[28]

The late 1960s witnessed the appearance of a new filmmaking trend—one in which fiction was presented in the guise of documentary. Joan Mellen gave a name to this genre, calling it the fictional documentary. In her words, those propelling this movement—politically conscious filmmakers like Bernardo Bertolucci, Costa-Gavras, and Gillo Pontecorvo—were operating under the assumption that there is truth in fiction, that "through fictionalizing history, we reexperience it more authentically."[29]

But what if we reversed this formula? What if it was not simply that there is truth in fiction, but the opposite, that there is fiction in truth? Seen in this way, the power of film derives not from its ability to replicate reality but from its potential to reveal reality's cracks. As Žižek writes, "The ultimate achievement of film art is not to recreate reality within the narrative fiction . . . but, on the contrary, to make us discern the fictional aspect of reality itself, to experience reality itself as a fiction."[30]

At first glance, the fictional documentary genre seems an appropriate category in which to place *Punishment Park* and *Vladimir et Rosa*—two 1971 films that use the chaining and gagging of Seale as a metaphor to address larger social tensions. Even though these films appear to have been written with pens dipped in the same political ink, upon closer inspection, important differences begin to emerge. While *Punishment Park* remains a fictional documentary, *Vladimir et Rosa* reverses Mellen's terms and becomes something else—a documentary fiction.[31] That is, while the former film locates truth in fiction, the latter discovers fiction in truth—a move that has profound implications for our conception of power and resistance.

Punishment Park presents a dystopian view of the United States. The war in Vietnam has spread, martial law has been declared, and dissidents are being sent to fascistic tribunals to be tried before a television audience. In lieu of prison terms, the condemned can elect to participate in a training exercise for law enforcement agents—the eponymous Punishment Park—in which they are chased on foot through sixty miles of desert. If captured, they will be sent to prison. If they reach a US flag positioned at the end of the course, they are promised freedom. As subsequent events make clear, however, nobody is allowed to reach that goal.

Peter Watkins, *Punishment Park*'s English director, had originally conceived the film as a re-creation of the Chicago Conspiracy Trial. Although this plan was eventually abandoned, the trial still retains a ghostly presence. As in the case of the Chicago Eight, the defendants are tried for conspiracy, and the actor who plays the tribunal head (Mark Keats) was selected for his resemblance to Judge Hoffman.[32] But the trial's

---

28   In Clavir and Spitzer, *Conspiracy Trial*, 175.

29   Joan Mellen, "Film and Style: The Fictional Documentary," *Antioch Review* 32, no. 3 (1972): 421. Although Mellen does not mention them in her discussion of fictional documentaries, one might also include Haskell Wexler's *Medium Cool* (1969) and Robert Kramer's *Ice* (1970).

30   Slavoj Žižek, *The Fright of Real Tears: Krzysztof Kieślowski between Theory and Post-Theory* (London: British Film Institute, 2001), 77.

31   Rancière uses this term in reference to Chris Marker's *The Last Bolshevik* (1993). Jacques Rancière, *Film Fables*, trans. Emiliano Battista (New York: Berg, 2006), 157–170.

32   Joseph A. Gomez, *Peter Watkins* (Boston: Twayne, 1979), 103.

influence is perhaps most apparent when Charles Robbins (Stan Armsted), a young black activist, is ordered bound and gagged.

Filmed in the style of newsreel documentary, *Punishment Park* presents two parallel stories: the members of Corrective Group 637 as they head through the desert and the members of Corrective Group 638 as they appear before the tribunal. Using cross-cuts and sound bridges, the film offers ironic juxtapositions, setting the two narratives against each other. A particularly dramatic example of this parallel editing takes place during the interrogation of Robbins. After the tribunal head castigates Robbins for not adhering to the nonviolence preached by Martin Luther King Jr., the film cuts to the desert, where officers gun down a white dissident who chose to fight back. A voice-over of Robbins serves as commentary: "Pigs are running madly through our community slaughtering off our children and our women." At this point, the officers in the desert murder yet another convict, unloading several rounds into the back of an unarmed black woman attempting to flee.

Like Seale, Robbins is incensed by his treatment, and he eventually resorts to outbursts, calling his interrogators "pigs" and "meatheads." The tribunal head responds in the fashion of Judge Hoffman: "Shut him up! Gag him!" Upon this command, four uniformed officers surround Robbins and physically restrain him—one at his legs, the other three around his head and torso. In a close-up shot, an officer covers Robbins's mouth with his hand. It is an image rife with symbolism: a white hand silencing a black face.

In *Punishment Park*, then, the image of Seale's chains is summoned to demonstrate the power of oppression. To be sure, the film showcases several forms of resistance—everything from principled pacifism to violent rebellion. But while the possibility of resistance is not obliterated, it is rendered impotent. Even those who reach the flag are not given their reward but are instead subjected to the officers' brutality. One can resist, *Punishment Park* seems to be saying, but the power of oppression is impossible to ever overcome.[33]

While *Punishment Park* splinters those who resist into factions, the ruling order displays no such cracks. Power is depicted as a well-oiled Orwellian nightmare, and any internal dissent is concealed. This is evident even at the level of sound, and throughout the film, the audience is constantly confronted with an incessant barrage of background noise—the sound of distant helicopters and gunfire. Like the film's depiction of power, this wall of sound is inescapable. In short, *there is no Real*. Such a portrayal of power is common to Watkins's oeuvre and can be found in his other films, including *Culloden* (1964), *The War Game* (1965), and *Gladiators* (1969). Thus, even though *Punishment Park* is critical of existing power structures, its depiction of them ironically replicates the propaganda peddled by the status quo's steadfast apologists. Either way, power is omnipotent and seemingly invincible.

This is not to say that *Punishment Park* should be dismissed in toto. On the contrary, a focus on oppression can combat the tendency to ignore it altogether. Watkins crafted *Punishment Park* with such a goal in mind, hoping that the film would, in his words, "act

---

33 For Watkins's response to charges of pessimism, see ibid., 120–121.

as a braking effect to the usual media portrayal of Western society."[34] But while Watkins may have intended to tear down those narratives that obscure oppression, his film does little in the way of forging new paths. To move beyond the film's implicit nihilism, one must transcend it—or, to put it in Hegelian terms, one must negate the negation, finding redemption in defeat and locating resistance in the Real.

Often, images of oppression are at the same time images of resistance. Whether they are perceived as such has less to do with any empirical data than with the ongoing battle for cultural hegemony. This hidden dimension constitutes what Dick Hebdige calls "a submerged possibility." It is real, but it cannot be measured scientifically— "you either see it or you don't."[35] Black history is replete with examples of submerged possibilities erupting into plain sight. Louis Agassiz's mid-nineteenth-century slave daguerreotypes—originally intended to prove African inferiority—are now displayed in museums and reproduced in books as demonstrations of the slaves' humanity; postcards celebrating early twentieth-century lynching spectacles were later circulated by black activists as part of their fight against apartheid; and the gruesome photograph of fourteen-year-old Emmett Louis Till's mutilated corpse was put to use by the instigators of the civil rights movement. Those who protested Jim Crow refused to let Till's death be turned into a defeat, and in this way, he did not die in vain. As Jesse Jackson later declared, his murder was transformed from "a crucifixion into a resurrection."[36]

Do Seale's chains likewise carry emancipatory value? An affirmative answer is suggested by the French film *Vladimir et Rosa*. In contrast to the grittiness of *Punishment Park*, the avant-garde methods and comic tone of *Vladimir et Rosa* seem hardly capable of instigating revolution. Critic Vincent Canby made this very claim, writing that the film was less likely "to inflame audiences than to put them immediately to sleep."[37] But while the film's various distanciation techniques might seem a far cry from the Lacanian call to traverse the fantasy, *Vladimir et Rosa* nevertheless articulates a nuanced view of resistance, using the chaining and gagging of Seale to explore power's disavowed foundations.

Directed by Jean-Luc Godard and Jean-Pierre Gorin (then working anonymously under the Dziga Vertov Group), *Vladimir et Rosa* involves a conspiracy trial directly patterned after the case in Chicago. Standing in for Judge Hoffman is Judge Ernest Adolf Himmler.[38] He overrules the defense with violent shouts, bangs his mallet for order, and mindlessly scribbles notes on nude centerfolds rather than paying attention to the proceedings—a crude habit that recalls the lechery of the justices in Franz Kafka's *The Trial*.[39] The Nazi connotations of his name are made explicit with his final

---

34 Peter Watkins, "*Punishment Park* and Dissent in the West," *Literature/Film Quarterly* 4, no. 4 (1976): 296.

35 Dick Hebdige, *Subculture: The Meaning of Style* (London: Methuen, 1979), 131.

36 In Christine Harold and Kevin Michael DeLuca, "Behold the Corpse: Violent Images and the Case of Emmett Till," *Rhetoric and Public Affairs* 8, no. 2 (2005): 276.

37 Vincent Canby, "From Malcolm X to Dan B," *New York Times*, May 28, 1972, D1.

38 Like the film's two directors, all the actors who appear in *Vladimir et Rosa* worked anonymously under the Dziga Vertov Group, and their names do not appear in the credits.

39 Franz Kafka, *The Trial*, trans. Breon Mitchell (New York: Schocken, 1998).

declaration to the jury: "Hitler may have been right; in our society, wild beasts should be destroyed."

The defendants pursue a variety of tactics in their attempts to subvert the proceedings. Godard and Gorin, who also play two of the defendants and serve as the film's narrators, comment on these modes of resistance, evaluating them for strengths and weaknesses. A special emphasis is placed on the tactics of the sole black defendant, a Black Panther activist whose name has a familiar ring: Bobby X. Like Seale, Bobby X's behavior in court is markedly different from that of his white codefendants. While they look for ways to defy the law, Bobby X seeks to identify with it.

This paradoxical position represents an example of what Žižek calls "overidentification"—the act of "taking power discourse at its (public) word, [and] acting as if it really means what it explicitly says (and promises)."[40] As a member of an excluded part of the community—Rancière's part with no part—Bobby X asserts an underlying equality by overidentifying with the law. Seale himself pursued such a strategy, and while his more colorful lines from the trial are the most quoted ones—his denunciation of the founding fathers as slave owners, for instance—his interruptions were more frequently appeals to the law.

In *Vladimir et Rosa*, Bobby X's overidentification results in the judge ordering him chained and gagged. Two marshals whose faces remain unseen push pistols against Bobby X's head as they violently move to gag him. Bobby X fights back, and there is hair pulling and head slapping as images of his face are interlaced with close-ups of his shackled hands and feet. He is then taken from the courtroom. But while Judge Himmler intends to silence Bobby X, his removal has the opposite effect. Bobby X's presence becomes even more conspicuous in his absence, and the film brings attention to it with two repeated images: a blank screen and an empty chair.

The void Bobby X leaves behind indicates a hole in reality. It is a stain in the visual field, a missing piece that proves false power's universal claims. Although this gap is constitutive of the Symbolic, it must be covered up or externalized if that order is to avoid collapse. It is through this lens that Césaire's words take on new relevance: "Europe, if it is not careful, will perish from the void it has created around itself."[41]

In *Vladimir et Rosa*, this absence, cinematically represented through an empty chair, threatens to overtake an already fragile power structure. In other contexts, power holds this threat at bay, projecting its own antagonisms onto an ideological whipping boy. This is the role played by the figure of the Jew in Nazism.[42] A more recent example of such ideological scapegoating can be found in the rabid rightwing hatred of Barack Obama. That his policies differ little from those of his Republican predecessor does not matter. Obama is vilified not because of his actual policies but because of a need arising from within his opponents' crumbling ideology. American conservatism paradoxically presents itself as representing the interests of both the white working class

40 Slavoj Žižek, "*Da capo senza fine*," in *Contingency, Hegemony, Universality: Contemporary Dialogues on the Left*, by Judith Butler, Ernesto Laclau, and Slavoj Žižek (New York: Verso, 2000), 220.

41 Aimé Césaire, *Discourse on Colonialism*, trans. Joan Pinkham (New York: Monthly Review Press 2000), 75.

42 Žižek, *Sublime Object of Ideology*, 47–49. On this point, we might also recall the anti-Semitism of Richard Nixon, who reportedly asked his chief of staff, "Aren't the Chicago Seven all Jews?" See Jonah Raskin, *For the Hell of It: The Life and Times of Abbie Hoffman* (Berkeley: University of California Press, 1996), 201.

and the capitalist elite. It is therefore fraught with potentially volcanic antagonisms—irresolvable contradictions that must be unloaded onto a foreign scapegoat: the immigrant, the Muslim, the welfare queen, or even the black president.

It is in this light that one can make sense of another empty chair that appeared in 2012, the prop used by Clint Eastwood when he addressed the Republican National Convention and repeatedly castigated and mocked an invisible Obama imagined to be sitting on stage beside him. Following on the heels of Eastwood's performance came even more empty chairs. In several reported instances, critics of the president voiced their discontent by hanging chairs from trees, thereby turning their manicured lawns into make-believe lynching scenes.[43] In this way, a ghost from the Jim Crow past returned to haunt the Tea Party present. In the reactionary imagination, Obama is an empty chair. Like Emmett Till, Bobby Seale, or other scapegoats like Assata Shakur, he is a fantasy screen upon which the conservatives project their own sins.

Whereas Eastwood kept Obama's empty chair at a distance, Judge Himmler is not so successful. Bobby X's absence serves to inspire further acts of resistance, first on the part of the other defendants and then within the power edifice itself. Soon, an important arm of the judiciary stops playing by the rules. The hitherto-silent jurors suddenly discover their own voices. Having witnessed the brutal treatment of Bobby X, they begin defying the court, exclaiming "Right on!" in support of the defendants. While Judge Himmler can gag Bobby X and evict him from the courtroom, he cannot reach the emptiness that takes the defendant's place. Like Seale, Bobby X's actions have effectively induced a hanging judge to metaphorically hang himself. The Real begins to engulf the Symbolic. Césaire's slave ship begins to crack.

Any discussion of *Vladimir et Rosa* that remains at the level of fictional documentary thus misses the mark. The film not only testifies to the idea that there is truth in fiction; even more, it demonstrates that there is fiction in truth. It does this by negating the negation and presenting a fantasy within a fantasy—the fiction of Bobby X's empty chair within the fiction of the film itself.

At the film's conclusion, Bobby X and the other defendants are behind bars. They have been found guilty and are given prison sentences. Like *Punishment Park*, *Vladimir et Rosa* concludes with defeat. But these two endings are hardly synonymous. A tragedy can contain within it the seeds of redemption, and the conclusion of *Vladimir et Rosa* is not bleak. The final scenes are given to Bobby X and another defendant, a women's liberation activist. From their prison cells, they call for continued community resistance and solidarity. Because their resistance emanates from a void—from a blank screen or an empty chair, from the nothingness beneath the chains—it cannot be stamped out. Whereas *Punishment Park* offers no hope, *Vladimir et Rosa* demands the impossible and stages an encounter with the Real. It transforms the struggle of Bobby X into a promise of what is yet to come, a future liberation whose seeds already exist

---

43 Katherine Haenschen, "Republican Lynches Empty Chair in Racist Presidential Effigy in Northwest Austin," *Burnt Orange Report*, September 20, 2012, http://www.burntorangereport.com/diary/12756/republican-lynches-empty -chair-in-racist-presidential-effigy-in-northwest-austin; Glenn W. Smith, "The Lynchings of Empty Chairs," *Huffington Post*, September 20, 2012, http://www.huffingtonpost.com/glenn-w-smith/empty-chair-lynched_b_1900843 .html; and Kim Murphy, "'No-Bama' Hanging Chair: Is It a Protest? Or a Symbolic Lynching?," *Los Angeles Times*, October 5, 2012, http://articles.latimes.com/2012/oct/05/nation/la-na-nn-nobama-chair-protest-20121005.

in the here and now, located in the absences that are present all around us and even within us.

We Are All Bound and Gagged: *Conspiracy* and *Chicago 10*.

The real must be exposed in a fictional structure. —Alain Badiou[44]

All black people are gagged and chained in Amerika's courtrooms. But because the gags and chains are invisible, we cannot see or experience them. Bobby Seale forced us to see and experience them directly. —Jerry Rubin[45]

If resistance is to be properly political, it must reach beyond the level of the individual subject. As Fredric Jameson has argued, "genuine revolt and resistance must take the form of a conspiratorial group."[46] One of the dangers hovering over any examination of the Conspiracy Trial is the risk of fetishization, the possibility of particularizing Seale's struggle and immortalizing him as an individual hero. Atomizing Seale in this fashion would inevitably come at the cost of taking him outside of history's "long fetch," causing one to disregard all of the shoulders upon which he stood.

This observation may lead one to question the viability of psychoanalysis as an explanatory framework for political struggle. If resistance emanates from the split subject, how does one account for collective revolt? It is on this point, however, that a Lacanian approach is helpful. Rather than restricting resistance to the individual, the Real provides a path out of the empirical prison house, allowing resistance to tap into the universal. It is therefore by rooting resistance in the Real that Seale can metaphorically break out of his chains.[47]

To date, there have been five major filmic reenactments of the Conspiracy Trial. Whereas *Punishment Park* and *Vladimir et Rosa* were fictional works that merely utilized selected elements of the trial, the reenactment films assert claims to historical authenticity. Indeed, all five use dialogue from the trial transcript, and several begin with a title card announcing the historicity of the depicted events.

But one would be amiss to assume that these films depict only the cold, hard facts. They also present audiences with something else—an extra layer giving them an aura of fiction. In some instances, this mythic dimension is easy to identify—the references to *Alice in Wonderland* in *The Great Chicago Conspiracy Circus*, for instance, or *Chicago 10*'s cartoonization of the trial. As the latter film's director openly admitted, "In animation, you're creating something that can't be objective history, but creating something more steeped in mythology."[48] Sometimes this surplus takes the form of a tiny detail—an editing decision or a protracted camera focus. It can therefore be found even in a

44 Alain Badiou, *The Communist Hypothesis*, trans. David Macey and Steve Corcoran (New York: Verso, 2010), 255.

45 Jerry Rubin, *We Are Everywhere* (New York: Harper and Row, 1971), 229.

46 Fredric Jameson, "Realism and Utopia in *The Wire*," *Criticism* 52, no. 3–4 (2010): 363.

47 Todd McGowan has recently provided a remarkable argument in favor of the emancipatory political potential of psychoanalysis. Todd McGowan, *Enjoying What We Don't Have: The Political Project of Psychoanalysis* (Lincoln: University of Nebraska Press, 2013).

48 Brett Morgen in Gina Piccalo, "Drawn into a Revolution," *Los Angeles Times*, February 28, 2008, E4, http://articles .latimes.com/2008/feb/28/entertainment/et-morgen28.

more straightforward retelling of the trial like the HBO-produced *Conspiracy*. Indeed, that film's phantasmal quality did not go unnoticed by the original defendants. Rubin remarked that *Conspiracy* was "creating a myth," and Hayden claimed it was "accurate as myth" but not "accurate in detail."[49]

One should avoid the historicist temptation to dismiss this phantasmal edge as a failure to stay true to history. Fantasy can serve more than one purpose, and rather than indicating a departure from reality, this surplus can also mark an intrusion by that part of reality that is more real than reality itself. Indeed, how else can one represent the unrepresentable except through fiction? Fantasy can act as a gateway into the impossible, and it is precisely through this protruding excess—Lacan's *objet petit a*—that the filmic depictions of Seale's struggle can attain the level of the universal.

Claims to universality, to be sure, have fallen out of fashion. One of the hallmarks of postmodernism has been a turn to the particular—a shift Hebdige traces to 1968's political defeats.[50] Universals are suspected of secretly harboring values saturated in particularity. As such, universal claims—even those made against oppression by certain articulations of feminism or Black Power, for instance—are often little more than underdog oppressors who fortify themselves by violently paving over their own internal differences.[51] While the universalization of a particular is indeed an exclusionary endeavor, however, fleeing its horrors by escaping into the arms of particularity is perhaps no less dangerous. By severing the particular's links to the universal, one may actually be complicit in its marginalization, ghettoizing in theory that which has already been ghettoized in reality.

There thus exists a need to walk a tightrope between these two poles, a need to discover a path that, in Lipsitz's words, manages to evade the dangers posed by "a disembodied universalism" on the one hand and "a parochial particularism" on the other.[52] Here again, it is important to recognize the centrality of failure—the failure of the subject to be subjectivized, the failure of power to constitute itself as a seamless whole. It is through failure that the road to the universal runs. Contrary to the assumptions of those who dismiss universality as a dangerous illusion, universals do exist. They just cannot be located in the world of particulars. As Joan Copjec claims, universals are not just real; they are *Real*.[53]

Here, the Lacanian Real begins to bleed into the work of Alain Badiou, whose attempt to reclaim universality for radical politics rests upon his distinction between particularity and singularity. While the former can be discerned by means of

49 Rubin in Stephen Farber, "Film on Chicago 8 Includes Originals," *New York Times*, May 14, 1987, C26, http://www
    .nytimes.com/1987/05/14/arts/film-on-chicago-8-includes-originals.html; Hayden in Lawrence Christon, "Movie
    Based on Chicago 8 Trial Draws Today's Chic Ex-Radicals," *Los Angeles Times*, May 18, 1987, F1, http://articles
    .latimes.com/1987-05-18/news/vw-410_1_chicago-conspiracy-trial.

50 Dick Hebdige, *Hiding in the Light: On Images and Things* (New York: Routledge, 1988), 186–190.

51 Prominent members of the BPP rejected the exclusionary nationalism often implied by Black Power, espousing
    instead what Huey Newton called "revolutionary intercommunalism" and what Fred Hampton envisioned as a "rain-
    bow coalition." During the Conspiracy Trial, Seale rejected the prosecutor's description of the clenched fist as a
    "black power symbol." He argued, "It's not a black power sign. It's a power to the people sign." Clavir and Spitzer,
    Conspiracy Trial, 120.

52 George Lipsitz, "Interview with George Lipsitz," *European Journal of Cultural Studies* 15, no. 3 (2012): 381.

53 Joan Copjec, *Imagine There's No Woman: Ethics and Sublimation* (Cambridge, MA: MIT Press, 2002), 4.

descriptive predicates (e.g., gender, race, even class) the latter renders such differences insignificant. A particularity is part of the field of knowledge, but a singularity bores a hole through knowledge. Like the Real, Badiou's singularity is a point of negation, a point that resists incorporation in existing power structures.[54]

As such, the singularity remains open for anyone to join, an empty chair in which anyone can sit. In Badiou's words, "Truth is open to all."[55] Partaking in it only requires a self-conscious act of political will. Žižek draws a similar distinction between the particularity of the working class and the singularity of the proletariat. "To be a 'proletarian' involves assuming a certain *subjective stance* . . . which, in principle, can be adopted by *any* individual."[56] Lipsitz makes the same claim apropos antiracist struggle. "We do not choose our color," he writes, "but we do choose our commitments."[57] This does not mean that the particular does not matter. Indeed, the singularity necessarily emerges in a particular context. But while a singularity can be known only through the particular, the particular itself can never be truly universal. In navigating the tension between universality and particularity, then, the task before us is not to ghettoize the particular but rather to universalize the ghetto.[58]

Seale certainly understood his predicament in universal terms. He saw his struggle as more than just a private affair and declared his bindings to be "a message to the world."[59] Seale openly identified his ordeal with the broader public, accusing Judge Hoffman of being in contempt of "the constitutional rights of the mass of the people of the United States."[60] He thus identified his position as a hole and equated it with the whole.

Importantly, one did not have to accept Seale as the uncontested spokesperson of the black community to perceive traces of this universality. Although the *Chicago Defender*—the city's main black daily—had maintained a relatively cool position toward Seale even after his indictment, its tone changed once he had been shackled. On the cover of the next morning's edition was a full-page cartoon of Seale, gagged and tied to a railway cart.[61] The next week, the paper published an editorial in which Seale was compared to a host of black heroes and martyrs—from Denmark Vesey, Nat Turner, and Frederick Douglass to Medgar Evers, Malcolm X, and MLK.[62]

---

54 Alain Badiou, *Theoretical Writings*, ed. and trans. Ray Brassier and Alberto Toscano (New York: Continuum, 2004), 144. See also Paul Eisenstein and Todd McGowan, *Rupture: On the Emergence of the Political* (Evanston, IL: Northwestern University Press, 2012), 167.

55 Alain Badiou, *Philosophy for Militants*, trans. Bruno Bosteels (New York: Verso, 2012), 27.

56 Slavoj Žižek, *The Ticklish Subject: The Absent Centre of Political Ontology* (New York: Verso, 1999), 227. Emphasis in original.

57 George Lipsitz, *The Possessive Investment in Whiteness: How White People Profit from Identity Politics*, 2nd ed. (Philadelphia: Temple University Press, 2006), viii.

58 One may be reminded of James Cone's scandalous rewriting of Christian universality in which he claims that Jesus *is* the ghetto. James H. Cone, *Black Theology and Black Power* (New York: Seabury, 1969), 66, 150.

59 Bobby Seale, "A Personal Statement," in *The "Trial" of Bobby Seale* (New York: Priam, 1970), 128.

60 Clavir and Spitzer, *Conspiracy Trial*, 175.

61 "Seale Chained, Gagged," *Chicago Defender*, October 30, 1969, 1.

62 Donald Mosby, "Now Comes Bobby Seale!," *Chicago Defender*, November 4, 1969, 5.

But Seale's struggle should not be reduced to the particularity of race alone. Shortly after he was gagged, Fred Hampton—the twenty-one-year-old chair of the Chicago branch of the BPP—spoke to a diverse crowd of protesters gathered outside the courtroom and asserted that Seale's chains had a universal relevance: "Every bus you get on, every building that you go into, they're talking about how cruel it is, the way they're treating Chairman Bobby Seale. And that's good, but what's not so good is that they don't understand that after Chairman Bobby Seale, it will be you and me and everybody else."[63] By connecting the dots between Seale's plight and the notion that one day others could likewise find themselves chained and gagged, Hampton was making a bold claim, treating Seale's chains as a short-circuit to the universal by asserting that *we are all Bobby Seale*. For Hampton, this grim prediction became prophecy when just one month later, a Chicago police squad acting in coordination with the FBI invaded the BPP's headquarters and murdered Hampton and fellow BPP member Mark Clark in their sleep. While Seale was able to resist his gag, US authorities made sure Hampton would not have that same chance.[64]

Hampton's declaration of universality was duplicated by the crowds before him, and it was reported that "a new symbol of protest appeared in the plaza outside Chicago's Federal Building: a plain white cloth wrapped around the mouths of demonstrators."[65] Those who identified Seale's struggle as their own saw in him something other than himself—a singularity, a gateway to the Real. In this way, Seale's bound figure momentarily came to occupy the same negative space as all those others who have been chained and gagged: from the legendary tales of Prometheus and Jesus Christ to those in the present whose exclusion is required by the dictates of power—people like whistle-blower Chelsea Manning, the illegally detained prisoners at Guantánamo Bay, those who are silenced not with a gag but a drone attack like sixteen-year-old US citizen Abdulrahman al-Awlaki, and more recent black martyrs like Trayvon Martin, Michael Brown, and Eric Garner.[66] Their place coincides with a hole in reality, a gap around which people can come together in protest, donning gags or holding placards declaring, "We are all bound and gagged" (or, in the wake of the police murder of Eric Garner, "I can't breathe"). This potential does not emanate from any particular positive traits on the part of the excluded but from exclusion itself. Thus, when the marshals carried Seale back into the courtroom, it was as if Prometheus himself had arrived in Chicago.[67]

63   Speech included in the film *Growing Up in America* (Morley Markson, 1988).

64   Jeffrey Haas, *The Assassination of Fred Hampton: How the FBI and the Chicago Police Murdered a Black Panther* (Chicago: Lawrence Hill, 2010).

65   J. Anthony Lukas, "Chicago Trial: It Has Become a Political Confrontation," *New York Times*, November 2, 1969, E7.

66   Lahav links the trial to Prometheus and Jesus. Pnina Lahav, "Theater in the Courtroom: The Chicago Conspiracy Trial," *Law and Literature* 16, no. 3 (2004): 417–418, 437.

67   To be sure, "we are all" assertions are not always radical, and they can also be used to reassert existing hierarchies—for instance, the chant "We are all Israelis" sometimes adopted by American Zionists or the slogan "*Je suis Charlie*" that appeared after the *Charlie Hebdo* shootings in early 2015. See Alex Lubin, "'We Are All Israelis': The Politics of Colonial Comparisons," *South Atlantic Quarterly* 107, no. 4 (2008): 671–690; Slavoj Žižek, "In the Grey Zone," *London Review of Books*, February 5, 2015, http://www.lrb.co.uk/2015/02/05/slavoj-zizek/in-the-grey-zone.

Talk of universality therefore slips easily from fact to fiction. Such is necessarily the case when one attempts to access that dimension of reality that cannot be symbolized. Here again, we find ourselves navigating the mystical terrain of submerged possibilities. While fantasy is often derided as a fool's fairy tale, as a whimsical deception that naturalizes oppression by papering up its cracks, it can also serve to bring attention to power's disavowed foundations. To quote Todd McGowan, "Fantasy creates an opening to the impossible."[68]

It is along these lines that one should approach the mythic specter haunting the filmic reenactments of the trial. *Conspiracy* and *Chicago 10* portray the trial in radically different ways. While one is a relatively straitlaced rendition, the other is a polemical cartoon. But despite their differences, something remains curiously unchanged between them. Both films mobilize fictional excess to depict Seale's struggle as an opening into a void, and it is by locating Seale in this chasm that his struggle becomes universal. Fiction, as it turns out, is not necessarily the hobgoblin of history, and sometimes the most faithful representations of history are those that delve most deeply into fiction.

Conspiracy's central antagonism is anticipated during the opening credits. The film begins with rolling footage of violence: a montage of jets, missiles, and napalm fire. Slowly, the camera pulls back, revealing these images to be newsreel footage playing on a television monitor in a storefront window. The trauma is thus domesticated, and absolute horror is transformed into an everyday object. This normalcy is shattered when marching antiwar demonstrators fill the street in front of the store. Their appearance serves to fold back the edges of the Symbolic, allowing us to catch a glimpse of the underlying trauma as the violence on the television monitor begins to spill into social reality. Suddenly, police officers appear and quickly descend upon the demonstrators with clubs. Whereas the demonstrators open up a void, the police act to close it.

This opening scene rehearses the film's main encounter with the Real. Even though it occurs less than halfway through the film, the confrontation between Seale (Carl Lumbly) and Judge Hoffman (David Opatoshu) is central. This scene is the film's emotional linchpin, and it is here that the presence of the Real becomes most prominent.

Forty minutes into *Conspiracy*, Seale is taken to be bound and gagged off-screen. Rather than following Seale, the camera fixates on a closed door. Like the television in the opening credits, the door is an ordinary object, but its ordinariness masks the presence of something extraordinary, an underlying antagonism. The camera then begins a complete 360-degree rotation. Lasting nearly a full minute, this single take curiously reveals the entire set: the lights, the cameras, and even the crew. All remain silent as they face the closed door. Thus, while we do not have direct access to the ongoing trauma, we witness it by means of distortions in the visual field. The camera reveals hitherto unseen spaces, demonstrating that social reality—in this case, the courtroom—is filled with mysterious gaps and hidden dimensions.

At last, the camera returns to where it started, the closed door. When it opens, the silence is broken as the marshals enter carrying Seale, who is now bound, gagged, and tied to a chair. The film pauses on Seale's struggling figure for a brief moment, cutting

---

68   Todd McGowan, *The Real Gaze: Film Theory after Lacan* (Albany: State University of New York Press, 2007), 23.

away to close-up shots of the mortified faces of the other defendants, their lawyers, and even the prosecuting attorney. As the marshals move to tighten the gags, the camera again leaves Seale, focusing on the drawings of a courtroom sketch artist. Once again, the trauma is revealed indirectly, through a mediated image, a fiction within a fiction. Appropriately, Seale's confrontation with the judge ends with a familiar sight. When Seale is taken from the court for the final time, we see the image that had been so important in *Vladimir et Rosa*—Seale's empty chair.

Chicago 10 does not share *Conspiracy*'s pretenses of historical authenticity. There are no talking heads, no spoken narration, and very little historical context. But what *Chicago 10* shares with its predecessor is the presence of an underlying antagonism. Both confront the spectator with an opening and a closing, with an eruption of a singularity and its violent repression. The film cuts between archival footage of the 1968 demonstrations and an animated version of the trial. While Seale is included in almost none of the footage culled from the archives, his struggle dominates the animated trial. Twenty minutes into *Chicago 10*, Seale (voiced by Jeffrey Wright) first requests the right to defend himself, and his conflict with Judge Hoffman (voiced by Roy Scheider) simmers for the film's remainder. The narration keeps coming back to it until Seale is finally gagged at the climax. Thus, while the footage from 1968 follows a day-by-day chronology, the trial is rearranged so as to achieve maximal dramatic impact.

Like *Conspiracy*, the film does not follow Seale when he is taken from the court. Whereas *Conspiracy* had dealt with this emptiness by revealing the hidden dimensions of the courtroom, *Chicago 10* deals with these gaps through editing cuts—a filmmaking technique that Paul Eisenstein and Todd McGowan contend to be the cinema's "most prominent manifestation of rupture."[69] The unseen trauma of Seale's gagging is revealed through footage of the 1968 protests. When Seale is taken from the court to have his gags tightened, there is a corresponding escalation in the conflict between the Chicago police and the demonstrators, and both narratives eventually explode in a crescendo of violence.

Upon *Chicago 10*'s debut, many veterans of the sixties voiced concern about its treatment of history. The author of a book about the 1968 protests criticized it for containing "no context. No connections. And no explanations."[70] Todd Gitlin claimed that the film "simplified the Chicago saga," arguing that "the events are hard to understand when you rip them out of their historical situation and cram them into melodrama."[71] And while original Chicago Eight defendant Tom Hayden praised the film for capturing the spirit of the era, he nevertheless warned that "there is a real danger in theatricalizing history."[72] By contesting theatricality, Hayden was being true to form. He had been the one of the defendants most strongly opposed to the

---

69 Eisenstein and McGowan, *Rupture*, 176.

70 David Farber, "The Art of Rebellion: Brett Morgen's Chicago Ten," *Sixties* 1, no. 2 (2008): 240.

71 Todd Gitlin, "Paraphrasing the '60s," *Los Angeles Times*, January 27, 2007, A21, http://articles.latimes.com/2007/jan/27/opinion/oe-gitlin27.

72 Liptak, "Recapturing the '60s," AR32.

theatricalization of the trial—a stance that provoked the ire of Abbie Hoffman, who later gave him the derisive moniker "Uncle Tom Hayden."[73]

Perhaps most remarkable, however, was the response of Bobby Seale. He criticized the film, complaining that "there are a lot of details that the animation just left out."[74] While *Chicago 10* may not remain faithful to the particularities of history, however, does not this criticism fail to account for singularity? What these commentators all seem to miss is *Chicago 10*'s chief accomplishment. The film links the struggles of the past to the problems of the present, positing that the cracks in power revealed in Judge Hoffman's courtroom still have contemporary relevance. In a 2008 interview, director Brett Morgen stated this intention quite openly. "I never thought I was making a film about 1968. I thought I was making a film about today and appropriating the iconography and the imagery from the sixties . . . to tell a story that was ultimately about the time I'm living in and about the war that I'm living through."[75] Morgen's efforts to connect the dots between the past and the present did not go completely unnoticed, and upon the film's release, one reviewer described the film as "an incendiary device to fan protest of the current war in Iraq."[76] By locating Seale's struggle in rupture, Morgen was able to identify its universality and to imbue Seale's act with a relevance penetrating beyond the barriers of time and space.

Just as *Conspiracy* and *Chicago 10* depict the opening and closing of ruptures, however, the films themselves are contradictory texts, and they occasionally threaten to undermine their own radicalism. *Conspiracy* director Jeremy Kagan claimed that he did not want his film to be a simple "re-creation of a historical event or a nostalgic exercise," but at times, his film is in danger of becoming exactly that.[77] By relying on interviews with the original defendants, *Conspiracy* risks creating a distance between the events of the trial and the present. This danger reaches its apogee during the end credits when the original defendants enter the courtroom and join their actor stand-ins. As the film ends, the camera pulls back, revealing that their image is on a television screen in a film studio. It is the same shot used in the opening credits, but if the earlier example had shattered the illusion that the trauma can be safely contained, the latter seems to suggest the opposite. There is no parade of protesters to compress the distance. Instead, order is restored as the events of the trial come to a neat conclusion. In this instance, historicization is accompanied by depoliticization.

If *Conspiracy* is in danger of closing up its radical encounter with the Real by placing it in the distant past, *Chicago 10* runs a different risk. It threatens to replace the traumatic singularity of Seale's struggle with white particularity. Indeed, the scenes in which Seale is gagged concentrate less on Seale's resistance than on the grandstanding rhetoric of Kunstler and the pointed barbs of the Yippies, a trait shared

73 Abbie Hoffman, *Soon to Be a Major Motion Picture* (New York: G. P. Putnam's Sons, 1980), 303.

74 In Tirdad Derakhshani, "It Was a Wild Time in the Windy City," *Philadelphia Inquirer*, August 26, 2008, D01, http://articles.philly.com/2008-08-26/news/25257390_1_infamous-chicago-seven-trial-brett-morgen-protests.

75 In "Political History Gets Animated in 'Chicago 10,'" *NPR*, February 26, 2008, http://www.npr.org/templates/story/story.php?storyId=37759288.

76 Carrie Rickey, "'Chicago 10' Lacks the Context of the Tumultuous Times," *Philadelphia Inquirer*, March 14, 2008, W08, http://articles.philly.com/2008-03-14/entertainment/25259493_1_protest-students-and-activists-brett-morgen.

77 Farber, "Film on Chicago 8 Includes Originals," C26.

with *Steal This Movie* and *The Chicago 8*. While a focus on the other defendants is not in and of itself problematic, it becomes so when Seale's struggle is hijacked and used as an opportunity to display white heroics—a tendency that recalls the troublesome legacy of civil rights dramas like *Mississippi Burning* (Alan Parker, 1988) and *Ghosts of Mississippi* (Rob Reiner, 1996).[78]

This shift to white redemption is also epitomized by posters for *Chicago 10* that features the bound and gagged face of an animated Abbie Hoffman. The best one can say about this substitution is that it testifies to the universal potential of Seale's struggle, but it does so at the cost of marginalizing Seale. One should contrast this whitewashed image with advertisements for Gillo Pontecorvo's *Burn!* (1969), which is emblazoned with the face of that film's anticolonialist hero (Evaristo Márquez)—a black slave–turned–peasant revolutionary—gagged with the Union Jack. Whereas posters for *Burn!* interpellates viewers from all backgrounds and asks them to identify with a black insurgent, posters for *Chicago 10* evacuate the gags of any racial content, bleaching Seale's struggle and grafting it onto a white face.

The portal into the Real is thus a tenuous one, forever in danger of slipping into its opposite. While *Conspiracy* and *Chicago 10* treat Seale's struggle as an eruption of a singularity, they also display opposing tendencies, healing the wounds they themselves inflict. The question of how one maintains fidelity to a radical act of resistance becomes even more pertinent as the dust begins to settle and the struggles of the past begin fading into memory.

From Revolution to Inclusion: *The Chicago 8*.

A political difference is always on the shore of its own disappearance: the people are always close to sinking into the sea of the population or of the race; the proletariat is always on the verge of being confused with workers defending their interests; the space of a people's public demonstration is always prone to being confused with the merchant's *agora* and so on.

—Jacques Rancière[79]

Oh, don't be so pessimistic. Our system isn't collapsing. Fellows as smart as you could do awfully well under this system.   —Judge Julius Hoffman[80]

With the passing of time, the memory of Seale's struggle seems to have largely evaporated. Unlike so many other figures from that era, Seale's image does not often appear on classroom bulletin boards, and his gagged face has never been featured on any commemorative stamp. It might therefore come as a surprise to learn that in

---

78   Jennifer Fuller, "Debating the Present through the Past: Representations of the Civil Rights Movement in the 1990s," in *The Civil Rights Movement in American Memory*, ed. Renee C. Romano and Leigh Raiford (Athens: University of Georgia Press, 2006), 167–196. See also the discussion in Lipsitz, *Possessive Investment in Whiteness*, 221–224.

79   Jacques Rancière, *Dissensus: On Politics and Aesthetics*, ed. and trans. Steven Corcoran (New York: Continuum, 2010), 39.

80   Clavir and Spitzer, *Conspiracy Trial*, 583.

recent years, the story of Seale's ordeal has been revived, appearing in several new films and even materializing in the midst of contemporary protest movements. For instance, when Woodstock veterans David Crosby and Graham Nash were asked to explain their support for Occupy Wall Street in late 2011, Nash answered by recounting the political events that had marked his own generation, including the chaining and gagging of Seale.[81]

Seale's struggle can thus be brandished as a political weapon. It constitutes what George Lipsitz terms "counter-memory"—a repressed artifact from the past that can be resurrected in the present and used to subvert dominant historical narratives. In Lipsitz's words, "Counter-memory forces revision of existing histories by supplying new perspectives about the past."[82] With counter-memory, it is hoped that voice can be restored to the seemingly voiceless and that those written out of history can be written back in.

Few endeavors are more noble than the task of bringing to the forefront those hidden historical relics that have hitherto been eviscerated from master narratives. Such acts of necromancy, however, can never be anything more than a first step. As Badiou writes apropos the Holocaust, "I do not doubt the necessity of remembering the extermination of the Jews . . . but I note that the neo-Nazi maniac harbors a collector's memory for the period he reveres, and that, remembering Nazi atrocities in minute detail, he relishes and wishes he could repeat them." For Badiou, then, "the problem is not one of memory but of truth."[83] To breathe new life into the forgotten struggles of the past does not guarantee how they are interpreted in the present—a fact confirmed by the widespread sterilization and sanitization in the US mainstream of such radical figures as MLK and Rosa Parks. Counter-memory does not always transform dominant culture. Perhaps even more frequently, dominant culture transforms counter-memory.

This danger of appropriation likewise hangs over Seale's struggle. Even when his gags were fresh, some blamed the victim, arguing that Seale had gotten exactly what he deserved.[84] This view has survived into the present, and when a defendant began speaking out during his April 2011 trial in Florida, a judge ordered his mouth taped shut. Asked to comment on the incident, a local law professor defended the decision by referring to the precedent set by the gagging of Seale.[85] Thus, resuscitating the memory of Seale's chains is not necessarily revolutionary, and it is worth noting that when Seale's contempt charges were eventually overturned, an appellate judge con-

---

81 "Legendary Folk Duo Crosby & Nash on Soundtracking Movements from the 1960s to Occupy Wall Street," *Democracy Now*, November 10, 2011, http://www.democracynow.org/2011/11/10/legendary_folk_duo_crosby_nash_on.

82 George Lipsitz, *Time Passages: Collective Memory and American Popular Culture* (Minneapolis: University of Minnesota Press, 1990), 213.

83 Alain Badiou, *Saint Paul: The Foundation of Universalism*, trans. Ray Brassier (Stanford, CA: Stanford University Press, 2003), 44; Badiou, *Communist Hypothesis*, 170.

84 See, for example, William F. Buckley Jr., "The Bobby Seale Show Had a Judicial Straight Man," *Los Angeles Times*, November 14, 1969, C7; Tony Fuller, "Panther Chief Bound, Gagged at Trial," *Washington Post*, October 30, 1969, A1, 6; "Shortcircuiting the Judicial Process," *Washington Post*, November 12, 1969, A22; and "The Strategy of Provocation," *Wall Street Journal*, November 11, 1969, 14.

85 Curtis Krueger, "In a Rare Move, Man's Mouth Taped in Court," *St. Petersburg Times*, April 14, 2011, 1B.

cluded the gag order to be an "authorized but drastic step."[86] The legality of Judge Hoffman's decision was not questioned. As Pnina Lahav attests, "the power to bind and gag an unruly defendant is indeed a part of the American justice system."[87]

Seale's resistance is thus forever in danger of slipping into its opposite—the Real into the Symbolic, a singularity into a particularity, counter-memory into just plain memory. Following the trial, such a fate appears to have befallen several of the defendants. Rennie Davis went from community organizer to venture capitalist, Tom Hayden from SDS radical to mainstream politician, and Jerry Rubin from Yippie to yuppie. So drastic was Rubin's metamorphosis that he was hesitant even to participate in the production of *Conspiracy*, fearing that fresh attention to his activist past might adversely affect his business investments.[88] Seale, too, seems to have undergone such a change. After his Black Panther days had come to an end, he appeared in advertisements for Ben and Jerry's ice cream and even authored a cookbook, *Barbeque'n with Bobby*.[89]

How, then, does one preserve the radicalness of Seale's stand and keep it from becoming a tool of the power structures it was meant to contest? How does one prevent a scene of emancipatory struggle from devolving into a set of localized grievances? How does one maintain fidelity to resistance across the distance of time and thereby keep the *counter* in counter-memory? For Jacques Rancière, these questions go to the very core of politics. Dispensing with the cliché that everything is political, Rancière argues that if everything is political, nothing is, and that, while no place is inherently political, any place can become political.[90] Accordingly, what most people call politics is, for Rancière, *the police*—a term that, in his parlance, signifies consensus. Police logic asserts that every part of the community has its own specific function and that there are no gaps. It hides conflict and obscures antagonism.

Whereas the police are involved in consensus, *politics* is a question of dissensus. It asserts what the police deny—that the natural order of the community is not natural at all and that there are holes and lapses that belie power's claims. Politics thus begins when an excluded part of the community—the part with no part—presupposes equality and identifies itself with the entirety of the community. It begins when a hole stands in for the whole.[91] Rancière's account of politics can therefore be compared to Badiou's singularity and Lacan's Real. While Badiou links politics to the emergence of a singularity, Lacanian theorist Todd McGowan claims that an "authentic political act has its origins in an encounter with the real."[92] The difference in terminology should not obscure a common basis in rupture, and, by presupposing equality in the midst of inequality, Seale was performing a properly political act.

86 Lahav, "Chicago Conspiracy Trial," 1336.

87 Ibid., 1333.

88 John J. O'Connor, "A Re-Creation of the Chicago 8 Trial," *New York Times*, May 19, 1987, C18, http://www.nytimes.com/1987/05/19/arts/tv-reviews-a-re-creation-of-the-chicago-8-trial.html.

89 Bobby Seale, *Barbeque'n with Bobby* (Berkeley, CA: Ten Speed, 1988).

90 Jacques Rancière, *Disagreement: Politics and Philosophy*, trans. Julie Rose (Minneapolis: University of Minnesota Press, 1999), 32, 41.

91 Ibid., 39.

92 Alain Badiou, *Metapolitics*, trans. Jason Barker (New York: Verso, 2005), 23; McGowan, *Real Gaze*, 17.

Counter-memory, then, is counterhegemonic precisely insofar as it disrupts the existing order and thereby remains political. Although counter-memory necessarily involves historical particularity, its radicalness derives from its attachment to singularity. The distinction between counter-memory and memory, between politics and the police, is thus a question of where one places the empty chair. Does one project it—as Clint Eastwood did—onto a stage to disavow it, or does one locate it at the heart of society itself? Thus, to neutralize Seale's struggle—to reimagine it as a story about the progressive march of the American dream, to treat it as a particular historical anecdote with little contemporary relevance, or to divorce it from history's "long fetch"— is to lose its radicalness and conform to the logic of the police. It is to depoliticize Seale's chains and divest them of their most important dimension. An identification with a point of negation must therefore be accompanied by a simultaneous *disidentification* with the Symbolic order. Otherwise, one succeeds not in overturning existing power structures but in expanding their reach. Césaire's slave ship does not crack but is merely made to hold more cargo.

It is with this view of counter-memory in mind that we can approach the most recent film portrayal of Seale's struggle, *The Chicago 8*. *The Chicago 8* is one of the most factually based depictions of the trial. It includes specific details that other versions gloss over (e.g., the fact that Seale was the only defendant to rise on the first day of the trial or the episode in which a jury member was relieved of duty after receiving a threatening letter allegedly sent by the BPP). Sometimes this attention to detail is quite commendable. For instance, *The Chicago 8* is the only version that includes Seale's muffled response to Kunstler after the latter rose to speak out against the gags: "You don't represent me. Sit down, Kunstler."[93]

But despite the film's apparent fidelity to history, it cannot escape fantasy completely. There are alterations to the trial chronology, and the film also offers ironic contrasts through parallel editing. For instance, to emphasize the severity of Seale's situation relative to his white codefendants who are out on bail, a scene of Seale (Orlando Jones) diligently studying law books in his prison cell is juxtaposed to images of the two Yippies engaged in frivolous sexual escapades. While other versions of the trial utilize fiction to draw attention to an underlying trauma, however, *The Chicago 8* deploys fantasy for a different purpose—not to point out the gaps in power but to fill them.

To be sure, traces of the void are still occasionally detectable. When Seale is first taken from the courtroom to be gagged, the film replicates the procedure of *Chicago 10*, cutting to footage of the 1968 police riot and thereby suggesting a subterranean depth to the violence. But such moments are fleeting, and while *The Chicago 8* cannot completely erase the rupture, it goes much further than *Conspiracy* or *Chicago 10* in closing it.

The film's primary method of depoliticizing the trial is humanization. It dilutes the underlying trauma by pathologizing it. Thus, while Seale is presented as a black leader struggling against racism, even more emphasis is placed on his role as a devoted husband and a loving father. His wife and young son come to the court to watch the proceedings. As Seale is led away from the courtroom, his son rushes to him, and

93 Clavir and Spitzer, *Conspiracy Trial*, 163.

they tearfully embrace. Seale's dramatic confrontation with Judge Hoffman (Philip Baker Hall) is presented as having more to do with his family's presence than any collective political struggle, and indeed, *The Chicago 8* provides even less context than *Chicago 10* regarding the Black Freedom Movement. In this way, Seale is defanged and domesticated. He is presented not as a singularity but as a father calling for integration, for an expansion of power rather than an overturning of it, for inclusion instead of revolution.

This depoliticization is even more pronounced in the film's treatment of Judge Hoffman. Lest it be forgotten, other versions of the trial like *Vladimir et Rosa* and *Chicago 10* had been concerned with the judge's symbolic role. Even in *Conspiracy*, the first glimpse offered of the judge focuses not on the man himself but on the portraits of the founding fathers behind him—pictures upon which footage of Chicago Mayor Richard Daley speaking at the 1968 convention is then superimposed. In this way, *Conspiracy* introduces Judge Hoffman by creatively linking him to a symbolic matrix of white, patriarchal authority. *Conspiracy* is not concerned with Julius Hoffman the individual but with Judge Hoffman the representative of power. Whether he was pleasant or wretched in his personal life is not as important as his symbolic authority. As Žižek writes, "A judge . . . may be a miserable and corrupt person, but the moment he puts on his robe and other insignia, his words are the words of Law itself."[94]

The Chicago 8, by contrast, shows us a different side of Hoffman, Julius instead of the judge. Twice, he is presented out of his robes and away from the bench. The first time, he is up late at night in his home, reading headlines about the trial. Clearly frustrated with the news coverage, he tells his wife that he believes the defendants are purposefully trying to make him look like a bigot. Later, he is in his office, talking to his secretary about the ongoing war in Vietnam. He tells her that the dying US soldiers are the real patriots—them and not the eight defendants. In these scenes, Hoffman is revealed to be a fragile old man, and while his views are clearly out of touch with the times, he harbors no malice. He is humanized as a well-meaning if misguided individual, and his harsh actions in the court can be reinterpreted as a result of simple miscommunication.

The Chicago 8 thus presents social reality as a neutral zone. Conflict stems not from the normal operations of power but from the idiosyncratic actions of individuals. Seale's struggle no longer represents a constitutive rupture but an incidental one. With its radicalness erased and its political significance diminished, Seale's stand is transformed into nothing more than an unfortunate hurdle in the long march of American progress. Such a conservative view of history has been openly stated by Pinchas Perry, the film's Israeli director. In an interview, he claimed that the trial demonstrates the greatness of the American system: "In spite of all the critics . . . it's only in America that such a trial [can] take place in front of a jury and a judge, and the press is free. You won't have such a trial in China, Russia, or some other places in the world. So . . . if the system's even not perfect here, it's the best we have and everything is in the

---

94 Slavoj Žižek, *The Plague of Fantasies*, 2nd ed. (New York: Verso, 2008), 80.

open."[95] The memory of Seale's chains can thus be resurrected not to disturb existing power structures but to perpetuate them, not to condemn them but to glorify them. To recall the words of Badiou, the problem here is not memory but truth. If dominant historical narratives of the 1960s have typically divided that decade into two opposing camps—a good 1960s versus a bad 1960s, a peaceful civil rights movement versus a militant Black Power, a romanticized MLK versus a demonized Malcolm X—*The Chicago 8* deals with Seale's saga by incorporating it into the former. Seale is rechristened as an integrationist and reclaimed as part of the "good" 1960s. His baptism into the canon of American history is marked by the film's grossly overstated finale in which black and white spectators in Judge Hoffman's courtroom join hands and sing that old civil rights anthem, "We Shall Overcome."

Seale's struggle is thus assimilated. His scandalous presupposition of equality against the court's inequality is turned into an apology for power. Counter-memory slips into memory, politics into the police. In this way, the film covers up the void and sews up the rip in the fabric of the Symbolic. In *The Chicago 8*, Bobby Seale is no longer Prometheus. Bobby Seale is just Bobby Seale. No longer rooted in the Real, his audacious act of resistance loses its disruptive potential and finally becomes "doomed to perpetual defeat." ✳

95 Pinchas Perry, interviewed in "The Making of: *The Chicago 8*," *The Chicago 8*, directed by Pinchas Perry (Warren, NJ: Passion River, 2013), DVD.

Projections of Diasporic Sensibilities through Travel: Wong Kar Wai in/and *My Blueberry Nights*

by Yi Wei Chew

Abstract: This article argues for *My Blueberry Nights* as a projection of Wong Kar Wai's diasporic sensibilities through the trope of travel. How does the film expand and problematize classical notions of diaspora within the discourse of transnational Chinese cinemas? As such, how does it expand the notion of Chinese diasporas within the context and constraints of transnational Chinese cinemas? How does it complicate the already intricate and tangled ideas of movement, stasis, and home? We can only hope to profitably answer these questions by understanding, first of all, the diachronic, multifaceted, and multispatial nature of travel.

> It is possible that this has everything to do with my transplant from Shanghai to Hong Kong at the age of 5. . . . For some time, I was totally alienated and it was like the biggest nightmare of my life. It might not be conscious, but certainly I have an intense feeling for geographical upheavals.   —Wong Kar Wai, quoted in "City Film Industry"[1]

My *Blueberry Nights* (2007) is arguably the most peculiar Wong Kar Wai film to date. Little, however, has been written about this film as compared to those that were released before it; for some reason, scholars have not given the film the critical attention it deserves.[2] Nonetheless, this article hopes to shed new light on this significantly underrated film by discussing its potential in contributing to the study of transnational Chinese cinemas by understanding it through the lens of diaspora.

1 Barbara Mennel, "City Film Industry: Hong Kong," in *Cities and Cinema* (Abingdon, UK: Routledge, 2008), 83–102.

2 See Lim Song Hwee, "Transnational Trajectories in Contemporary East Asian Cinemas," in *East Asian Cinemas: Regional Flows and Global Transformations*, ed. Vivian P. Y. Lee (Basingstoke, UK: Palgrave Macmillan, 2011), 19; Kenneth Chan, "Visualizing Hong Kong: Diasporic Cinematic Gaze on the 1997 Handover," in *Remade in Hollywood: The Global Chinese Presence in Transnational Cinemas* (Hong Kong: Hong Kong University Press, 2009), 36.

Yi Wei Chew has just completed her PhD at the National University of Singapore. Her thesis focuses on diasporic and transnational Chinese cinema.

© 2015 by the University of Texas Press

Before we do that, however, it is important to discuss Wong's directorial ethos. Wong Kar Wai is a director with a distinctly sharp sense of play, protraction, and creation. Anyone with more than a perfunctory knowledge of Wong's films can say at once that his films never speak or stand alone; instead they constantly allude to of each other. Following this logic, we can refer to the maverick director's films as a choppy continuation, a cacophony of "multi-logues" (as opposed to dialogues)—an oblique, slippery series. Ackbar Abbas states, "Every film then is a fragment, incomplete in itself; a return to a site whose features have been glimpsed before, but only partially."[3]

That Abbas posits a "return" to a previous filmic site, or filmic sites, is significant for the understanding and unfolding of this article. What makes *My Blueberry Nights* so loaded and sophisticated is its connection, remote or palpable, to Wong's older films, and this fact alone is significant when subjecting it to close textual analysis. With this knowledge, it would then be logical to describe Wong's particular obsessions. Stephen Teo, for example, has crowned Wong Kar Wai as the "Auteur of Time,"[4] and rightly so, as all of Wong's films deal with temporal abstractions, urgencies, and anxieties. Recalling Abbas, who ingeniously invokes the metaphor of space with his use of the word *site* as a double entendre to describe the cinematic sites and/or sights of Wong's films (i.e., Wong's choice of location when shooting and his manipulation of diegetic space), as well as the film medium as a kind of extradiegetic site, a space for analysis, the director as such is not only an auteur of time but an architect of space. Spatiotemporal relations and dynamics are thus key concerns in any and every Wong Kar Wai film. If his individual films make up one long and incomplete film, then *My Blueberry Nights* is but the ellipsis at the end of an unfinished sentence.

Second, as the epigraph to this article reminds us, Wong is also a director with an unmistakable consciousness of himself as a diasporic individual. The use of the word *transplant* is painfully significant. Because Wong considers his move from Shanghai to Hong Kong a kind of transplantation, it can then by extension result in not just replacement but also a violent displacement and hence transformation to adapt, assimilate, and suit the new body, the *terra nova*. Because of the passing of time and Wong's association with Hong Kong today, we can fairly consider Wong a Hong Kong citizen; nevertheless, we must not dismiss what had happened before the fact of his move:

> Wong has spoken of feeling isolated as a Shanghainese child living in Cantonese-speaking Hong Kong, and it may be said that this perception has translated into his status as a maverick film-maker in the Hong Kong film industry. On the other hand, like most mainland migrants who grew up in

---

3 Ackbar Abbas, "The Erotics of Disappointment," in *Wong Kar Wai*, ed. Jean-Marc Lalanne, David Martinez, and Ackbar Abbas (Paris: Dis Voir, 1997), 39–40.

4 Auteur theory is of course given to much controversy and provocation in film scholarship. But I grant a place of privilege to the director of any given film. Having said this, I do not discount the efforts by the rest of the creative team, but the director as the one who establishes the film's vision should not be undervalued. There is a reason film journals like the aforementioned *Journal of Chinese Cinemas* (the cited issue being one that focuses solely on Tsai Ming Liang) as well as reputable conferences like the Asian Cinema Studies Society's Conference 2012 still devote entire issues and panels to individual directors, with the 2011 issue of *Journal of Chinese Cinemas* focusing on Tsai Ming Liang and the ACSS conference devoting a panel to Zhang Yimou. This phenomenon is all the more pertinent in the discourse of diasporic filmmaking in transnational Chinese cinema because the diasporic sentiments of each of these directors do somehow figure into their films, be they pronounced or not.

Hong Kong, Wong has integrated into Hong Kong Cantonese society, and his films also reflect this condition.[5]

At the same time, however, we must not fail to mention Wong's dilemma about the Shanghainese or, by implication, the Chinese roots that conspicuously belie his identity and films. To complicate matters, he is deliberately known by his Cantonese name Wong Kar Wai, rather than the Chinese Hanyu Pinyin Wang Jia Wei—with the former now a global brand of repute.[6] Stephen Teo then asks, "How do we [in this vein] understand Wong as a Hong Kong film-maker? How do we reconcile Wong's global standing with his local roots?"[7] Autobiographically, therefore, Wong is by no means a creature of uncomplicated identity; he is in every sense a collection of contradictions as well as a constant metamorphosis of being: "The name of Wong Kar Wai, taken in itself, is like a riddle wrapped in an enigma."[8] An admixture of alienation, assimilation, foreignness, and familiarity still lingers, and this is only too apparent in all his films. *My Blueberry Nights* together with Wong's earlier works reflect this predicament and, as such, reveal a deep concern with what it means to be a diasporic Chinese. More precisely, they are Wong's way of engaging with his own diasporic identity vis-à-vis his characters and their cinematic universes. By this token, then, the films are in themselves cultural and social practices—through their production characteristics and thematic concerns—that mirror Wong's identity as "Hong Kong–Chinese."[9] He is a member of one of the many kinds of Chinese diasporas, a diaspora that could well be prefixed, prefaced, and pronounced first with a code that resonates with nationality and then with a secondary inflection of ethnicity. The label "Hong Kong–Chinese" undoubtedly drips with traction and controversy, especially when we talk about Wong Kar Wai as a diasporic Chinese within a transnational context. This is additionally entangled with Wong's seemingly umbilical remembrance of himself as Shanghainese, uprooted from one port city to another.

Wong's quandary is itself amplified in light of recent events, making this issue not just one that is germane to him but also one that ossifies the reality of what it means to be a Mainlander and a Hong Konger today. An incident of topical interest that transpired between Mainland tourists and Hong Kong locals on the territory's Mass Transit Railway highlights the increasing tension between the two groups. A Hong Konger reprehended a group of Mainland tourists for eating a pack of instant noodles on the train and was shockingly met not with an apology but with irreverent mockery for his inadequate Mandarin. Hong Kongers themselves have expressed little tolerance for and identification with their Chinese compatriots and refer to them disparagingly as "locusts," insects that invade and destroy crops: by inference, people who infiltrate their land, driving up property prices, tainting and unethically selling milk powder unfit for consumption, and poisoning Hong Kong society with their bad habits and self-serving

---

5 Stephen Teo, *Wong Kar Wai: Auteur of Time* (London: British Film Institute, 2005), 5.

6 Ibid., 1.

7 Ibid.

8 Ibid.

9 Ibid.

attitudes.[10] Mainland Chinese, in contrast, deride the Hong Kongers for their inferior Mandarin and accuse them of being jealous of Mainlander affluence. Professor Kong Qing Dong, a Peking University academic known to be a vocal, trenchant critic of Hong Kong, unabashedly and with much chutzpah labels Hong Kongers as "'dogs trained by colonialists,' 'worshippers of the West,' and 'bastards.'"[11] These are but a few such examples that characterize the mutual resentment both have toward each other; more cuttingly, it bespeaks an almost unbridgeable transnational cultural divide. To back this with numbers, a recent poll found that only 16.6 percent of Hong Kongers see themselves as Chinese citizens first, compared with more than 38 percent three years ago. Instead, more and more consider themselves to be Hong Kong citizens or Hong Kong Chinese."[12]

Hong Kong, therefore, finds itself in a remarkably ambiguous and ambivalent position. While it grudgingly recognizes that it is a part of China, it also remains a distinct national entity, with a history, geography, and culture of its own. It would therefore not be a stretch, under such circumstances, to classify Hong Kong as a (kind of) Chinese diaspora in spite of its being part of China. The familiar principle of "one country, two systems" indubitably goes beyond the territory's economic and political autonomy from China. Truly, the parsing of the numerical "one" betokens a fabric that is more fragmented than fused, more combative than complementary, and certainly more complex than clear cut. What lies between China and Hong Kong, then, is a diaspora—a (former) colony-nation of Chinese people with a varying historical trajectory; a child, once given away, now reluctantly found but still separated from its parent by the Shenzhen River. With this logic, we can then understand diaspora to be a condition that happens on both geographical (spatial) and historical (temporal) planes; it is a processional phenomenon that changes with place, space, and time.

In an interview with Song Hwee Lim and Wai Siam Hee in a recent issue of *Journal of Chinese Cinemas*, Tsai Ming Liang had this to say: "You must believe that there is an author behind every film, and you are here today precisely to watch the film of this author."[13] Such a statement, no doubt controversial, confirms plainly that the concept of the author or auteur is very much alive. Applying this to Wong Kar Wai, we can reasonably assert that reading Wong both "auteur-biographically" and autobiographically is perhaps one of the most substantive ways we can understand his films in their entirety. Auteur-biographically, his position as a famed international art-house director should not be taken for granted, as this very signature is crucial in influencing the way he negotiates with his identity, or indeed identities—his autobiography, as it were. On the same note, however, we must be circumspect in relegating Wong's characters to being mere functional mouthpieces; they are instead always in dialogue with him despite his auteur-biographical and autobiographical investment in his films.

10 Cheong Ching, "Growing Colder towards the Motherland," *Straits Times*, February 4, 2012, A34.

11 Ibid.

12 Ibid.

13 Tsai Ming Liang, interview by Lim Song Hwee and Hee Wai Siam, "'You must believe there is an author behind every film': An Interview with Tsai Ming-liang," *Journal of Chinese Cinemas* 5, no. 2 (2010): 181–191.

One of the most palpable ways Wong annexes his auteur-biographical and autobiographical concerns, like those of the Hong Kong new wave, exists in tandem with the territory's history and politics.[14] Vivian P. Y. Lee posits: "The New Wave films [used] Western cinematic techniques and narrative strategies to address local issues and subject matter; New Wave films . . . became an important arena for the articulation of a local subjectivity in times of social change and political uncertainties."[15] A specific and recurrent example is the constant fixation on Hong Kong's very eventful timeline—its historical trajectory, with 1997 as a milestone year and event, both politically and cinematically. To illustrate my point, we could usefully recall some of Wong's older films: if we could, in brief, read *In the Mood for Love* (2000) as being intransigently fixated on and located in Hong Kong's past, and *2046* (2004) as projecting a grave uncertainty in and about Hong Kong's future (i.e., a future marked by the past, by memory), then *My Blueberry Nights* sits, debatably, somewhere between the two.[16] Indeed, the latter film shares with the initial two a curious obsession with time and temporality as well as space and spatiality by moving along the 1997 route, despite all three films being made post-1997. We can almost track the attitude and ethos toward time and space as *In the Mood for Love* progresses to *My Blueberry Nights*—a temporal movement analogous to Hong Kong's moving further away from the pivotal and indelible nexus of June 1997.

What other Wong film reminds us of *My Blueberry Nights*? Here, we must refer again to Abbas's observation on the relationality of Wong's films. *Happy Together* (1997) is arguably more intimately related to *My Blueberry Nights* than *In the Mood for Love* and *2046* are. This is so for a few reasons. First, *Happy Together*, like *My Blueberry Nights*, is the only other film to be shot fully on location in places—Buenos Aires and Taiwan— outside of Hong Kong and China. In the earlier film, the pair of traveling lovers, Lai Yiu-Fai (Tony Leung) and Ho Po-wing (Leslie Cheung), leave Hong Kong for Buenos Aires. Wong himself reveals his intentions in making *Happy Together*. He, much like his protagonists Lai and Ho, wanted to leave Hong Kong to "escape reality."[17] Second, and more significant, Wong admits that Hong Kong's historical destiny—the question of Hong Kong's handover to China on July 1, 1997—plagued him continually, so much so that he eventually got "sick of the constant questions about [it]" (the handover).[18] Yet his aversion to the impending date of Hong Kong's return to the Mainland was not to last, as the further he traveled away from Hong Kong, the more the city figured in his immediate directorial and cinematic concerns. In his own words, Wong opines that the "more [I] wanted to escape, the more [I] became inseparable from Hong Kong. No matter where [I] went, Hong Kong was always with [me]."[19] The need to get away, the craving for distance qua travel, is therefore inevitably tied to the almost visceral

---

14 See Teo, *Wong Kar Wai*, 135.

15 Vivian P. Y. Lee, "The Hong Kong New Wave: A Critical Reappraisal," in *The Chinese Cinema Book*, ed. Lim Song Hwee and Julian Ward (London: Palgrave Macmillan, 2011), 131–140.

16 Wong Kar Wai, interview by Mighty Ganesha, *Filmstarr Celebrity Interviews*, April 1, 2008, http://www.thedivareview .com/My_Blueberry_Nights_Wong_Kar-Wai_Interview.html.

17 Stephen Teo, "Wong's Buenos Aires Affair: Happy Together," in *Wong Kar Wai: Auteur of Time* (London: British Film Institute, 2005), 98–113.

18 Ibid.

19 Ibid.

need to look back to Hong Kong; the greater distance from Hong Kong, the greater difference in time zones, the greater extent of time spent away from the colony serve only to compound and exacerbate Wong's separation anxiety—indeed, he remains inseparably and umbilically attached to the city. In *Happy Together*, the lovers leave Hong Kong to start their broken and destructive relationship afresh—to "start over" as it were—but they end up in a vicious cycle of patching up and breaking up, only to be permanently separated in the end. The preponderance of failure, heartache, pessimism, and loss are characteristic of Wong's films, and this motif is suggestive of the edginess Wong feels toward Hong Kong's return to China: Would the relationship between Hong Kong and China be epitomized by this already anticipated sense of loss (of real autonomy on Hong Kong's part, of Hong Kong's already fraught sense of identity as an ex–British colony to yet another dramatic negotiation with what it means to be a territory under Chinese rule)? Would this new, post-1997 relationship also signify a pessimism and insecurity about Hong Kong's future? That Wong has to make a detour traveling from Hong Kong to Buenos Aires, then back to Taipei, in *Happy Together* without actually returning to Hong Kong underscores travel as a kind of postponement of return as well as an apprehensive transition to an inevitable historical deadline and destiny. The fact that the lovers never find any sort of belonging or happiness (as the titular *Happy Together* ironically intimates) in a faraway land shows too that travel is but a temporary getaway, not a solution to the potential problems that a post-1997 Hong Kong might be subject to. On another level, the unhappy and exiled state of the lovers may reflect Wong's permanent state of geographical upheaval, as is stated in the epigraph to this article: his constant feeling of being an outsider in a foreign place. His being Shanghainese in Hong Kong remains indelibly a part of his identity; this renders him, ipso facto, the perennial outsider in a place that has become his putative home. It is this diasporic complex, this assembly of contradictory feelings of alienation, assimilation, foreignness, and familiarity that has also come to make up his autobiography, hence governing his cinematic universe.

Ten years on, in 2007, *My Blueberry Nights* leaves the imagined futuristic Hong Kong of *2046*, as seen from the animation that dominates the end of the film, for various cities in America, New York in particular. The film recalls Wong's auteur-biographical sojourn in Buenos Aires in 1997 and travels once again from Hong Kong to the other side of the world. The deterritorialization and transnationalism that the idea of travel elicits in these films show Wong to be a mobile, traveling subject, both autobiographically and auteur-biographically. Indeed, his cinematic oeuvre and his life represent one long arc of travel(ing): the search for a sense of belonging in Hong Kong and the world, as well as the questioning of what home really means. Traveling as such, for Wong, is a complex amalgam of discovery, mobility, empowerment, dislocation, and insecurity. In significant ways, Wong's travels mirror his diasporic identity as a Shanghainese who has moved from Shanghai to Hong Kong, and now as a Hong Konger who has politically returned, as it were, to China, post-1997. Wong's autobiographical and auteur-biographical life seep into each other with his traveling from Shanghai to Hong Kong to Argentina to New York, and now, after *The Grandmaster*, to China and finally back to Hong Kong again—this route emblematizing his transnationalism as a director and his diasporic identity as a well-heeled, highly mobile Hong Kong Chinese. Wong Kar Wai and Hong Kong are still very much engaged with the impact of 1997, and this fixation characterizes Wong and Hong Kong as a diasporic individual and diasporic community, respectively. The ability to travel is but symbolic of the kind of Chinese diaspora Wong belongs to, one whose restless search for home is born out of his ability to travel and his persistent feeling of dislocation which ironically provides him the opportunity to question what home means to him.

The themes of travel and hence encounters with foreign cultures so prominent in *My Blueberry Nights* are similarly pronounced in *Happy Together*, which is touted as Wong's most political film to date.[20] This point segues nicely into the next: first, travel elicits notions of space as well as time, and the two conditions are core points of interest in both films, despite Wong's different treatments of the subject matter. Second, travel exists in a zone of slippage between the global and the local; one's *objectif*—one's lens or perception, in other words—cannot but be multifariously colored before, during, and after the journey. This article does not in any way seek to undertake a close analysis of the above-mentioned films, except *My Blueberry Nights*. However—in the parlance of Abbas, through whose work I have established that all of Wong's films are fragments of each other—they serve as useful juxtapositions when thinking about Wong's handling of travel, space, and time.

As international travel inevitably proffers a meeting with other cultures, we need to ask ourselves just how 1997, time, space, and travel are deeply intertwined with and connected to Wong's diasporic sensibilities. Clearly, all the films mentioned earlier deal in one way or another with the political status of Hong Kong via the route of its history. Routes are marked by travel and travel by both time and space. In addition, routes also speak of movement and motion, with the beginning and end of any given journey being at best elusive possibilities and at worst unknowable aporias. Hong Kong's history is a fluid conflation of past, present, and future; it is spatialized and dimensionalized. History cannot exist except in time and space. The foregoing films therefore display a fraught anxiety with Hong Kong's future through their intense preoccupation with the past. While the nervousness manifests temporally, it is also reflected and refracted spatially. Through travel, space is scattered, place is deterritorialized, and as a result filmic narratives are as well; Wong therefore uses spatial flux and difference to tell the story of Hong Kong, both within the territory itself and outside of it.

Travel can be, though not necessarily always is, a transnational condition, and the kind of Chinese diaspora Wong belongs to is a transnational, mobile, and well-traveled one. Clearly, the concepts of travel, transnationalism, and diaspora are imbricated with one another, despite their rather tenuous differences. As an auteur whose works are given to cross-border production and distribution, Wong's identity and cinematic opus are indisputably transnational. Yet his works do not simply remain at the superficial production-driven level of transnational funding. Wong moves in toward the level of the national while negotiating the "trans": traveling can certainly mean moving beyond the borders of one's country, as Wong's forays into Argentina and the United States

---

20   Allan Cameron, "Trajectories of Identification: Travel and Global Culture in the Films of Wong Kar-wai," *Jump Cut: A Review of Contemporary Media* 49 (2007), http://www.ejumpcut.org/archive/jc49.2007/wongKarWai/text.html.

prove. Yet the level of the national is tackled specifically when we think about Wong's autobiographical identity as a diasporic individual dealing with Hong Kong's identity, first as a British colony (pre-1997) and then as the Special Administrative Region at once under the political sovereignty of China yet holding the dubious and ambiguous status of an autonomous region. Indeed, the word *Special* is but a euphemism for the complex definition of *autonomous*—Hong Kongers' dicey form of self-governance and national identity as Chinese citizens, or indeed as post-1997 Hong Kong citizens, and finally as citizens of a global metropolis (perhaps a post-post-1997?). Wong travels out of Hong Kong so that he can discuss cinematically what it means to be in Hong Kong; he transcends Hong Kong's national and geographical borders so that he is able to engage with what is within those very same borders. Travel is a tool of exploration and negotiation between the transnational and the national. It is also between the borders of the transnational and the national that Wong's diasporic identity resides. As a diasporic Chinese who left China for Hong Kong, Wong has literally traveled from an old home to a newer one. However, 1997 saw the political return of Hong Kong to her "rightful home" in China, and this historical (de)tour de force pushes Wong to question whether he has in a way been compelled to return home to China as well—hence his very confused and complicated diasporic Chinese identity, and his constant querying of what home really means for diasporic Chinese individuals like himself.

My Blueberry Nights reflects on the nuanced yet rich differences between travel, the transnational, and diaspora. It conflates Wong's autobiographical diasporic Chinese identity and his auteur-biographical transnational identity by taking a trip out of Hong Kong ten years after 1997 and *Happy Together*. No previous research has discussed this film at length or from the perspective of the transnational, using diaspora as a theoretical framework. This article therefore contributes immensely to the way we approach Wong's films and offers wider notions of what home can mean to different Chinese diasporas. Thus, in light of all that has been discussed already, I argue for *My Blueberry Nights* as a projection of Wong's diasporic sensibilities through the trope of travel. Travel is the apparatus used in the film to underscore his predilection for diasporic concerns and his profoundly strong sense of diasporic sensibilities. How indeed does the film expand and problematize classical notions of diaspora within the discourse of transnational Chinese cinemas? As such, how does it expand the notion of Chinese diasporas within the context and constraints of transnational Chinese cinemas? How does it complicate the already intricate and entangled ideas of movement, stasis, and home? How does Wong's transnational proclivity as a director affect his diasporic identity as a person who left China for Hong Kong, only to be forcibly sent back by the returning tides of history? We can only hope to profitably answer these glaring questions by understanding, first of all, the diachronic, multifaceted, and multispatial nature of travel.

Round Trip / Multiple Destinations? Hong Kong–New York / New York-Beyond / New York–Hong Kong? When purchasing a plane ticket, the choice of destination and mode of flying reveals the travel considerations of any individual—whether making a round trip (which suggests a return to the destination one departed from, home or otherwise) or going to and ending up in places one did not set out from, again home or otherwise. The point here, however, is to think about diasporas in terms of travel and place(s): how indeed is the *moving* from one place to another—the journey—and the *landing*—the destination(s)—homologous to diasporas? More precisely, how does *My Blueberry Nights* perform and project Wong's diasporic sensibilities, his diaspora in terms of the (traveling) journey, the traveler, and the destination(s)? Does he end up complicating and educing greater and more important questions about what it means to be a Hong Kong–Chinese auteur-director who was born on the Mainland but bred in the Special Administrative Region (SAR)?

Although it is indeed tempting to launch into an excursus regarding the above questions on travel and diasporas in *My Blueberry Nights*, it also pays to exercise some conceptual caution lest the argument veer out of control. Avtar Brah notes incisively, "Diasporas are not synonymous with casual travel. . . . [D]iasporas emerge out of migrations of collectivities, whether or not members of the collectivity travel as individuals, as households, or in various other combinations."[21] Similarly, other theorists, like Jana Evans Braziel and Anita Mannur, probe the limits of diasporas by asking, not delineating, "how . . . odyssey, sojourn, and travel differ from migration, diaspora and exile."[22] Song Hwee Lim also identifies the tenuous boundary between the two with his question, "How long does it take for a traveler to become diasporic?"[23] Our responsibility is not to provide an answer to these very pertinent questions; what is paramount instead is to query why such issues are relevant, why such questions are being asked in the first place, and why an issue is being made about the imbrications between travel and diaspora. What further ideas can we hope to achieve with this continual dialogue involving both notions within the discourse of transnational Chinese cinemas qua *My Blueberry Nights*? How does the film, in its engaging with travel and diasporas, expand and enrich our understanding of both concepts? My contention therefore is that travel cannot simply be identified with diaspora; travel as a lived experience of diasporic subjects nevertheless presents a very constructive, innovative trope and tool in helping us appreciate the disjunctures and dissonances in diasporic identities, the uneasy coexistence of territory and deterritorialization, and most of all, diasporas as ongoing movements—as "new points of becoming."[24]

The peculiar thing about travel in *My Blueberry Nights* is that it at once assumes seemingly polarizing ideas of home(s), places of belonging, the journey, the return, the finding and/or losing of one's direction, the tyranny and the liberation of distance, stops and starts, motion and stasis, fluxes and fixities. Yet upon deeper scrutiny, we find these ideas to be engaged in dialogue rather than locked in dichotomy. Wong, through dialogue with his characters, uses several associations to do with travel that his diasporic sensibilities can be colorfully projected onto. First, and most important, it is the relational dynamics of Hong Kong and New York that form the core of Wong's

21 Avtar Brah, "The Homing of Diaspora, the Diasporizing of Home," in *Cartographies of Diaspora: Contesting Identities* (Abingdon, UK: Routledge, 1996), 190–195.

22 Jana Evans Braziel and Anita Mannur, "Nation, Migration, Globalization: Points of Contention in Diaspora Studies," in *Theorizing Diaspora*, ed. Jana Evans Braziel and Anita Mannur (Malden, MA: Blackwell, 2003), 1–22.

23 Song Hwee Lim, "Travelling Sexualities: Wong Kar Wai's *Happy Together*," in *Celluloid Comrades: Representations of Male Homosexuality In Contemporary Chinese Cinemas* (Honolulu: University of Hawai'i Press, 2006), 99–125.

24 Braziel and Mannur, "Nation, Migration, Globalization," 3.

travel, through the character of Elizabeth (Norah Jones). This brings to mind the import of the city as a cognate of travel in the film. Do the characters find home in the city? Where is home, or for that matter, does home even exist? Second, Wong includes the all-too-familiar act of journaling during the process of travel through Elizabeth. Why is there a need to detail our days when we travel, and how is this reflective of Wong's diasporic consciousness? Third, and as a corollary to the previous point, how is the narrative structure of the film, together with its visual metaphor, also paradigmatic of the way diasporic space and diasporic time can plausibly be perceived? Last, and by way of concluding, encapsulating the discussion would be Wong's cinematic sojourn toward Hollywood: What indeed does this quintessential transnational enterprise tell us about his diasporic identity? How is the diegetic world of *My Blueberry Nights* semiotically intertwined with Wong's filmmaking practices, and what does this say about his diasporic position? These issues do not of course exist in isolation; we must instead discuss them as a synthesis of relations so that a fuller understanding—of Wong's projection of his diasporic sensibilities through travel—can be realized.

The City. In 2008, a special report in *Time* commented on

> the extent to which New York City, London, and Hong Kong, three cities linked by a shared economic culture, have come to be both examples and explanations of globalization. Connected by long-haul jets and fiber-optic cable, and spaced neatly around the globe, the three cities have (by accident— nobody planned this) created a financial network that has been able to lubricate the global economy, and, critically, ease the entry into the modern world of China, the giant child of our century. Understand this network of cities—Nylonkong, we call it—and you understand our time.[25]

Later, the article goes on to herald them as a single "interconnected tripartite city [that] greases the wheels of trade and development."[26] The clunky coinage of New York, London, and Hong Kong as "Nylonkong" notwithstanding, it is beyond doubt that the latter, despite being the only Asian city in the triptych, is dynamically a member of the holy trinity of globalization. Leung Ping Kwan's historical observation that Hong Kong has always had an "unconditional identification with the West" further reinforces the contemporary bearing of the *Time* article.[27] With foreign influence being extremely strong in the 1960s, what with the popularity of Western movies, TV series, music, books, and magazines, it is thus of little surprise that local (Hong Kong) culture was inexorably shaped by these external influences.[28] Gina Marchetti calcifies Leung's point: "Hong Kong is a city of immigrants and the children of immigrants,

25 Michael Elliot, "A Tale of Three Cities," *Time*, January 17, 2008, http://www.time.com/time/magazine/article /0,9171,1704398,00.html.

26 Ibid.

27 Leung Ping Kwan, "Urban Cinema and the Cultural Identity of Hong Kong," in *The Cinema of Hong Kong: History, Arts, Identity*, ed. Poshek Fu and David Desser (Cambridge: Cambridge University Press, 2000), 227–251.

28 Ibid., 233.

people with multiple passports and global connections."[29] In Marchetti's terms, it seems reasonable to suggest that Hong Kong is a place that is generationally, globally, and genetically predisposed to centrifugal forces, plural identities, and invisible conduits linking it to the rest of the world; the metonymical and material possession of "multiple passports" grants Hong Kongers access to an excess of travel and mobility. That Hong Kong is located in such an enviable geographical position as a city surrounded by a natural harbor reinforces this idea. The porosity of Hong Kong's borders was, of course, fueled by its being a British colony: In contrast to China before Deng Xiaoping implemented the open-door policy post-1978, the West has long been a big part of Hong Kong's global relations and cultural identity.

In relation to *My Blueberry Nights*, then, it is not difficult to understand the connections between Hong Kong and New York and, in turn, between Hong Kong and the West and Hong Kong and the world. The Asian port city as such shares the global allure, cultural vibrancy, and economic stature of New York. Under such auspices, we cannot but mention that the film begins in New York. How is this related to Hong Kong and why should it, for that matter, have any relevance to the Special Administrative Region? We must first understand the world of the film before the wider implications of this question can be adequately dealt with.

Jeremy (Jude Law), a charming, good-natured marathoner from Manchester, England, hangs up his running shoes and ends up operating a café in the Big Apple, to ground himself to put a stop to all that motion. Enter Elizabeth, a nubile and angst-ridden young woman who has just experienced a failed relationship. She steps into the cafe and strikes up a conversation with Jeremy. A friendship ensues and before long, Elizabeth decides to go on a trip across America to "find herself," as it were. During her journey, Elizabeth becomes embroiled in a string of events; she updates Jeremy as the two of them correspond. Eventually, Elizabeth returns to New York, and the two somehow, as the film seems to intimate, take their relationship to a romantically deeper level. The plot sounds simple enough, unremarkable and hackneyed perhaps. Yet its locational circularity is patently underscored and as such warrants our attention: the film opens and closes in New York.

New York exists in *My Blueberry Nights* both materially and metaphorically. On one level, the film is literally shot on location in New York; New York thus doubles as the diegetic world and the extradiegetic one. On another, perhaps more abstract level, New York is at once a place of travel (site) as well as a place of projection (sight)—it is both an image projected on the cinematic canvas and an actual physical site, a travel destination, representing Wong's diasporic sensibilities. Film as a medium and practice is as such intimately linked to its representative powers. Wong has said in an interview that Hong Kong is, for him, a base. With Hong Kong as base and springboard, there is in consequence much ease of travel between both cities. Because of their apparent concatenation, one cannot help but find Hong Kong (projected) in New York or at least locate the critical and ideological connections between them. As part of the second generation of new wave directors, Wong, like his counterparts, is thematically and

---

29 Gina Marchetti, "Cinemas of the Chinese Diaspora," in *The Chinese Cinema Book*, ed. Lim Song Hwee and Julian Ward (London: Palgrave Macmillan, 2011), 26–34.

innovatively "linked to the social and political issues facing Hong Kong as well as an artistic impetus."[30] These sociopolitical issues are inextricably tied to the urban culture so embedded in Hong Kong. Barbara Mennel notes that "urban culture centrally defines Hong Kong's identity and differentiates it from mainland China."[31] How much more so, when New York is visually and thematically implanted in this narrative? Both cities are therefore visual counterparts of each other, functioning as visible, material images (New York) and invisible, metonymic projections (Hong Kong).

Wong is known for his innovative reconstruction, reconfiguration, and representation of the city. Rather than focus on urban exterior spaces, he zooms in on the interior, more intimate, even claustrophobic spaces. One would expect perhaps a fixation on the iconicity of New York, but Wong does not bother with such embellishments. What we see instead is just a passing glimpse of the Empire State Building. Relegated to the background, the spectacular building is flattened and one-dimensionalized in an otherwise crowded and darkly lit mise-en-scène that contains anonymous streaks of light from passing cars and a railway line as well as other urban accoutrements. Nowhere do we see anything particularly foregrounded; in fact, passing trains and sinews of light often obstruct the view of the building. Exterior urban spaces are configured by movements and intersecting architectural structures; they are never unblocked or unhindered (Figure 1). Other than shots of trains and narrow streets, the rest of New York is basically centered on Jeremy's café.

Walter Benjamin highlights the mercurial character of urban space in a pithy phrase: "Now a landscape, now a room." Indeed, Wong's peripatetic movements

Figure 1. The Empire State Building, one-dimensionalized and flattened in *My Blueberry Nights* (Block 2 Pictures).

around New York reflect not so much the differences but the similarities between New York and Hong Kong: New York's uniqueness as compared to Hong Kong is not as important for Wong as is its ubiquity.[32] A familiarity with what is commonplace in any global city is of greater significance to him than a fascination with what is distinctive. The café as recurring motif emphasizes not just the comfort Wong feels in relation to this type of location; it also underscores the intimacy that can transpire in such a setting. Abbas once wrote cynically about Wong's city films engendering a social relation of "proximity without reciprocity."[33] The portrayal of the café in *My Blueberry Nights*,

30 Elizabeth Wright, "Wong Kar Wai," *Senses of Cinema* 20 (2002), http://www.sensesofcinema.com/2002/great-directors/wong/.

31 Barbara Mennel, "City Film Industry: Hong Kong," in *Cities and Cinema* (Abingdon, UK: Routledge, 2008), 83–102.

32 Walter Benjamin, "Baudelaire, or the Streets of Paris," in *Walter Benjamin: Selected Writings, Volume 3, 1935–1938*, ed. Howard Eiland and Michael W. Jennings (Cambridge, MA: Belknap Press of Harvard University Press, 2002), 32–49.

33 Abbas, "Erotics of Disappointment," 54.

however, apparently challenges this claim. We note that it is within the café, a space given to considerable contradictions, that Elizabeth and Jeremy meet and mingle. Very unlike his older films where relationships are often impossible because of the inhospitable, obtrusive layout of the city, where people simply say hello and wave good-bye, Jeremy and Elizabeth seem to form and plausibly take their relationship in a newer and perhaps happier direction.[34]

Nevertheless, just as we are tempted to rush headlong into the intoxicatingly happier ending, we must be wary of the outwardly affirmative associations the film places in the café. As mentioned earlier, it is a space of paradoxes. While it is the place in which Elizabeth and Jeremy's relationship starts, it is also the place where many other relationships end. Keys, at once a metaphor for entrances, arrivals, and accessibility, are at the same time a metaphor for exits, departures, and inaccessibility. And the café serves as a repository for people to leave and lock away their sad memories as the metropolis continues with its incessant hum and rapacious speed. Cafés are also places where people come and go with little or no attachment. Like the bar, the café is "the urban space, above all others, where unattached members of the city meet, exchange with each other, and then go their separate ways."[35] With this logic, the café, despite being an interior space, is simultaneously a liminal zone, a conduit, a tunnel between outside and inside, between public and private. As a smaller space within the wider urban world of New York, the café doubles as a microcosm of the metropolis. A point to illustrate this is the diegetic sound of the city constantly penetrating, infiltrating the café as its door incessantly opens and closes. Trains and traffic, in this case, permeate the auditory world of the café, annexing the wider world of the metropolis to the café's smaller world. The city meets the café, through the door and the transparent windows, "transitional object[s] that [have] two senses, two orientations: from inside to outside, and from outside to inside. Each is marked in a specific way, and each bears the mark of the other. Thus [doors and windows] are differently framed outside (for the outside) and inside (for the inside)."[36] Visually and audibly, the transition from inside to outside, and vice versa, and the ephemerality of the café are heightened by these structural paraphernalia. Relationships are germinated or terminated spatially. I highlight here a scene from the film that evokes the paradox of the café. At the end of the film, Elizabeth and Jeremy are seen, with a view from the top, kissing (Figure 2). The shot is long and lingering, with the camera almost enjoying and indulging in the moment as much as the lovers. Elizabeth seems to have finally found her "home" in Jeremy's café. The café and/in New York, at the outset, proffers a sense of home. It is the place that Elizabeth unquestionably returns to. The familiarity with New York's global ubiquity seems to engender a sense of comfort—the city and the café seem to be under Wong's skin. Even travel, apparently, does not do anything to undermine this assimilation with

34 A host of very good, albeit pessimistic, readings of Wong's earlier films are available. For better examples, see Teo, *Wong Kar Wai*; Jean-Marc Lalanne, David Martinez, and Ackbar Abbas, eds., *Wong Kar Wai* (Paris: Dis Voir, 1997); Janice Tong, "Chungking Express: Time and Its Displacements," in *Chinese Films in Focus II*, ed. Chris Berry (Hampshire, UK: British Film Institute, 2008), 64–72; Jean Ma, "Chance Encounters and Compulsive Returns," in *Melancholy Drift: Marking Time in Chinese Cinema* (Hong Kong: Hong Kong University Press, 2010), 123–146.

35 Barbara Mennel, "The Dark City and Film Noir," in *Cities and Cinema* (Abingdon, UK: Routledge, 2008), 46–60.

36 Henri Lefebvre, "Spatial Architectonics," in *The Production of Space* (Oxford, UK: Blackwell, 1991), 169–228.

Figure 2. Elizabeth and Jeremy, lips locked, in the latter's New York café (Block 2 Pictures).

city life. The slow camera work also performs a kind of being at p(e)ace with the place, as such suggesting that home may not be an improbability after all.

Or so this all seems. We, however, experience a nondiegetic interruption. As the kiss unfolds, Norah Jones's voice enters plaintively and playfully: "I don't know how to begin / 'Cause the story's been told before . . . I guess it's just how it goes / The stories have all been told before." Here, we return to Wong's older work, his auteur-biographical predilections. The story—the Wong Kar Wai story—has been told before; there is an intimation here that old affinities might again arise: the teasing converging of song and image confer an ambiguity that makes the possible failure of this relationship hard to resist. With the kiss happening in the transient space of the café and with the song—in spite of its drowning out the city noises from the outside—pervading the mise-en-scène, we can once again potentially slip precariously into the zone of great uncertainty and disquiet at best, and at worst, into the "erotics of disappointment" and failed relationships.[37] Underlying this overt optimism of finding one's way (home), of finding the person waiting on "the other side" of the street, as Elizabeth quips, is a bubbling nebulousness that reveals an anxiety, a questioning of the existence of home as opposed to the surety that there is indeed a place called home. The slowing down of time as manifested cinematographically, as if to savor the present, does not prevent the future from being fraught with doubt. Indeed, the unstoppable pace and pulsation of the city with its speed of life, where time roars forward into the future, will not cease for the present. Global metropolises like Hong Kong and New York, because of their connectivity and speed, make only impossible homes.

Elizabeth's present with Jeremy is constantly and always already threatened by the uncertain future and by the supposedly better, safer past—as goes the story in all of Wong's older films. Released ten years after the 1997 handover, the film seems to project a more optimistic outlook on the future by focusing on the here and now instead of the there and then. Upon deeper scrutiny, Wong's nervousness about time has not yet been transcended nor placated; one could argue that this apparent happier ending is Wong's way of adapting and catering to the taste of an American audience

37 Abbas, "Erotics of Disappointment," 39.

accustomed to a diet of Hollywood happy endings, but understanding his films as vestiges of one another will cause one to pause for thought at just how optimistic the film actually is. The year 1997 still resonates, albeit more subtly, in *My Blueberry Nights*. If home is a place of temporal continuity and spatial coherence, then *My Blueberry Nights* unsettles this supposition "at a moment when the assurance of temporal continuity erodes under the pressure of historical rupture, globalization, and a discrediting of the narrative's ability to impose a stable order upon the experience of time," and space, for that matter.[38] In the beginning of the film, for example, we see a medium close-up of Jeremy inhabiting a mise-en-scène that is constantly given to shaky camera movements and jump cuts (Figures 3 and 4). Jump cuts not only articulate a destabilized time but also enunciate a temporal anxiety, as if the time-world within the image is given to a kind of irregular palpitation. The medium close-up does not guarantee a space-time unity for Jeremy. The space behind him is blurred and restless, rendering the café a space that fidgets haphazardly along with time. The café, much like the city, is not a place that allows one to experience seamless time and consistently unadulterated space. Time fractures space, while temporal experiences scatter spatial unanimity. The slow-

ness of the camera at the end of the film does not mitigate this quietly powerful and revealing opening scene. Rather, they coexist in a curious ambiguity, making it nearly impossible for us to state with any certainty that home has indeed been found and embraced. Ultimately, the search for home and the knowledge of its elusiveness continue to pervade the narrative through the time-space (dis) articulations of the

Figures 3 and 4. Jump cuts of Jeremy in the café telling the brokenness of time. Blurred space in the background of the mise-en-scène exposes an inchoate and disoriented space (Block 2 Pictures).

café in/and the city. Hong Kong, because of its being plugged into a global network of cities and subject to temporal-spatial disruptions of globalization, is still very much in a diasporic identity crisis. The specter of 1997 lingers on ten years after in *My Blueberry Nights*: broken or destabilized time connotes the Hong Kong Chinese diasporic temporal experience in a global metropolis where travel, traveling, and constant movement are the modus vivendi more than stasis and stability. Hong Kong's qua New York's

---

38   Ma, "Chance Encounters and Compulsive Returns."

experience of time is fragmented, with the former constantly looking back and looking forward, where the present is but an agitated and jumpy moment trapped between the nostalgia of a better past and the anxiety of an unpredictable future.

Journaling and Narrative Structure. Hamid Naficy, in his book *An Accented Cinema: Exilic and Diasporic Filmmaking*, proposes a fitting framework for reading what he terms "exilic and diasporic"—"accented"—films. The films that Naficy chooses to analyze are by and large appropriate for his model. However, my contention here is that while Naficy has indeed contributed significantly to the scholarship of "accented" films, effectively turning them into a genre, his framework does not lend itself suitably and flexibly to similar films (like *My Blueberry Nights*) that somehow do not fall into the prescriptive categories of "diasporic" and/or "exilic" films. Nevertheless, some of what he says is useful in a discussion of how *My Blueberry Nights* complicates notions of diaspora through performing the act of journaling the journey during travel. How is journaling represented cinematically and visually through the use of mise-en-scène, or what Naficy calls "diegetic staging"?[39] Are Wong's diasporic sensibilities projected through distance and detailing? How is time reconfigured through distance, and as such, what does it say about the experience of Wong's diasporic identity?

First, Naficy identifies one key characteristic of accented films. He states that self-inscription is typical of accented filmmakers; and his observation is not inaccurate in the case of Wong Kar Wai: "In the modality of performativity and doubling the filmmakers appear in their own films, visually or on the sound track only, either as themselves or as fictional characters. . . . [A]utobiography is a strong motif of the accented cinema. It is woven into the idea of film as performance."[40] I stated earlier that Wong's authorial and autobiographical authority do not escape his films. As a way of "doubling," Elizabeth and Jeremy and Wong participate in a three-way conversation, exploring through diegetic and extradiegetic staging the vagaries of Chinese diasporic identity.

Elizabeth leaves New York and begins a process of detailing her journey, first through writing in her journal and second through corresponding in letters with Jeremy. Jeremy in turn journals her absence, his time without her, by responding to her letters. According to Naficy: "Film-letters inscribe letters and acts of reading and writing of letters by diegetic characters."[41] The letters that Elizabeth and Jeremy write to each other are given visuality and visibility; what results is a letter-within-a-film—a physical, embodied, tactile, corporeal calligraphic text within the mise-en-scène. This creates a *mise-en-abyme*: it is Elizabeth's letter within Wong's film; it is Elizabeth's form and/or act of writing within Wong's. That a letter is itself a form of recording and journaling also provides a sense of narrative autonomy and subjectivity. Elizabeth writes her journey and hence gives it life and meaning through her own act of journaling, and

39 Hamid Naficy, "Journeying, Border Crossing, and Identity Crossing," in *An Accented Cinema: Exilic and Diasporic Filmmaking* (Princeton, NJ: Princeton University Press, 2001), 222–287.

40 Ibid., 277.

41 Naficy, "Epistolarity and Epistolary Narratives," in *An Accented Cinema: Exilic and Diasporic Filmmaking* (Princeton, NJ: Princeton University Press, 2001), 101–151.

as such, so does Wong. His travels outside of New York are inscribed—with inscription being another act of writing and recording—in the form of Elizabeth. If travel is understood as a sort of movement, and as Avtar Brah says so eloquently and aptly, if the "image of a journey" is indeed that which "lies at the heart of the notion of diaspora," then the diaspora is therefore a process that constantly reconfigures one's act of self-understanding.[42] One literally writes oneself into being in the diaspora. While we could ascribe to letter writing a kind of immediacy and spontaneity on the part of the writer, we must not forget that it takes time for the letter to reach the receiver. In addition, the act of letter writing implies a looking back or looking away from one's current location. Time is therefore of great importance here, should we not want to oversimplify the diasporic experience as a temporally cogent, smooth, and uninterrupted one. That Elizabeth makes it a point to correspond with Jeremy, who is based in New York, could well intimate a sense of remembering the place and/or the person who is far away. However, this distance is not bridged successfully by time, because Elizabeth is constantly on the move and thus her distance from and destinations between New York fluctuate. Jeremy, on the other hand, is fixed at one particular location. To ensure that his postcards reach her, to increase the chances of successful correspondence, Jeremy preserves time, as it were, by repeating his words on different postcards; he repeats and relives the moment through identical words and wording. Real and actual time may pass, but the repeatability of words freezes a particular moment in time. Jeremy prolongs the moment to prevent the mutability of distance (space) from separating him and Elizabeth any further. Yet this attempt at securing the moment is already doomed to failure because time never waits. What should matter is not so much Jeremy's success or failure at preserving time; rather, it is the realization of the very act of *wanting to own* time, of making time immutable, that reveals the missing of or longing for a moment and a constant looking back to a better time. As Figures 5 and 6 show, the shot that comes directly after Jeremy's stack of postcards is that of a sun setting behind

Figure 5. Jeremy's stack of postcards (Block 2 Pictures).

mountains in an undisclosed anywhere, suggesting a sense of vastness and unlocatability, and in turn, the possible expanse of space that keeps Jeremy and Elizabeth apart: the stack of postcards may not eventually reach her. Time lags are associated with waits and delays largely due to the tyranny of space. Time as such does not belong to Jeremy or Elizabeth—or Wong.

To add to this epistolary act as a kind of recording, of journaling, Wong overtly intervenes by adding intertitles, detailing the time and distance away from New York. Elizabeth's private countdown is shared by Wong to detail his own journey away from New

42 Brah, "Homing of Diaspora," 192.

York. Intertitles, says Naficy, are inscribed using the "film's frame as a writing tablet on which appear multiple texts."[43] That Wong interposes these a few times throughout the course of the film is not surprising; it high-lights his diasporic

Figure 6. The shot of a sunset in an undisclosed anywhere (Block 2 Pictures).

sensibilities and the way in which he foregrounds these sensibilities using the materiality of the image. We know Wong to possess a curious obsession with time and space, and his intertitles reflect this tellingly. New York is shown to be the epicenter of relations, a round-trip made around America back to the Big Apple. For example, the intertitle that proclaims a countdown of "185 days and 3906 miles since New York" defines the city as a starting point demarcated by time with the use of the word "since" as a temporal preposition. This could perhaps trigger thoughts about New York as a place that one returns to. Yet as discussed in the previous section, the city and the café are themselves sites of transience. The calcified idea of home as a place of belonging is therefore out of the question. What then could Wong be hinting at, with his insertion of this intertitle between Elizabeth's writing to Jeremy and an unspecified train station, another space of impermanence? Is he bestowing upon New York the title of "home," or is he actually being more indirect, questioning rather than answering what "home" really means? Judging by the ethos of his work, the latter seems more probable. Although the intertitle seems to liken New York to Elizabeth's home, it is placed among a patchy order of shots, disrupting the continuity of "since." As Figures 7 and 8 show, the sequence of shots indicates an editing frenzy, starting with Elizabeth writing to Jeremy from Tennessee (Figure 7). Cut to the next shot and a view of an undisclosed mountainous location is seen, presumably from a passing train. This alternates with an unnamed city, seen with much obstruction and obfuscation, and then gives way to the intertitle (Figure 8), finally, before cutting to Elizabeth writing to Jeremy again from an anonymous train station. We do not know if this sequence of shots happens in chrono-logical time, given Wong's capacity to throw chronology out of sync by spreading out his locations randomly and ambiguously. Time as linearity and sequentiality is given over to disorder and a sense of the inchoate; the supposed starting place of home, and by association its harmony of time, is disrupted.

It would be fruitful to note that journaling can also take the form of mechanical repeatability. Here, another *mise-en-abyme* is evinced. The clever use of the camera-within-a-camera literally records the happenings of the day in sound and image, a feat not possible with the mere act of writing. Wong's camera is positioned strategi-cally behind Jeremy's security camera, and both are conflated into a single recording

43 Hamid Naficy, "Situating Accented Cinema," in *An Accented Cinema: Exilic and Diasporic Filmmaking* (Princeton, NJ: Princeton University Press, 2001), 10–39.

Figure 7. Elizabeth writing a letter to Jeremy from a diner in Tennessee (Block 2 Pictures).

Figure 8. Intertitle (Block 2 Pictures).

device. A blue-tinged mise-en-scène with characters moving mechanically around in the café is reminiscent of a video recorder in the fast-forward mode, albeit without the speed. The people in the mise-en-scène seem to be slightly behind the speed of actual movement, hence their hazy images. Moreover, the blue tinge of the mise-en-scène magnifies the recorded-ness of the moment, playfully straddling the diegetic world of Jeremy's café and Wong's very own extradiegetic observation of the action. Wong is in effect making a recording of a recording, a double detailing of sorts to underscore his obsession with preserving time. Jeremy sums up the presence of the camera by saying contemplatively that the camera is "like [his] diary," a form of capturing the passing of time and life in a city not quite his own into recorded immortality.

Last, we could broaden Naficy's idea of film letters. Arnie (David Strathairn), the uxorious and heartbroken cop in Tennessee, dies in a horrific car accident after a fight with his estranged wife, Sue-Lynn (Rachel Weisz). He leaves behind only an unpaid bar tab, which the camera captures in a close-up. In this example, the calligraphic text, that is, the tab, is neither epistolary nor journalistic; rather, it is the form of handwritten bar tabs or bills that belong to the now-dead Arnie. Sue-Lynn asks Elizabeth to keep Arnie's "bills hanging so that they don't forget him too soon." Forgetting is another reminder of time's stride. Remembering, as opposed to forgetting, ensures that what is past is not relegated to nonexistence. Elizabeth then ruminates in her voice-over: "I wonder how people would remember Arnie. When you are gone, all that's left behind are the memories you created in other people's lives." Just when she ends her contemplation, the shot cuts to Arnie's tabs, now clipped to a board. The phrase strategically enters this mise-en-scène, thus solidifying Arnie as a memory, embodied in his last orders in the bar. The camera moves slowly, scanning the bill, as if in tribute to and remembrance of him, immortalizing him by his debt, once owed, now paid by his wife who will never see him again. The time lag in paying off his debt corresponds to his death; he never sees it paid, and thus his gratification of getting back with Sue-Lynn and being debt-free is perpetually delayed. Sue-Lynn pays his debts for him—she owes him nothing now—but the reconciliation is, like Arnie's gratification, forever deferred. That the camera deliberately moves down his bills underscores Wong's penchant for keeping tabs, literally, on past events and keeping them alive by journaling and immortalizing them in word and image. Capturing the past and never letting it go is one of Wong's main thematic concerns; likewise, memory and its elusiveness are always prevalent when we think about diasporas. Wong's preserving of memory projects the diasporic sensibility of looking back to a better time, and the only reliable way that this can be achieved is through the certainty of repeatability via the camera's recording.

It is plain to see that diaries, postcards, letters, and even bar tabs are mnemonic objects in the film. They represent, corporeally, a piece of past time kept alive by memory. Because the past is always already out of reach, the only way to properly hold on to it would be to journal it, to detail it in tactile form. We could read all this somewhat pedagogically: Wong is perhaps suggesting that diasporic time can never be changeless and immediate. Time is itself already subject to constant motion, fluxes, fluidities, and lags in distance and space, even more so in diasporic experiences, when spaces are subject to further dispersal and constant change. Under such volatile circumstances, the act of journaling then becomes an attempt at keeping time. Only by detailing the day's events can we ascertain some sort of eternity; the performativity of Elizabeth's and Jeremy's acts of journaling—be it to themselves or to each other—suggests an anxiety over losing a moment. By the same token, Wong's film—*My Blueberry Nights*—is itself Wong's diary, Wong's filmic journal in sound, words, and images, where he self-reflexively inscribes his time in America through himself and, at other times, through his characters. That the title is unsurprisingly sealed with the pronoun *my* also implies a sort of ownership, a personal recounting of Elizabeth's and Wong's blueberry nights.

Also, why nights? This could well refer to the difference in time zones. America's night is Hong Kong's day. The titular reference to the nocturnal world hints at the travel condition of jet lag. Indeed, the idea of antipodal time and space, so pronounced in *Happy Together*, is once again represented here. Geography is real, and geography influences temporal perceptions and experiences. Hong Kong, though not present in the film, is recalled through the trope of jet lag. More important, jet lag, or the temporary inability to adapt to a different time zone, is indeed a facet of diasporas. Not all diasporas are assimilated temporally and spatially. Wong's world and that of his characters form a double layer, and these two layers often overlap, turning the film into a protracted dialogue about recording a temporality that mercilessly marches into the unfathomable future, forever.

This concern with disrupted and disconnected temporality is replayed in the narrative structure of *My Blueberry Nights*. Editing is used in the film not only as a means of performing ruptures in space and time; it also performs the film's narrative. The episodic structure of the film is unmistakable. If Elizabeth's journey can indeed be broken down into parts, then it is done episodically. Episodes do not perform seamlessness; rather, a sense of disjointedness characterizes the narrative. At the outset, Elizabeth seems to move from place to place, with each place constituting an episode. However, these episodes can stand alone; they do not necessarily have to be part of a larger, longer continuum. The supposedly continuous flow of time is therefore given to fracture. Naficy quotes Janis Stout: "There is a pattern to journey narratives, based on the 'direction of the journey, motivation for journeying.'"[44] Should we conceive of the diasporic journey in this vein, as a sort of metanarrative with clear motivations and transitions, until Wong intervenes to tell us otherwise? While the voice-overs of Jeremy and Elizabeth seem to suture the narrative, they are undercut by the recurrent and erratic choppiness and disconnectedness of the various episodes. The apparent subjectivity and autonomy of the voiceovers do nothing to stitch the narrative into an orderly, linear whole. Rather, the voices are disembodied from the traveling and stationary bodies of Elizabeth and Jeremy, respectively. This disembodiment reads against consecutive, full-bodied time. The temporal world of the speaking voice does not share a simultaneity with the present body; in fact, the latter is divorced from the more freely floating other—voices can fluidly inhabit a thought-world of letters and postcards emancipating themselves from belonging solely to the body, which is constrained by space. The certainty of presence and the present is therefore disturbed. Elizabeth's wandering and drifting accentuate the disconnectedness in the narrative. Drifting presupposes an attenuation of direction, or perhaps even a complete lack of it. She wanders into random episodes and finds herself stumbling into various subplots. Although the people and incidents she encounters teach her a thing or two, she does not enter into them knowingly or consciously. Character motivation and hence narrative continuity are missing. The capriciousness of travel is therefore represented through the drifting body and, to that end, the drifting, spasmodic, episodic narrative. If diasporas are consonant with the travelling journey, they can be just as unpredictable, ruptured, and discontinuous. Theme and fragmented narrative converge to perform the randomness of time as conceived and experienced in diasporas qua travel. The vicissitudes of diasporic identities as marked by such structural and temporal arbitrariness of the narrative are as a consequence also performed. Jean Ma sums it

---

44 Naficy, "Journeying, Border Crossing, and Identity Crossing," 222.

up well: "Characters acquire new identities . . . and narrativity itself is fractured in order to be reconstituted to a non-linear format."[45]

Conclusion: The Hub. We have established that diasporic time and space are fragmented, irregular, lagged, sporadic, and discontinuous. In keeping with the experience of diasporas, the entire film questions the very feasibility and existence of home. Undeniably, Wong's projection of his diasporic sensibilities has made an issue of this concept; in the film, he swings from the familiarity of the city to the jerkiness and disorderliness of time and space. He has teasingly proffered a slippery notion of home through Elizabeth and Jeremy's final discovery of some sort of comfort and belonging in the café. Yet, this certainty, as we have seen, is mitigated by the transience of the café itself and the global city. He has also made a reference to Hong Kong through the significations of jet lag. On a similar note, his frenzied fixation with journaling exposes his anxiety over preserving time. If home is symbolized by temporal-spatial unity, then New York and Jeremy's café are by no means homes at all. As such, what is at stake? It would not be preposterous to suggest that *My Blueberry Nights*, in light of the tensions that it generates, rejects the idea of the homeland as an ideal, utopic space, a geographical place where one can always find solace, that one can securely return to. Hong Kong and New York, plugged into the global matrix, are centers for globalization and cannot possibly be unequivocal homes or homelands, certainly not in this film at least.

Rather, *My Blueberry Nights* offers up the idea of a hub as opposed to a home. A hub is a place of ceaseless exchange, a place where people come and go, where time is elusive, erratic, and fractured. It is given to perpetual jet lag because it welcomes people from all over the world at all times of the day; it is a conflation of time zones. A hub is not a regional space but a place characterized by entrances and exits, mobility, metropolitanism, centrality without commitment, assembly without gathering; it is a node of relations yet without a core, a place of gravitation and liberation, a nexus—an alluring, exciting center, completely unbound, and permeated by two-way forces of centrifugal and centripetal mobility. The ephemerality of the hub is epitomized by its constant movement of people and places—of routing as opposed to rooting. I attach the suffix *-ing* to *route* because it performs the constant mutability of time in the space of the hub. Roots and rooting, unlike routes and routing, perform in contrast the acts of moving toward permanence. The hub, of course, does not allow for that. While it is geographically a fixed place, its spatiality is varied and volatile, its pace fast and relentless. Time and space meet in a complex dynamic of relations; the hub never stops and never sleeps. Globalization is fueled and fed by the very presence of the hub; globalization simultaneously produces and is produced by the hub.

Wong's feeling "at home" in the city does not mean that it is "home" for him. His is a Chinese diaspora of mobility, a diaspora that inhabits the metropolis. As noted above, Wong has said that Hong Kong is his base. A base is a launch pad, a place he would most likely buy a return ticket to; but such a base functions more like a hub than

45 Ma, "Chance Encounters and Compulsive Returns," 136.

a home. Aihwa Ong has often been quoted as saying that many Hong Kong Chinese possess "flexible citizenship"; this reiterates what was said earlier about their having multiple passports and hence multiple, roaming identities.[46] By this token, Esther Yau could be right when she says that this state of affairs "relatively frees [Hong Kong cinema] from obligations of national self-representation."[47] However, for filmmakers like Wong Kar Wai, national self-representation remains a concern that must be dealt with, albeit subtly and innovatively. "Light doses of Chineseness," antidotally prescribed as a kind of national self-representation, is perhaps too simplistic a "panacea" for Wong with regard to issues of identity.[48] Not only is the connectivity of Hong Kong to the world represented in *My Blueberry Nights* through New York; the American city is a statement of a kind of traveling global Chineseness. No longer does Chineseness need to be confined and defined by a predestined belonging or return to the Mainland. While the territorial presence of China should not be underestimated, what it means to be Chinese is subject to constant reconfigurations.

Wong's diasporic sensibilities are projected lucidly on the (screen of the) film not through a diasporic individual who desires a home, but one who has been at the center of the action in the hub. His concern with preserving time does not simplistically mean that he seeks a home; more likely, Wong is more concerned with the difficulty of remembering (in) the hub. His remembrance of China and his fixation with the idea of transplantation from place to place do reflect an undeniable diasporic proclivity. But at the same time, we cannot assume that he wishes to return to Shanghai, nor does he say anywhere that he considers Shanghai home. Hong Kong and New York as hubs not only reveal a disposition toward the world but also open up the possibility of Wong's future filmic directions: a direction toward Hollywood, the West, and the rest of the world. This trend is also coterminous with Wong's relations with the Chinese film industry. One plausible reason *My Blueberry Nights* suffered at the box office was because many saw the film as a cop-out on Wong's part; it pleased neither Wong fans nor American and Western audiences, with the latter vilifying it for being "wildly unrealistic," slow, and boring.[49] These mixed, uneven reviews of the film parallel Wong's diasporic status—at best, it reflects teething problems and a bumpy transition into a new filmmaking ethos; at worst, both could reflect teething problems and a bumpy transition into a new filmmaking ethos; at worst, permanent inability to assimilate and belong in their twinned auteur-biographical journeys to the West. As the Chinese cinema industry continues to expand, transnational film practices will persist in being the norm. As such, more questions will beset the Chinese people in and outside of China. Hong Kong, as a Chinese diaspora and as a global hub, will continue to face questions about its identity.

46 Aihwa Ong, *Flexible Citizenship: The Cultural Logics of Transnationality* (Durham, NC: Duke University Press, 1999).

47 Esther Yau, "Introduction: Hong Kong Cinema in a Borderless World," in *At Full Speed: Hong Kong Cinema in a Borderless World*, ed. Esther Yau (Minneapolis: University of Minnesota Press, 2001), 1–30.

48 Ibid.

49 A. O. Scott, "On the Road, with Melancholia and a Hankering for Pie and Ice Cream," *New York Times*, April 4, 2008, http://movies.nytimes.com/2008/04/04/movies/04blue.html. See also Xan Brooks, "*My Blueberry Nights*, Directed by Wong Kar Wai," *Guardian*, May 16, 2007, http://www.guardian.co.uk/film/2007/may/16/cannes2007 .cannesfilmfestival1.

My Blueberry Nights, with its projections of diasporic sensibilities, is only the start of this long and unpredictable process. Does it spell a different direction for Hong Kong filmmakers? Does it herald Hollywood's becoming a staple in Hong Kong film production? Does it retain or reject the validity and valence of Hong Kong national cinema? By virtue of its being made by a diasporic Hong Kong Chinese filmmaker starring a foreign cast, can it be considered a "nationalistic triumph" for both Hong Kong and China? Historically speaking, can the film open up the possibility of the 1997 connection being reconfigured and reworked, signaling a post-post-1997 era of Hong Kong filmmaking? *My Blueberry Nights* is only the beginning of a potentially new and incomplete sentence.[50] ✱

50   Chris Berry, "Transnational Chinese Cinemas Studies," in *The Chinese Cinema Book*, ed. Lim Song Hwee and Julian Ward (London: Palgrave Macmillan, 2011), 9–16.

"Useful Cinema," of What Use? Assessing the Role of Motion Pictures in the Largest Public Relations Campaign of the 1920s

by PAUL MONTICONE

Abstract: Using testimony and subpoenaed exhibits published in the seventy-two-volume record of a Federal Trade Commission investigation, this article traces the role of motion pictures in the private utility industry's public relations campaign against municipal ownership and federal regulation in the 1920s. This article reconstructs the utility companies' decision to employ films in its campaign; the production, distribution, and exhibition strategies for its motion pictures; and the relationship of producers to sponsoring organizations. Ultimately, the article argues that the use of film in this campaign was experimental and, relative to other media, limited, but by investigating such experiments with film, we can identify institutional agents struggling to find a "use" for cinema, thereby enabling media historians both to identify what determinants might cause an organization to find cinema more or less useful at different historical moments and to better assess cinema's changing cultural status and social functions.

Perhaps inspired by research tracing early cinema's interaction with a broad field of cultural institutions, media scholars have recently turned their attention to sponsored or "useful" cinema produced after the medium assumed its dominant cultural function of popular entertainment. The period of Hollywood's dominance has, these scholars believe, too often been equated with the feature-length fictional entertainment film.[1] Haidee Wasson and Charles Acland have most clearly articulated the historiographical stakes of this project. They ar-

---

1   The eleventh annual Domitor conference was dedicated to such networks during cinema's first two decades; the proceedings are collected in Marta Braun, Charlie Keil, Rob King, Paul Moore, and Louis Pelletier, eds., *Beyond the Screen: Institutions, Networks and Publics of Early Cinema* (Bloomington: Indiana University Press, 2012). Recent collections tracking cinema's use by a broader range of institutions include Vinzenz Hediger and Patrick Vonderau, eds., *Films That Work: Industrial Film and the Productivity of Media* (Amsterdam: Amsterdam University Press, 2009); Charles R. Acland and Haidee Wasson, eds., *Useful Cinema* (Durham, NC: Duke University Press, 2011); Devin Orgeron, Marsha Orgeron, and Dan Streible, eds., *Learning with the Lights Off: Educational Film in the United States* (Oxford: Oxford University Press, 2012).

Paul Monticone is a PhD candidate in the Department of Radio-Television-Film at the University of Texas at Austin, where he is a coordinating editor of Velvet Light Trap. *His dissertation is an institutional and cultural history of the Motion Picture Producers and Distributors of America during the studio era. An earlier version of this article won the Society for Cinema and Media Studies Student Writing Award in 2014.*

© 2015 by the University of Texas Press

gue that long after the mid-1910s—the moment of "a stabilization of the cinematic apparatus" and victory of the theatrical "mode"—motion pictures "operated as mobile and flexible cultural materials."[2] For scholars studying useful cinema, film has "long been implicated in a broad range of cultural and institutional functions, from transforming mass education to fortifying suburban domestic ideals."[3] Importantly, Wasson and Acland offer a definition of "useful cinema" that transcends film studies' familiar systems of classification; more than a mode of production, genre, or exhibition venue, the term identifies "a disposition, an outlook, and an approach toward the medium on the part of institutions and institutional agents."[4] This understanding of "useful cinema" suggests a project broader than we have yet seen in this subfield's existing scholarship.

Much of the research to date has focused on the filmmaking output available in particularly well-stocked corporate archives, and such work, drawing on the films left behind by institutions already convinced of the medium's utility, can safely assume the efficacy of cinema.[5] But film scholars should be careful to not allow the accidents of film survival or the commitment of a few farsighted or eccentric companies to color their general conclusions about cinema's purported use. Moreover, at present much of the "use" to which useful cinema has been put is as a heuristic that permits scholars to move from the textual properties of films—and extratextual material indicating audience addresses—to the communicative functions pursued by public and private institutions and the ideological interests underpinning these communications.[6] While such scholarship admirably places previously neglected forms of filmmaking on the agenda of film studies and takes up Wasson and Acland's call to "integrate moving-image culture into a fuller spectrum of historical analysis to reveal the intricate relations among films, institutions, and exhibition locations," extant research does not sufficiently pursue another historiographical challenge posed by this "provocative paradigm."[7] If the "disposition . . . outlook, and . . . approach" represented by "useful cinema" is to have explanatory value to film and media historians, it should allow us not only to better understand the uses to which film was put but also to identify and explain changing, historically specific conceptions of what is "useful" in different periods and for different institutions.

This article will provide a much-needed case study of a cooperative business organization's identification and exploitation of "useful" cinema, taking as its focus a context and an institution—a nationwide public relations campaign organized by the trade association of the electric utility industry—that should be expected to have had a use for film but for which an existing body of films does not, from the outset,

---

2 Haidee Wasson and Charles Acland, "Introduction: Utility and Cinema," in *Useful Cinema*, 2, 6.

3 Ibid., 3.

4 Ibid., 4.

5 Companies prominent in the literature for demonstrating the use of cinema for corporations include Ford, International Harvester, and National Cash Register, all of which had motion picture or visual instruction departments.

6 For exemplary work in this vein, see, for example, Stephen Groening, "'We Can See Ourselves as Others See Us': Women Workers and Western Union Training Films in the 1920s," in *Useful Cinema*, 34–58; and Lee Grieveson, "The Work of Film in the Age of Fordist Mechanization," *Cinema Journal* 51, no. 3 (2012): 25–51.

7 Wasson and Acland, "Introduction," 13, 3.

prove an interest in or the importance of the medium. Moreover, this article takes up a period understudied in the nontheatrical film literature: while the utopian experiments and ambitions of Progressive Era reformers are increasingly well documented and state-sponsored filmmaking during the Great Depression has long been understood as foundational in establishing alternatives to commercial cinema, the 1920s remain something of a lacuna. How were cinema's broader functions understood at the moment the commercial film industry stabilized into an oligopoly and its product, the "movies," became identified with the medium of film?

The subject of the intersection of the utility industries and cinema during this period is not entirely uncharted territory in film history. As is well known, the commercial film industry emerged as a modern business enterprise during the 1920s, first by rationalizing its systems of production, distribution, and exhibition, and second, by vertically integrating them. Models for such a transformation were found in the period's other modern business enterprises, most notably, as is known from Douglas Gomery's work, chain stores for film exhibition.[8] Somewhat less frequently cited is Donald Crafton's suggestion that another model was found in the utility industries. Like the gas, electric, and streetcar services, the commercial film industry "'distributed' an intangible product to the masses" and was sensitive to interest rates, thus these businesses seemed to offer appropriate financing and management templates.[9] At the same time that Hollywood looked to modern business enterprises like the electrical utilities, these industries looked to the modern communications medium of motion pictures for their own purposes (Figure 1). The public debates over the government's proper role in the US electrical system that raged throughout the 1920s pitted the trade association of private utility companies, the National Electric Light Association (NELA), against a coalition of progressive politicians and reformist civic groups, which agitated for public ownership of the utilities.[10] Seeking to outmaneuver the advocates of public ownership of the utility system, NELA waged a fierce public relations campaign—one that often verged on underhanded propaganda—to convince the broader public that private ownership of utilities was both natural and inevitable.

This campaign is today remembered for its often-outlandish use of virtually every form of communication then available: from pamphlets inserted in monthly bills to passages inserted into civics textbooks, to essay-contestant schoolchildren inserted into their neighbors' inadequately illuminated parlors (Figure 2). This public relations campaign was, by some estimates, the largest and most extensive of the decade—so extensive, in fact, that it attracted the attention of the Federal Trade Commission (FTC), which, at the end of the decade, conducted an investigation of the industry's publicity activities, which were detailed in an eleven-thousand-page, seventy-one-volume

8   Douglas Gomery, "Film and Business History: The Development of an American Mass Entertainment Industry," *Journal of Contemporary History* 19, no. 1 (1984): 89–103.

9   Donald Crafton, *The Talkies: American Cinema's Transition to Sound, 1926–1931* (Berkeley: University of California Press, 1999), 182.

10 A note on terms: the phrase "public ownership" was, during this period, contested. NELA and its allies used it to refer to the present arrangement, where private citizens were free to purchase utility securities, while reformers insisted that the government owning the utilities would be properly "public" ownership.

report (Figure 3).[11] According to the testimony of one utility executive, the campaign neglected "only one" medium, "and that is sky-writing."[12] And indeed, motion pictures also played a role in NELA's activities, although perhaps not one as prominent as scholars of useful cinema might expect.[13] In *The Talkies*, Crafton is quick to note that the "rationalization [imported from the utilities] was more of an ideal than a reality, and good business practices in other industries did not always work in Hollywood."[14] And just as the film industry did not find a perfect model in the utilities, the utility industry did not find an ideal medium for its message in motion pictures. Although filmmaking activity can be located in the FTC report, in the trade organization's and utility industry's own publications, and in the nontheatrical film catalogs

Frank A. Barnes, Brooklyn Edison Co.

Prompt Service Gains the Acclaim of the Public

Figure 1. A cartoon in the utility industry's trade publication likens public relations to the exhibition of motion pictures. *N.E.L.A. Bulletin*, June 1930.

and trade press, these activities were nevertheless intermittent, widely dispersed, and unevenly distributed.[15] The traces of lost films and the discourse surrounding them and films not made suggest that cinema's "use" was not at all obvious to those organizing NELA's public relations campaign. However, this material allows us not only to reconstruct what filmmaking activity there was but also to uncover the several determinants that conspired to leave motion pictures a not-fully-exploited medium for the dissemination of NELA's message.

11 US Senate, *Utility Corporations*, 1928, 70th Cong., 1st sess., document 92. In addition to the testimony of utility executives involved in the public relations campaign, this report reproduces correspondence, internal reports, budgets, and meeting minutes subpoenaed by the FTC in the course of its investigation.

12 NELA's director of public relations, George Oxley, in answer to Judge Healy's question whether there was any form of publicity neglected by the association; *Utility Corporations*, pt. 3, 214. The line was widely quoted in popular accounts; see Ernest Gruening, *The Public Pays: A Study of Power Propaganda* (New York: Vanguard Press, 1931), 221.

13 It should be noted that, during this period, corporations and industries found uses for film beyond publicity and advertising; these included training employees and increasing their efficiency, aiding in sales to distributors, and building company morale as the size and scope of economic institutions separated workers from management. All these are part of a company's internal communications network, although the line between internal films and public relations films is often blurred. For a useful schematization of these internal communication functions, see Hediger and Vonderau, "Record, Rhetoric, Rationalization: Industrial Organization and Film," in *Films That Work*, 35–50.

14 Crafton, *Talkies*, 182.

15 This publication is the *N.E.L.A. Bulletin*. In addition to it, I've consulted *A.E.R.A.* and *Gas Age*, the publications of the two other utility company trade associations, as well as *Electrical World*, *Electrical West*, *Public Service Management*, *Electric Railway Journal*, *American Gas Engineering Journal*, *System*, and *Journal of Electricity*.

Figure 2. A home lighting contest was among the most notable aspects of NELA's campaign. Instructions for local power companies were printed in the *N.E.L.A. Bulletin*, July 1924, 417.

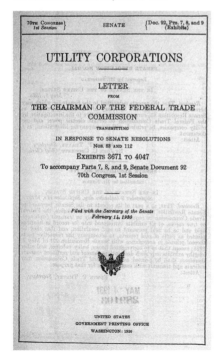

Figure 3. Cover to parts 7, 8, and 9 of the seventy-one-part FTC report.

This article situates the sponsorship and circulation of public relations films by NELA within broader developments in the "nontheatrical" filmmaking field to highlight three principal factors that shaped NELA's limited use of motion pictures. Some of these factors characterize the fields of industrial filmmaking and nontheatrical cinema in the 1920s generally, whereas others seem unique to NELA and the objectives of its public relations campaign. First, a survey of how film projects were initiated and produced suggests that NELA itself—a trade organization composed of, but by no means controlling, companies that enjoyed local monopolies—limited the association's attempts to sponsor film production and made the organization a difficult one for industrial filmmakers to work with, even though they were more than eager to acquire new clients. Second, in my discussion of the distribution and circulation of these films, I argue that the nontheatrical film market, whether as the desired outlet for these films or as a necessary ancillary market once theatrical venues were exhausted, was not sufficiently developed to justify extensive film production. Finally, a consideration of the political objectives of and audiences targeted by the campaign's other activities suggests that the audiences that could have been reached through commercial theaters—the exhibition outlets that had sufficiently developed material infrastructures to reliably show films—were not the ones NELA was most interested in influencing. However, before assessing how widespread filmmaking and exhibiting activity was and attempting to explain its relatively minor role among NELA's other public relations activities, it is necessary to outline NELA's broader campaign and establish what sorts of films would function within it.

NELA and the Public Utility Wars of the 1920s. In 1925, on orders from the US Senate, the FTC began an investigation into the ownership structure of the electric utilities, which preceded a second inquiry focusing on their propaganda activities. Over the previous decade, the electric utility business consolidated its power as the number of corporate entities multiplied. Of particular note were holding companies, which were entities "not directly engaged in the business of producing and distributing commodities or services, but which [control] such a business through the ownership of stock in operating companies."[16] The effect of such entities in an industry is to create a pyramid structure where a single company at the top, controlled by a few individuals and with a relatively small investment, exerts control over and reaps the majority of the financial rewards from the smaller, regional companies at the bottom.[17] The private utility interests insisted that the holding company was a necessity for financing and developing a large technological system, permitting ease of organization, decentralized management, and a dispersed liability to creditors. But advocates of public power "did not accept that they were either inevitable or necessary. Instead, they thought that greed motivated individuals to maximize profits at the public's expense."[18] These advocates perceived in the holding company's dense organizational chart a strategy of avoiding state regulation by locating components of the business, such as stock and bond sales or electricity rates, in states where regulation of that component was lax. Further, these state-level regulatory boards were, according to public power advocates, undermined by the utility companies: "Private power[, they charged] controlled commissions through the selection of commissioners and the manipulation of the political process and the media."[19] The image of the many-tentacled octopus, used years earlier to characterize Standard Oil, found another use in the critiques of the private utility industry's organization.[20] The 1925 FTC investigation of the economic structure of the utility industry that uncovered these facts led to a second investigation, focusing solely on the industry's attempts to influence public opinion.

---

16 Jay L. Brigham, *Empowering the West: Electrical Politics Before FDR* (Lawrence: University Press of Kansas, 1998), 29.

17 For a detailed description of this corporate and investment structure and the flow of capital within an organization so structured, see Brigham, *Empowering the West*, 28–34.

18 Ibid., 36.

19 Ibid., 56.

20 Frank Norris invoked the image to characterize the Southern Pacific Railroad in his *Octopus: A Story of California* (New York: Doubleday, 1901), and muckraking journalist Ida M. Tarbell used similar imagery in her exposé of John D. Rockefeller's trust, which was serialized in *McClure's* and later published as *The History of the Standard Oil Company* (New York: McGuire, Philips, 1904). The most iconic image of a trust as an octopus is Udo J. Keppler, *"Next!"* illustration, *Puck*, September 7, 1904, from Library of Congress Prints and Photographs Online Catalog, http://www .loc.gov/pictures/item/2001695241/.

Like many large and dispersed industries, the utility industry had formed a national trade association, the National Electric Light Association, ostensibly to exchange technology and ideas on best practices, thereby increasing efficiency throughout the industry.[21] Although it included electrical engineers, NELA was a commercial association, comprising standing committees devoted to advertising, marketing, sales, and competition, and composed of smaller regional and state associations.[22] Critics of the utility companies saw the complexity of the industry's associations much like the holding companies described earlier, as purposefully concealing its true activities, and "charged that the organization went beyond mere forums for exchanging ideas and operated as propaganda machines intent on destroying public power sentiment in the United States."[23] An early exposé that preceded the FTC investigation contended that NELA's own 1927 advertising expenditures were $10 million, a sum that its regional subsidiaries and member companies nearly trebled, bringing the total to double what the industry's advertising budget had been five years prior.[24] In light of such facts, those in the Senate who had pushed for the investigation of the utility companies' financial interrelations began clamoring for another investigation.

The resolution that finally passed and directed the FTC investigation was known as the Walsh Resolution, after Senator Thomas Walsh (D-Montana), who had successfully pursued the Teapot Dome Scandal several years prior. He, along with his allies against private utilities, such as Senators George Norris (R-Nebraska) and Robert La Follette Jr. (R-Wisconsin), had hoped for Senate hearings on NELA as well, and the resolution he initially put forward in December 1927 called for a five-senator commission to be convened for that purpose. But given the certainty of a presidential veto from Calvin Coolidge, a compromise was offered that the FTC handle the investigation. Many of the public power advocates feared this legislative compromise would not only deprive the investigation of publicity but also compromise the investigation itself; the pro-business commission would, it was feared, not pursue the matter vigorously and bury whatever findings resulted.[25] Despite their fears, the FTC report revealed a great deal about the private utility companies' activities. The FTC's seventy-one-part report would not be fully published for seven years, in 1935, but by the early 1930s liberal writers such as Ernest Gruening, then a journalist associated with the *Nation* but later a prominent New Dealer and territorial governor of Alaska, and Carl D. Thompson, a Wisconsin minister, socialist politician, and then secretary of the Public Ownership League of America began writing sensationalistic accounts—bearing such

---

21 On the emergence of trade associations and their developing functions, see Louis Galambos, *Competition & Cooperation: The Emergence of a National Trade Association* (Baltimore: Johns Hopkins University Press, 1966); Lyn Spillman, *Solidarity in Strategy: Making Business Meaningful in American Trade Associations* (Chicago: University of Chicago Press, 2012), 29–70.

22 On the early history of NELA, see David Nye, *Electrifying America: Social Meanings of a New Technology* (Cambridge, MA: MIT Press, 1990), 173.

23 Brigham, *Empowering the West*, 39.

24 H. S. Raushenbush and Harry W. Laidler, *Power Control* (New York: New Republic's Dollar Books, 1928), 25. In 2014 dollars, the utility industry's total 1927 advertising budget was more than $500 million, five times the cost of presidential elections during the period.

25 Brigham, *Empowering the West*, 35–61.

titles as *Confessions of the Power Trust* and *The Public Pays*—of the investigation's findings.[26] These works drew from the testimony of NELA's and its constituent companies' officers to construct a damning account of the organization's vast and coordinated publicity efforts.

In 1918, the electric utility industry launched its concerted effort to turn public sentiment against threatened public ownership or burdensome federal regulation.[27] These efforts originated with Samuel Insull (Figure 4), president of the Middle West Utilities Company, a holding company that had, before World War I, facilitated electrification of the Midwest and soon thereafter began expanding, acquiring interests in utility companies throughout the country. During World War I, Insull had been placed in charge of the Illinois Council of National Defense—a Creel Committee—and immediately after the war, he converted a state propaganda organization into an information bureau to protect his private interests. As these investments spread nationally, Insull rose to prominence in the national trade association, and in 1918 he encouraged the industry to expand the public relations work done by Middle West to a national scale. State and regional public utility associations formed their own information departments and public relations committees, which coordinated with those of the national organization. Over the next decade, NELA engaged

Figure 4. Sam Insull on the cover of *Time* magazine, November 29, 1929.

in an enormous public relations campaign to discredit state ownership of utilities and convince the public of the wisdom and efficiency of "proper"—that is, easily avoided—state-level regulation.[28]

Their activities ranged widely, from advertising on billboards and in newspapers to fliers inserted into their customers' electric bills, but the activities that most concerned the FTC and the authors of popular-press summaries of the investigation were elements of NELA's concealed propaganda campaign. The private utilities secured the support of banking institutions by making large deposits in interest-free accounts and enlisted the services of professors and researchers—members of the so-called

26 Carl D. Thompson, *Confession of a Power Trust* (New York: E. P. Dutton, 1932); Gruening, *Public Pays*.

27 On the period of "sharply critical" attitudes toward large corporations that followed World War I, see Louis Galambos and Barbara Barrow Spence, *The Public Image of Big Business in America, 1880–1940: A Quantitative Study in Social Change* (Baltimore: Johns Hopkins University Press, 1975): 193–221.

28 This background is drawn from Alan R. Raucher, *Public Relations and Business, 1900–1929* (Baltimore: Johns Hopkins University Press, 1968), 80–83.

"starveling professions"—by writing checks during the lean summer months.[29] These third parties, of course, did not divulge their association with NELA when promoting its political objectives. The most egregious tactics involved influencing the content of teaching materials—publishing books for school libraries and influencing the content of textbooks—and of local newspapers. To accomplish the latter, NELA supported wire services that supplied national news to local papers, and local editors often published articles authored by NELA's publicity men as "news," effectively publishing advertising for free and legitimating the interested communication as disinterested reportage.[30] None of these public relations techniques was unprecedented: railroad companies employed advertising and financial patronage at the turn of the century, and the Bell System was concurrently making use of fraudulent newswire services and manipulating textbook material.[31] But the scale of NELA's campaign, its necessity for cooperation among corporations whose management—if not ownership—did not overlap, its often-concealed nature, and the public opprobrium that resulted were unprecedented. Like the Bell Systems' campaign against public ownership of the telephone system, NELA's campaign achieved its political objectives—the federal government did not take control of the provision of electricity to its citizens—but NELA attracted public scorn and a federal investigation such that the campaign was long a source of embarrassment to the public relations field; according to Edward Bernays, one of the field's pioneers, "the new profession received a bad name from which it did not free itself for years."[32] So discredited was NELA by the propaganda scandal that in 1934 the organization dissolved and reformed under a new name, Edison Electric Institute.[33]

The Utilities on the Screen. Having established the scope, general features, and aims of NELA's public relations campaign, I now turn to the question of what sort of films were thought best to deliver NELA's message. Unfortunately, the films themselves are difficult to evaluate, as they appear not to have survived the past ninety years. Whether these films were destroyed when NELA dissolved in 1935 or were, without the stability of a corporate archive, simply lost to neglect when their immediate use

---

29 "Starveling professions" is from an address made by Dr. C. A. Eaton, president of the American Educational Association and a manager of industrial relations at General Electric, to the NELA convention in 1924. His remarks are published in *Utility Corporations*, pt. 71A, 149.

30 Summaries of NELA's campaign can be found in Raucher, *Public Relations and Business*, 82–90, and David E. Nye, "Public Relations as Covert Political Communication: The Debate over Public vs. Private Utilities in the United States," *American Studies in Scandinavia* 16 (1984): 21–35.

31 On these public relations programs, see Raucher, *Public Relations and Business*, 36–45, 75–79.

32 Bernays interviewed in Scott M. Cutlip, *The Unseen Power: Public Relations; A History* (Hillsdale, NJ: Lawrence Erlbaum Associates, 1994), 108. See also Kevin Stoker and Brad L. Rawlins, "The 'Light' of Publicity in the Progressive Era: From Searchlight to Flashlight," *Journalism History* 30, no. 4 (2005): 177–188.

33 Also contributing to the renaming of NELA was its association with Samuel Insull, whose seventy holding companies collapsed during the Depression—resulting in $2–3 billion dollars in losses to investors—which led to a fraud indictment and Insull's fleeing to Europe. These events are covered in Forrest MacDonald's sympathetic biography, *Insull* (Chicago: University of Chicago Press, 1962), and in Thomas Parke Hughes, *Networks of Power: Electrification in Western Society, 1880–1930* (Baltimore: John Hopkins University Press, 1983).

was exhausted cannot be established.[34] However, we can establish something more of the features of these films than that they were "frankly produced 'from the standpoint that public utilities must be privately owned in order to obtain the greatest efficiency in operation.'"[35] Reviews published in the nontheatrical trade press provide detailed synopses of industrial films, summarizing—appropriately enough for a publication for educators—their "lessons." Further, the utility companies' first forays into production inspired some internal discussion as to how the films should be organized, and this can provide some insight. For example, a utility executive's report to the Pacific Coast Electric Association's Publicity Committee on a film he was attempting to produce reminds his listeners that they had agreed to eliminate "any element of direct advertising," understood as title cards identifying a particular company's plant, and instead focus on the broader story of progress by emphasizing "that the industrial and economic miracles wrought have been the result of private initiative."[36] The content of the utility industry's films was continuous with the aims of their broader propaganda campaign—to promote not the service provided by particular companies but the service provided by private enterprise and to convince the public that public ownership was not preferable to the existing state of affairs—and one of its films, *Back of the Button*, seems to have been conceived to echo and amplify NELA's printed institutional advertising (Figure 5).[37] What remains to be explored is how the NELA films' formal properties—particularly their narrative design—fulfilled what Lee Grieveson has termed, in a discussion of the *Ford Animated Weekly* and *Ford Educational Weekly*, these films' "communicative, rhetorical, and pedagogic function."[38]

From existing descriptions and titles, two genres that proved especially well suited to promoting private enterprise without directly engaging the public-ownership groups' arguments were history films and process films. The former trace the development of a particular industry or activity to a point that culminates in electrification. In such films, history is arranged to occlude the complex processes of technological development by associating it with revered public figures.[39] The process films, in contrast, show the viewer how aspects of life that he or she takes for granted are the product of complex

34 The simpler explanation has numbers on its side: film archivists estimate that 85–90 percent of silent fiction films no longer exist. The numbers for films made by ephemeral industrial film producers are estimated to be even worse. For a discussion of survival rates, see David Pierce, "The Legion of the Condemned—Why American Silent Films Perished," *Film History* 9 (1997): 17n1.

35 This quote comes from a June 26, 1923, letter from J. A. Prosser of the Society of Visual Education, a producer of ostensibly educational films, to W. S. Vivian of the Middle West Utilities Co. Vivian circulated this proposal to other members of NELA's Public Relations committee. *Utility Corporations*, pt. 2, exhibit 378, 342–344.

36 *Utility Corporations*, pt. 10–16, exhibit 4223, 595.

37 On the "institutional style" in advertising, see Roland Marchand, *Creating the Corporate Soul: The Rise of Public Relations and Corporate Imagery in American Big Business* (Berkeley: University of California Press, 1998), 164–201.

38 Grieveson, "Work of Film," 27.

39 *All the King's Horses* (1926), made by Jam Handy for the Philadelphia Electric Company, is an excellent example of the type, and it not only has survived but is available online at *Archive.org*: http://www.archive.org/details/all _the_kings_horses. I've been unable to locate any material in the FTC report, educational film materials, or *N.E.L.A. Bulletin* on this production; thus, it seems not to have been part of the national campaign. Making more extensive use of the image of Franklin are two films discussed by Grieveson in his study of the films of Ford Motors' Motion Picture Department. See Grieveson, "Work of Film," 33–34.

processes best left to the private companies.[40] *Yours to Command* (Rothacker, 1924) is an example of the latter genre, and it was the subject of a detailed review in *Educational Screen*.[41] The film begins by asking viewers to consider "how electricity makes possible most of the comforts, luxuries, and conveniences we of this age enjoy," and it demonstrates how electricity is responsible for the filming, developing, printing, and projection of the film the viewer now watches. From the comfort of the cinema, *Yours to Command* moves on to demonstrate uses of electricity "in industry, in commerce, in offices, and in homes." Having progressed from society's largest organizations, industry, into the personal realm, the film displays the benefits to be derived from electricity in the home.

But *Yours to Command* is not, in the end, interested in demonstrating the domestic applications of electricity, and the film's final section proceeds back from the hearth out "to views of the service crew stringing cables and laying underground conduits, to scenes in the substation, and then to the generating station which is in turn dependent on the supply of coal." Here, the film presents the source of "this age we enjoy" as a complex, infrastructure-intensive, networked system requiring extensive capital investment and a specialized workforce. While the review does not mention any overt propaganda—according to the review, no mention is made of public ownership as a threat—the film concludes with a suggestion that public ownership would be redundant: "It is suggested in the end that the whole organization . . . really belongs to the public at large since they are chiefly financed by the money of a number of people, made available by the deposits in banks." The film, then, does not defend "private ownership" but instead redefines it as "public ownership," leaving the reformers' "public ownership" to refer to something else: government, state, or political ownership, implicitly. Articles arguing for the promotion of what was also known as "shareholder ownership" can be found throughout the *N.E.L.A. Bulletin* during the latter half of the 1920s: "The term public ownership in the mouths of demagogues usually means Government, State or City ownership and operation. . . . [Customer ownership] is a public ownership that takes politics out of business, that fosters thrift and that makes for a more secure state resting on a foundation of better citizenship."[42]

Beyond the content of the intertitles, which the review is likely paraphrasing, the very structure of the film functions to promote the private utility system, a system in which the broader public has a particular, circumscribed role. The initial positioning of the spectator as a consumer who "enjoys" the benefits of electricity separates him from the vast operation necessary to provide the "conveniences of the age," and his participation in the provision of electricity is limited to funding this system but not determining either its shape or function. If this point seems a bit obscure or conspiratorial and the organization of *Yours to Command* completely natural, we might briefly consider Joris Ivens's *Power and the Land* (1940), which proposed a different role for the beneficiary of electricity and possessed a very different form of address.

---

40   On films of industrial processes, see Frank Kessler and Eef Masson, "Layers of Cheese: Generic Overlap in Early Non-Fiction Films on Production Processes," in *Films That Work*, 75–84.

41   The following account of the film is derived from Review of *Yours to Command*, *Educational Screen*, May 1924, 199.

42   H. M. Addinsell, "A New Era of Public Ownership," *N.E.L.A. Bulletin*, June 1924, 376–377.

Although Ivens's New Deal documentary, produced for the Rural Electrification Administration (REA), was made in quite a different historical moment with different stylistic devices (notably, sound) and in a different style, considering *Yours to Command* in relation to it can clarify this industrial film's communicative function at the level of narrative organization, spectatorial positioning, and audience address.[43]

Power and the Land begins and ends with a day on the farm—the first without electricity and the second after electrification.[44] The film makes clear the benefits of electricity to the farmer by showing how every activity, from washing and cooking to harvesting and preserving milk, is improved with electrical technologies. In showing the viewer the "before" and "after" images, the narrator addresses the spectator directly. This spectator is assumed to be an urban or small-town resident who would be shocked that farm children blind themselves attempting to do homework by oil-lamp light. Moreover, the narrator insists that the viewer's well-being depends on the farming family and that they are owed the benefits of civilization: "Good people, hard-working people, deserve the best tools man can make." And while the presumed viewer is sustained by the farmer's labor, rural families have "earned" their meals "not by easy tasks but with their strength and their toil." The film's political address is clearly to the nonrural population, whose political support was necessary for the Roosevelt administration's rural electrification program. But in addition to this overt political message, the film's structure also presents a vision of the political process in relation to complex networks such as the electrical utility system.

The crucial section of the film is between the segments showing daily life on the farm, and this middle sequence depicts what brings electricity to rural America—not the inevitable march of scientific progress, but the actions of the farmers. The narrator recites a poem over images of them harvesting the crop, and this agri-chanty presents the farmers' sense of solidarity in physical labor: "When we get together, we're hard to stop. . . . We can get the power and the light, we can get the things we want today." During a break in the work, they discuss a new program that might allow them to receive electricity, and in the next scene the issue is debated in a town-hall meeting. Agreeing that the REA is not offering charity, the farmers decide to form an electrical cooperative. After a brief sequence representing the scale of the electrical system, the scene preceding the modern day on the farm shows the farmer and his neighbors connecting his farmhouse to the nearby transmission lines.

The constellation of images—maps, generating stations, electrified homes, and power lines—is not dissimilar from what appeared in the private utility films, but the arrangement of the images, and the role for the viewer implied, is quite different. Rather than shifting *out* to a monumental system, the film moves from its synoptic view to the farming community, showing local citizens exerting control over their own utility. Moreover, the complex network and vast system represented by electrification does not

---

43 On the emergence of a documentary style in the 1930s, and its reliance on the interplay of image and sound, see Charlie Keil, "American Documentary Finds Its Voice: Persuasion and Expression in *The Plow That Broke the Plains* and *The City*," in *Documenting the Documentary: Close Readings of Documentary Film and Video*, ed. Barry Keith Grant (Detroit: Wayne State University Press, 1998), 119–135.

44 In this, the film is not dissimilar from Ford's *Farm Progress*, which connects industrial processes to a narrative about an individual farm. See Grieveson, "Work of Film," 34.

overwhelm local community institutions but is integrated into them. Instead of taking electrification as a transcendent force, its provision and funding are here a decision that local citizens—through an idealized democratic institution—are fit to make. The technological system in the New Deal film may not be entirely understood, but here, this does not prevent an understanding of and deserved stake in the control of the electric power system. Such is not the case in *Yours to Command*. In NELA's film, all the average citizen has to command are his appliances, and all that he is free to direct is whatever excess income he may have to invest. The system of utility corporations— how it is financed, sets rates, and shops for favorable regulatory venues—does not bear mentioning at all.

NELA behind the Screen: Filmmaking Activities of the Electric-Utility Industry.

In March 1921, M. H. Aylesworth, then NELA's publicity director but soon to be president of NBC, received unanimous approval from NELA's Public Informa-

tion Committee to commission a series of films, "The Romance of Electricity." NELA's National Information Bureau was directed to appropriate the $3,000, in addition to $42,000 to be provided by fourteen other utility companies, necessary to fund production of the first films and the making of prints.[45] Neither the trade association nor any of its member companies, with the exception of New York Edison, maintained permanent film departments.[46] Thus production was handled by Chicago's Rothacker Film Manufacturing Company, a motion-picture processing lab that had recently opened an industrial film division, which several years later would be spun off into Rothacker Industrial Films Inc. (Figure 5).[47]

Figure 5. Rothacker expanded its laboratory business to include industrial film production. Rothacker Film Manufacturing advertisement from *Exhibitors Trade Review*, December 31, 1921.

The first film NELA sponsored, *Back of the Button*, premiered at the industry's Chicago convention in

---

45 Thompson, *Confession of a Power Trust*, 413.

46 David Nye has discussed the coordination of NELA with General Electric, a company with a two-hundred-person publicity department, in the production of advertising art and illustrated lectures, but there is no evidence that GE's film department similarly coordinated with NELA. See Nye, "Public Relations as Covert Political Communication," 21–35.

47 For an account of this company, see Arthur Edwin Krows, "Motion Pictures—Not for Theatres," *Educational Screen*, May 1940, 193–197.

1921, and the next film, *Yours to Command*, was shown to conference attendees in Atlantic City in 1922. Public Relations Committee chair Martin Insull introduced the latter film in his annual address and reported on the promise of motion pictures "in public education work."[48] One of the purposes of showing these films at the annual convention was to allow local companies to ascertain the appeal of the film, much like other products, practices, and plans that were showcased at trade association conventions. Insull's address sought to convince his audience of film's public relations value. The sixty-seven prints of the first film distributed, *Back of the Button*, had been seen, he said, by nearly two million people, and at a total cost of $14,000, the cost of advertising through a short film was seven-tenths of a cent per viewer, giving films an advantage over more expensive print advertisements.[49]

That films cost the utilities little more than the funds for production and print-making was not their only appeal. In an effort to encourage NELA members to see the value in film advertising, the *Bulletin* reprinted an article, previously published in *Journal of Electricity*, by a Portland Electric Power Company land and tax agent who had recently been involved in making and distributing a film promoting the local company. The advantage of film advertising, the author argued, stemmed from its receiving "the undivided attention of an audience that is relaxing and enjoying itself. In no other form of publicity is the mind of the audience so completely concentrated on the subject matter."[50] This distinguished films from print advertising, which could be skipped over by the reader. An editorial from a Nebraska operator similarly lauded motion pictures as "intelligent advertising," which could bring the facts of the industry to the "working" population and had, the writer observed, "aroused much interest on the part of the movie fans."[51]

And yet despite the apparent successes of *Back of the Button*, *Yours to Command*, and scattered films made by local utility companies, and enthusiastic coverage in the *Bulletin*, two years elapsed before "The Motion Picture Committee"—not a permanent committee within NELA, but an ad hoc subcommittee within the Public Relations section—reported any progress on the development of a third film.[52] In the articles about film published in the *N.E.L.A. Bulletin* throughout this period, the promise and potential value of motion pictures are highlighted, and preliminary successes always trumpeted, to justify further experiments in the field. These articles, promising the thorough exploitation of film, are found alongside others that publicized the more concrete accomplishments of the newspaper wire services, speaker bureaus, textbook

---

48 Martin Insull, "Address of Chairman Insull Presented at the Atlantic City Convention," *N.E.L.A. Bulletin*, July 1922, 440.

49 Ibid.

50 George J. Kelly, "The Motion Picture—a Medium for Public Utility," *N.E.L.A. Bulletin*, January 1925, 25.

51 *N.E.L.A. Bulletin*, January 1924, 38–39.

52 *N.E.L.A. Bulletin*, April 1924, 202. There is no evidence this third film was made. The only other film funded by NELA was *The Great Surprise* (Atlas, 1924), an adjunct of NELA's "home lighting contest." On the contest, see "Some School Child Will Win This Home," *N.E.L.A. Bulletin*, July 1924, 411–414. This featured the story of a "younger sister driven away to seek her good times elsewhere" by bad home lighting. See the review of *The Great Surprise*, *Educational Screen*, September 1924, 279. This contest was conceived by General Electric's Bruce Barton both to promote increased consumption of electrical appliances and to ascertain market data. See Nye, *Electrifying America*, 268–277.

commissions, and print advertisement departments, all of which were centrally coordinated programs sustained by standing committees. Motion pictures, when made, seemed to perform satisfactorily for NELA, but coordination and development of these motion picture experiments were not among the hallmarks of this campaign. As late as 1931, Mr. Oxley, of NELA's Department of Public Information, took to the pages of the *Bulletin* to request that member companies submit a list of films they had in their possession or had made, and information as to "if such films will be loaned or rented and under what conditions."[53]

As a trade organization whose publicity activities were funded through its member companies, NELA had to convince those members of the value of its endeavors. These companies did have print advertising departments and forged relationships with the local business community, so newswire bureaus, print advertising campaigns, and speaker bureaus would likely integrate well with their existing promotional operations. Motion pictures, in contrast, might not have had widespread support. The number of articles in the *N.E.L.A. Bulletin* devoted to convincing members of the value of public relations advertising suggests any such work of NELA's was resisted, or at least treated indifferently. Moreover, it appears that even the more familiar forms of public relations work had to overcome such indifference. Insull, in his 1922 address, attempted to explain why his committee had not accomplished more: "While the industry as a whole seems to very much appreciate the necessity of a better understanding on the part of the public of the problems of the industry, the individual of the industry does not yet seem to understand that in order to accomplish this he or she must make it their individual job."[54] Asking individual companies, which most often enjoyed local monopolies, to see themselves as part of a larger institution—an industry—and contribute to its well being by advertising the institution finds its nearest analogy in Roland Marchand's discussion of General Motors, founded as a holding company for relatively independent manufacturers that did not see themselves as part of the GM "family." Since GM's "funds ultimately derived from moneys 'taxed' away from the individual producing division, [Alfred P.] Sloan and other corporate executives recognized that the divisions would resist a diversion of funds for corporate publicity."[55] Although NELA's members were not, as GM's divisions were, competing to sell goods to the same consumer market, NELA's centrally produced motion pictures still may not have held sufficient appeal to its members to justify such a tax, given that the return on investment of a national public relations campaign designed to "tell the story" of an industry was far removed from the promotion of electrical appliances and home lighting, both of which more directly benefited companies' bottom lines.

Further, the very complexity of the public utility industry and the corresponding complexity of its trade association seem to have stymied nontheatrical filmmakers who might have offered their services to NELA and initiated more filmmaking activity. The production companies that did work with the national organization—Atlas, the Society for Visual Education (SVE), and Rothacker—were based in Chicago, the

---

53 "Information Wanted on Motion Picture Films," *N.E.L.A. Bulletin*, March 1931, 207.

54 Insull, "Address of Chairman Insull," 438.

55 Marchand, *Creating the Corporate Soul*, 133.

stronghold of the Insull group, which dominated NELA.[56] SVE's Harley Clarke, who presented the most ambitious motion picture plan, was a utility industry insider and so presumably knew where to find interested parties.[57] The preserved correspondence of other companies, outside or only distantly connected with the Insull group, suggests the futility that film producers based outside Chicago must have felt when they attempted to supply NELA's propaganda campaign.

In October 1925, Edward Stevenson, the president of Visugraphic, an industrial and educational film producer based in New York, attended a utility conference where a paper titled "Fundamental Work to Be Done in Education Area" was delivered.[58] The next month, Stevenson cited this paper in a proposal to make an educational film for the Missouri Committee on Public Utility Information, but he was told "the time does not yet appear to me to have arrived . . . when [the public-utility industry of Missouri] can make use of motion pictures as agencies of education in the public schools."[59] The letter continued to detail the indifference of local managers to the educational portion of the committee's campaign and the general poverty of the "state committees on public-utility information."[60] A month later, Stevenson tried again, this time pitching the film to the director of the Pennsylvania Public Service Information Committee. The director of this state committee did not complain about a lack of funds but replied: "Such a film would be an excellent thing but our committee is not the instrument through which or by support of which it should be produced. A film of the nature you propose would more properly be sponsored by the national and State utility associations."[61] Stevenson did produce films for several local utility companies—for example, he worked with the Virginia Electric & Power Company on a historical booster film for the Richmond region in 1929 (Figure 6)—but there is no evidence in the FTC report or other trade publications that Stevenson tried a third time or succeeded in finding the appropriate sponsoring organization for an educational film for broader industry use.[62] The efficiencies claimed by the defenders of the private

56 On Samuel Insull and his role in the development of the private utility system, see MacDonald, *Insull*.

57 *Utility Corporations*, pt. 2, exhibit 379, 342–343. In March 1924, SVE proposed a series of twenty-six films. Though production plans seem to have been far along, there is no evidence that they were actually made or why they were not. Clarke's fortune had been made in the previous decade by investing in an Indiana utility company and then an increasingly complex series of utility holding companies that finally encompassed fifty different entities that stretched into Canada and England. See "Harley Clarke, Utility Giant, Dies in Home," *Dixon* (IL) *Evening Telegraph*, June 7, 1955, 7. A particularly celebratory account of Clarke's activities in nontheatrical cinema, crediting him as an educational visionary and canny businessman, estimates his business interests at this time as amounting to "$401 million dollars worth of securities." See Krows, "Motion Pictures," 334–336. Clarke would go on to earn himself a footnote in Hollywood history as the investor who pushed William Fox out of his namesake company in 1930; see Upton Sinclair's sympathetic biography of Fox, *Upton Sinclair Presents William Fox* (Los Angeles: Upton Sinclair, 1936), subtitled "A Feature Picture of Wall Street and High Finance."

58 *Utility Corporations*, pts. 5–6, 113–114.

59 Ibid., 330.

60 Ibid., 331.

61 Ibid., 968.

62 On the Virginia Electric & Power Co. film *For the Old Dominion*, see "Historic Virginia on the Screen," *Electric Railway Journal* 73, no. 15 (1929): 681. The film seems to have been a municipal booster film, a nonfiction genre that was, by the beginning of the 1920s, in decline. For a discussion of this and other local film genres, see Martin L. Johnson, "Main Street Movies: Local Films in the United States, 1909–1934" (PhD diss., New York University,

Ready to shoot "For the Old Dominion"

Figure 6. *Electric Railway Journal* 73, no. 15 (June 1929): 681.

utility holding companies seem not to have been realized by filmmakers confronting their inscrutable organizational structure.

Distribution and Exhibition of Utility-Industry Films. The FTC report and other primary sources allow us to attend to how the films NELA made were distributed. Though films about industry or for education—that is, genre categories denoting subject matter and textual properties—are often labeled "nontheatrical," it was not always the case that such films were shown exclusively in exhibition settings distinct from commercial film theaters. While endorsing the terms *theatrical* and *nontheatrical*, Gregory Waller has recently described the division between them as often being "qualified, contingent, porous," noting that "one of the most historically significant aspects of this binary is precisely how and when and to what degree it has proven to be permeable, and when it has been contested and redefined."[63] The exhibition history of the NELA films suggests that they circulated in a moment when the border between *theatrical* and *nontheatrical* was contested. In the first years of the campaign, the border seems to have been porous; however, by the mid-1920s, nontheatrical venues were the only ones available to the campaign films. And because the nontheatrical circuits were themselves in a state of early development, the distribution possibilities open to NELA may have militated against the production of more films.

The two early films sponsored by the national association, *Yours to Command* and *Back of the Button*, both "premiered" at NELA's annual conventions, after which they were to enter a local distribution system. Interested utilities and regional associations would purchase a copy from either the producer or from NELA, which they would then arrange to have shown locally.[64] Events similar to trade organization conferences—county fairs and expositions—proved ready exhibition outlets for subsequent

2012).

63 Gregory A. Waller, "Locating Early Nontheatrical Audiences," in *Audiences : Defining and Researching Screen Entertainment Reception*, ed. Ian Christie (Amsterdam: Amsterdam University Press, 2012), 84.

64 The Louisiana-Mississippi Committee on Public Information, for example, purchased copies of *Yours to Command* and *Back of the Button* in January 1924. See *Utility Corporations*, pt. 4, 878.

screenings.[65] Regional utilities also had some success in placing these films in theaters. The film made by the Portland utility, *Modern Pioneers* (George J. Kelly, 1924), seems only to have played locally, first at Portland's largest commercial theater, the Liberty. This film's use of the local scenery seems to have impressed theatrical exhibitors, and George Kelly proudly quotes one: "The picture's presentation of Oregon's gorgeous scenery, coupled with a graphic demonstration of the utilization of some of our state's vast resources, makes it one of the best scenic and educational subjects I have ever seen."[66] Once theatrical outlets were exhausted, the film moved on to the local nontheatrical circuit, including venues such as "private gatherings, lectures, dinners."[67]

As with *Modern Pioneers*, NELA's films were to be placed by local utility men in the venues available to them. During the 1923 Chicago meeting of NELA, a correspondent from Boston reported his success in having the films exhibited:

> The use of the association films *Back of the Button* and *Yours to Command* brought forth a lengthy discussion. Companies that had used these films reported splendid results. Mr. Gibbs, of Boston, stated that he originally felt the films were poorly gotten out and a useless expenditure of money. He stated that after using them he had changed his opinion and was now enthusiastic over them. He stated he was still using them and had no trouble in getting them in all the moving-picture theaters without expense.[68]

The Boston correspondent's enthusiasm runs somewhat against the experience of educational and industrial film producers, who were often only "nontheatrical" because such venues were rarely open to them. But advertisements from local newspapers indicate that *Back of the Button* and *Yours to Command* were screened at small-town theaters in New Mexico, Iowa, Pennsylvania, and Michigan (Figure 7).[69] The apparent receptivity of exhibitors indicates that utility operators benefited in several ways from the divergent interests of Hollywood's producer-distributors and theater owners who were not associated with the major studios. First, short subjects provided by the major Hollywood distributors were not provided for free, as the films sponsored by NELA were; independent theater owners were likely as pleased to get a free and projectable film as Mr. Gibbs was to get a free advertising venue.[70] Second, the sensitivity of theater owners to criticism directed at the frivolousness and supposed immorality of their main product, Hollywood entertainment films, was a consistent theme in the exhibitor trade publications during this period, and this might explain their eagerness to associate

65 *Utility Corporations*, pts. 10–16, exhibit 4223, 595. On the prominence of sponsored screenings at public fairs and expositions, see Waller, "Locating Early Nontheatrical Audiences," 87–90.

66 Kelly, "Motion Picture," 26.

67 Ibid.

68 *Utility Corporations*, pt. 4, exhibit 1999, 448.

69 These advertisements were found through *newspaperarchive.com*, a pay website with sporadic holdings. See, for example, *Deming* (NM) *Headlight*, January 27, 1922, 4; *Davenport* (IA) *Democrat*, July 18, 1922, 3; *Altoona* (PA) *Daily Mirror*, March 1, 1922, 15; and *Ironwood* (MI) *Daily Globe*, September 28, 1922, 6.

70 On the quality of prints received from distributors by independent exhibitors, see Richard Koszarski, *An Evening's Entertainment: The Age of the Silent Feature Picture, 1915–1928*, ed. Charles Harpole, History of the American Cinema 3 (Berkeley: University of California Press: 1990), 163–210.

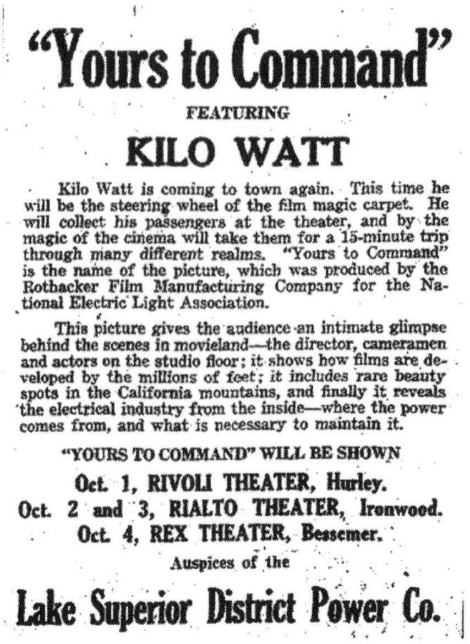

"Yours to Command"

FEATURING

KILO WATT

Kilo Watt is coming to town again. This time he will be the steering wheel of the film magic carpet. He will collect his passengers at the theater, and by the magic of the cinema will take them for a 15-minute trip through many different realms. "Yours to Command" is the name of the picture, which was produced by the Rothacker Film Manufacturing Company for the National Electric Light Association.

This picture gives the audience an intimate glimpse behind the scenes in movieland—the director, cameramen and actors on the studio floor; it shows how films are developed by the millions of feet; it includes rare beauty spots in the California mountains, and finally it reveals the electrical industry from the inside—where the power comes from, and what is necessary to maintain it.

"YOURS TO COMMAND" WILL BE SHOWN

Oct. 1, RIVOLI THEATER, Hurley.

Oct. 2 and 3, RIALTO THEATER, Ironwood.

Oct. 4, REX THEATER, Bessemer.

Auspices of the

Lake Superior District Power Co.

Figure 7. Advertisements for NELA's *Yours to Command* appeared on the entertainment pages of local newspapers and invoked the rhetoric of commercial film advertising. *Ironwood* (MI) *Daily Globe*, September 28, 1922.

themselves with industry and education in order to deflect such criticisms.[71] For the local movie theater, NELA's educational films may well have provided a note of uplift, just as they "aroused much interest in the movie fans" for the industry.

But the motion-picture theater appears not to have remained available to NELA throughout the period. In the summer of 1922, Will H. Hays, head of the newly founded Motion Picture Producers and Distributors of America (MPPDA), and exhibitor trade organizations negotiated standard exhibition clauses and a code of ethics that included a provision eliminating direct advertising films.[72] Also that summer, one of the exhibitor groups resolved to send a delegate to the convention of the Associated Advertising Clubs of the World (an advertisers trade association) to deliver a message "condemning the sale of worthless film stock to the public," and Hays dispatched Courtland Smith, the MPPDA's secretary, to the convention to encourage advertisers to seek alternate venues.[73] Thus, by mid-1922, a film like the SVE's proposed advertisement for utility securities would have had some difficulty finding a venue among movie fans.[74] While the filmmaking activity under consideration here eschewed the promotion of particular products or services, the ban seems to have had a chilling effect on industrial and educational film production companies.[75] In the case of NELA's films, the commercial industry's campaign against using commercial screens for anything but Hollywood entertainment seems to have closed these venues to the utility industry by early 1924.[76]

---

71 For a discussion of independent exhibitors' often strained relations with Hollywood producers, see Kathryn Fuller-Seeley, "'What the Picture Did for Me': Small-Town Exhibitors' Strategies for Surviving the Great Depression," in *Hollywood in the Neighborhood*, ed. Kathryn Fuller Seeley (Berkeley: University of California Press, 2008), 186–207.

72 For a discussion of the industrywide ban on advertising films and its effect on noncommercial cinema's distribution systems, see Katherine H. Fuller, *At the Picture Show: Small-Town Audiences and the Creation of Movie-Fan Culture* (Washington, DC: Smithsonian Institution Press, 1996), 94–95.

73 "Final Session of MPTOA Convention," *Exhibitors Trade Review*, May 27, 1922, 1861; "Work with Hays," *Film Daily*, June 15, 1922, 1.

74 *Utility Corporations*, pt. 2, exhibit 379, 342–343.

75 See Leon Pelletier, "Useful Cinema, Films Genres, and Screen Networks: The Story of Canadian Films Limited (1919–1920)," *Moving Image* 11, no. 1 (2011): 56–97.

76 This is the latest advertisement for any NELA-sponsored film I've been able to locate through local newspapers available through newspaperarchive.com. Also notable is that this was shortly after Ford's Motion Picture Department shifted its attention to the nontheatrical market and coincident with the department's ceasing production of films.

The general public's theatrical amusement sites were not the only cultural spaces in which NELA's films were screened. After engagements in these venues, NELA's films then moved to the nontheatrical circuit of lecture halls, churches, and schools. In this, NELA and its associate and subsidiary organizations had two options. First, the prints maintained by the local companies or regional associations could travel with lecturers from their own speaker bureaus or be loaned to schools through their educational committees. NELA's Great Lakes Division, seeking to forge "cooperation with educational institutions," sent films, among other teaching materials, to colleges. As to the speaker bureaus, all of NELA's films were expected to be of use not only on motion-picture screens but also to accompany local utility speakers' presentations to various civic organizations, as such nontheatrical venues were sometimes thought to be the primary venue for its films: "Companies will find this film useful for showing before their employees, at meetings of boards of trade, Rotary Clubs, church organizations, civic bodies, and various other local groups—*it will also be possible in many cases* to arrange with the management of motion-picture houses to put the film on as part of the regular entertainment."[77] A contemporary account reports that the "various other local groups" included churches and YMCAs.[78] These venues constituted not only the lecture circuit for utility company speakers but also the nontheatrical-film exhibition circuit that the variety of educational film companies servicing the utilities had hoped to access. Several of these organizations provided for distribution of their clients' films by maintaining circulating libraries, and this is the second option NELA had for accessing the nontheatrical circuit.

In March 1923, Oxley reported that *Yours to Command* had been placed with the DeVry Circulating Library, the YMCA, and "others," and was "receiving considerable circulation."[79] Almost five years later, in March 1928, Oxley reported the film had been placed with "a circulating library run by the Rothacker Film Co., which made the film, and that reports received to date covering three months show a circulation of over 10,000 for *Yours to Command* and about 10,500 for *Back of the Button*."[80] Films were also distributed by the Motion Picture Bureau of the YMCA, a significant distributor of nontheatrical films during this period, and it is under this distributor's cover that NELA's *The Back of the Button* appeared on Dunwoody Industrial Institute's classroom film schedule.[81] In such instances, NELA's distribution strategy would seem to be of a piece with the campaign's infiltration of civic institutions such as women's clubs,

---

See Grieveson, "Work of Film," 46.

77 *Utility Corporations*, pt. 3, exhibit 984, 1074, emphasis added. This Information Service bulletin is from June 1921, suggesting that the nontheatrical venues listed were considered important, in some quarters of NELA, before theatrical venues were closed off.

78 Gruening, *Public Pays*, 226.

79 *Utility Corporations*, pts. 10–16, exhibit 4138, 224.

80 Ibid., 209. It is unclear from the source what exactly "circulation" measures, but almost certainly, this figure represents rentals from the library, not an estimate of viewers. Although some nontheatrical lending libraries produced documents that approximated the number of viewers—a sample slip was printed in the *N.E.L.A. Bulletin*—the sizes of audiences who saw any film is difficult to establish in this period, and this problem is compounded by the variety of exhibition venues for these films.

81 *Educational Screen*, March 1926, 143.

fraternal organizations, local newspapers, and schools. The circulating libraries permitted NELA's films to move into the sorts of organizations it sought to reach through its speaker bureaus and educational committees.

It should be noted, however, that this distribution circuit was far from fully developed in this period. Despite several interesting case studies, there is not yet sufficient research to settle the question of whether film technology was widespread in churches, clubs, and schools. Though theatrical 35mm projectors were available to such institutions, the complexity of the machine and combustibility of nitrate film prints required trained and sometimes unionized operators, as well as, depending on one's municipality, a variety of safety devices, and the regulations conspired to limit the diffusion of this technology.[82] The nontheatrical film market was in the midst of a decade-long transformation, switching from the theatrical 35mm gauge to the smaller, more portable, and less combustible 16mm acetate standard. But competing formats still proliferated, which resulted in many institutional buyers delaying adoption of any of the new technologies, and this likely slowed the development of centralized distribution systems and other infrastructural supports necessary for cinema to achieve everyday and everywhere ubiquity.[83] As a result, during the 1920s, this new substandard gauge and constellation of portable technologies were still primarily sold as luxury consumer goods for the home and may not have been widely found in churches, schools, or Rotary clubs.[84]

Given this, NELA companies could have purchased their own portable projectors and provided a full-service screening system, and there is evidence that at least one company in California did as part of its educational campaign to reach schools and clubs.[85] However, even if a utilities representative did show up with film and projector, other, more basic necessities might still be missing. In April 1926, the secretary of the Missouri Public Utility Information section wrote to the president of a local power company: "It is important that schools shall, wherever possible, be lighted by electricity. Education by motion picture is progressing. I give a little lecture, illustrated with slides, which many schools have wanted, but owing to the fact that they did not have electricity I was unable to give it to them."[86] The material contained in the educational trade magazines was, at this point, aspirational, far outpacing the diffusion of technology necessary to sustain the new industry.[87] Production companies and

82 SVE's Harley Clarke gave up producing films once he realized the market was not yet sufficiently developed, and he invested instead in designing the material infrastructure of projection equipment that would create this market.

83 On the slow diffusion of 16mm from the perspective of the YMCA's Motion Picture Bureau, see Ronald Greene, "Pastoral Exhibition: The YMCA Motion Picture Bureau and the Transition to 16mm, 1928–1939," in *Useful Cinema*, 219–221.

84 On 16mm as a consumer good for the modern home, see Haidee Wasson, "Electric Homes! Automatic Movies! Efficient Entertainment! 16mm and Cinema's Domestication in the 1920s," *Cinema Journal* 48, no. 4 (2009): 1–21.

85 *Utility Corporations*, pts. 10–16, exhibit 4189, 398.

86 *Utility Corporations*, pts. 5–6, 291.

87 For the diffusion and promotion of 16mm in the 1920s and 1930s, see Wasson, "The Reel of the Month Club: 16mm Projectors, Home Theaters, and Film Libraries in the 1920s," in *Going to the Movies: Hollywood and the Social Experience of Cinema*, ed. Richard Maltby et al. (Exeter, UK: University of Exeter Press, 2007), 217–234; Gregory Waller, "Projecting the Promise of 16mm," *Useful Cinema*, 125–148, which makes the point about the nontheatrical trade press's being "aspirational." Waller indicates that in 1931, only 30 percent of schools had

distributors did not often last more than a few years, leaving what market there was short of content. By the end of the 1930s, this situation would be quite different, and private industry would, at this point, make more extensive use of 16mm filmmaking and nontheatrical venues.[88] If NELA's strategy for distribution had assumed a robust nontheatrical circuit, either as a primary or as a secondary outlet for films, it would have arrived too soon, and on discovering this, NELA might have sensibly scaled back operations. By the fall of 1927, the motion-picture work had fallen, according to one executive, into a state of "innocuous desuetude."[89]

Of Limited Use: The Limits of NELA's Use of Motion Pictures. Between the two popular accounts of the FTC investigation I have consulted, accounts of motion-picture propaganda constitute fewer than a dozen—albeit outraged—pages in works that, together, run nearly one thousand pages. In both, the vast majority of space is devoted to the private utilities' manipulation of the press and of nonvisual education. This distribution of attention is nearly proportional with the attention paid to motion pictures in the FTC report's seventy-one volumes, of which fewer than one hundred pages are devoted to film. The report contains advertising budgets for NELA and its nearly eight hundred member companies, separating motion picture expenditures from newspaper, radio, and other advertising. The number of associated companies functioned to conceal the scale of NELA's activities by distributing the costs of any advertising among a number of companies, and, since the different categories of spending are not in a constant proportion across the various companies, summarizing the total advertising expenditures throughout NELA is difficult. Nevertheless, a sample of companies indicates that motion picture advertising budgets were rarely more than 5 percent of any member company's advertising budget, perhaps totaling enough to produce three or four films per year, and that motion pictures were mostly utilized from 1922 to 1926, but not extensively thereafter.[90] One should be careful not to confuse the account of those carrying out and publicizing the investigation of the utility companies' propaganda activities with an accurate representation of those activities, and as we have seen, the motion picture was appealing precisely because it required relatively little investment. Nevertheless, a survey of multiple sources has turned up only three films directly sponsored by NELA: the two discussed above, *Back of the Button* and *Yours to Command*, and *The Great Surprise* (Atlas, 1924). In the context of the broader campaign and its objectives, why were films not more fully utilized? A

projectors, and, with Wasson, concludes this was the result of a market flooded with competing small-gauge, safety-stock formats (16mm, 28mm, 9.5mm, and more).

88 In 1938, *Business Screen*, a new trade publication for specifically business and industrial uses of film, was launched. And even then, recent research has suggested that the institutional small-gauge circuit did not fully blossom until the infusion of funds from a large federal program, the National Defense of Education Act (1958). See Devin Orgeron, Marsha Orgeron, and Dan Streible, "Introduction: A History of Learning with the Lights Off," in *Learning with the Lights Off*, 41.

89 *Utility Corporations*, pt. 3, 872.

90 *Utility Corporations*, document 92, reference figures for Alabama Power Company (pt. 30, p. 432), San Joaquin Light & Power (pts. 33–34, p. 1684), Cleveland Electric Illuminating Company (pts. 33–34, p. 1666), and Dallas Power & Light (pt. 25, p. 913). Estimate of films NELA could produce per year assumes an average budget of $45,000, the budget for the film indicated above.

consideration of NELA's political objectives and targeted audiences suggests that those most easily reached by motion pictures in the 1920s were not, ultimately, the people NELA was most interested in influencing.

Generalizing from NELA's manipulation of the press, David Nye has sought to explain the relative absence of imagery of any sort in the NELA campaign by arguing that the dynamics of covert communication worked against the inclusion of images in NELA's campaign: "Not only were photographs unnecessary in the newspaper, which itself was the guarantor of objectivity, but photographs could even raise questions of credibility. . . . Unusual photographs . . . particularly if taken inside factory gates, could arouse the very suspicion of bias, which the use of the newspaper was to allay."[91] Nye addresses still images, though his argument can be extended to those that move. This explanation is suggestive, neatly fitting Nye's communications model of public relations; here, the combination of two "ideological forms that masquerade as objective truth" cancel each other out.[92] Of course, images have been used in public relations, all the while preserving the masquerade, so I suspect Nye is closer to a satisfactory explanation when he attends to the particular objectives of NELA's campaign. Elsewhere in his article, Nye observes that NELA's covert communications sought to disrupt "the earlier processes [that] Americans had used to arrive at generally held opinions."[93] These processes imply locations and institutions not necessarily reached by cinema, an emerging mass medium, and nascent portable technology.

Cultivated debate and public oratory, the ideal media for democracy in nineteenth-century American political traditions, took place in and were sustained by specifically local civil institutions. These were precisely the institutions most often and most outrageously targeted by NELA: the school, the Rotary club, the local paper, and so on. We've seen above that several utility men valued cinema's ability to reach the "working man" and "movie fans," but NELA's broader public relations campaign was composed of a variety of campaigns targeting more specific groups: financial leaders through deposits in their institutions, editors through fraudulent newswire services, college professors and technical school instructors through altered textbooks and summer pay, and prominent citizens reached through Rotary Club lectures and "grand dames of the women's clubs cruising about the country on power trust subsidies."[94] Local institutions such as these constituted what Robert Weibe called "island communities." During the nineteenth century, communities could be described as "islands" because the "weak communication" between them "restricted interaction among these islands and dispersed the power to form opinion and enact public policy."[95] This understanding of community became a threatened ideal between the late nineteenth and early twentieth centuries, as the scale of new institutions—principally corporations—dwarfed these smaller institutions, and this anxiety over lost self-determination, for Weibe, lay behind

91 Nye, "Public Relations as Covert Political Communication," 31.

92 Ibid., 33.

93 Ibid., 26.

94 "Manufacturing Public Opinion," *New Republic*, December 9, 1931, 102.

95 Robert H. Wiebe, *The Search for Order, 1877–1920* (New York: Macmillan, 1967), xiii.

anti-monopoly sentiment in the early twentieth century.[96] The reaction to NELA's public relations campaign resulted not only from its size relative to local institutions but also from the fact that it had covertly infiltrated and undermined them. All together, the many smaller groups targeted by NELA might have added up to a large number of people, but this was not a "mass audience," insofar as these different groups were not targeted by a single media form that addressed the entirety of this audience.

In the more skeptical discourse surrounding NELA's sponsoring films, the utility men understood the cultural function of cinema to be equivalent with "the movies" and valued the medium's ability to reach a mass audience composed, mostly notably, of members of the middle and lower classes: "Mrs. Electricity Customer," the "working man," and "movie fans." And NELA's public relations films certainly traded on motion pictures' appeal to the "movie fan." Their screenings were announced in local newspapers' entertainment sections (see Figure 7), and their advertisements promised that its star "Kilo Watt is coming" to a nearby theater.[97] As a technology that was perceived to most easily reach this audience, motion pictures were of use in some corporate information campaigns, such as the Ford Motor Company's, the aims of which Grieveson neatly summarizes: "Ford's moving pictures were imagined as a pedagogic medium distinct from commercial cinema that was capable of shaping new modalities of 'useful' consciousness and conduct for working-class and immigrant groups who would form populations fitted to the new era of mass production."[98] Though the form and address of Ford's films were thought distinct from commercial cinema, the campaign—especially in its early years when the movie theater was the primary exhibition site—was nevertheless directed at the assumed audience of the movies: the working-class and immigrant population. Dissenting voices within the utility industry's discussion of whether and how to use motion pictures emphasized that this was not the audience the campaign needed to reach: "It is true that a great many people patronize 'the movies' but it is also true that the great number who do not . . . are of the most assistance to the utility business."[99]

Experiments in producing films for the commercial cinema's audience gave way, by the mid-1920s, to attempts to circulate existing films as the campaign increasingly targeted specific segments of the population, and these attempts were limited by the unsettled state of the nontheatrical field. The motion picture was, for the campaign's purpose, not yet sufficiently "mobile" and "flexible" and, at this historical moment, too closely associated with mass entertainment. No one, utility executives skeptical of the film campaign claimed, went to the movies to be educated. The "thinking man"

96   Ibid., 52.

97   Advertisement for *Back of the Button* in *Deming* (NM) *Headlight*, January 27, 1922. In his discussion of film in rural America during the 1930s, Gregory Waller notes the similar associations with "the movies"—though there located at the level of film form—sought by films designed for the instruction of farming communities. See Gregory A. Waller, "Free Talking Picture—Every Farmer Is Welcome: Non-Theatrical Film and Everyday Life in Rural America during the 1930s," in *Going to the Movies*, 248–272.

98   Grieveson, "Work of Film," 28.

99   Bernard J. Mullaney (director, Illinois Committee on Public Utilities Information), "Circulation Must Have First Consideration in Working Out Film Plan," *Electric Railway Journal* 56, no. 19 (1920): 971.

was not to be found there.[100] Thus, this communications medium was of less use in a campaign that sought to subvert the traditional organs of civil society than club lecturers and newspaper editors. Twenty years before the popularization of the two-step flow model of communication—which proposes that, even in a mass-mediated society, experts and opinion leaders mediate the messages of mass communications to influence broader opinion—utility executives and their public relations operatives did not perceive the mass medium of the movies to have much use in influencing broader public opinion.[101] In this respect, a quintessentially modern, multimedia information campaign remained at least partly rooted, in its understanding of public opinion and how it informed the political process in an earlier era.

Conclusions. NELA's public relations campaign, to the extent that we identify it with the national organization, seems not to have involved itself very heavily in film and did not view the medium as "useful" for convincing the public of its cause, as it did other media. This is not to say that other private utility companies within the organization did not produce their own films—in fact, several companies brought films to the 1927 convention for display to other members of the industry—but it is not clear from national trade journals and the record of the federal investigation that these films were part of the national association's coordinated public relations campaign against federal intervention. At the level of the national organization and what projects we can see it initiating, filmmaking, distributing, and exhibiting activities were frequently experimented with and used in a variety of different departments, but these were never developed along a particular line to have a particular effect, as was the case with the newswire services and pamphlets studied by Nye and Raucher.

Considered in the context of the entire campaign, film was used only slightly more than "sky writing." That film was only an interesting experiment peripheral to a very large, very multimedia advertising campaign—a campaign in which we might expect to find films—demands explanation. And Wasson and Acland's construction of useful cinema not as a genre or a body of films but as an approach to the technology by institutional agents encourages us to find explanations for the failure of the cinema to find a use in institutions. The reasons for this failure, as this account has shown, were several: constraints placed on the national organization by members indifferent to moving-picture propaganda; the difficulty that film producers had in locating the appropriate sponsoring body; the disorder in the industrial film market precipitated by the film industry's code of advertising ethics and the uncertainty over which would be the preferred small-gauge film technology in the nontheatrical market; the absence of centralized distribution in the nontheatrical market generally; uneven infrastructural

---

100 Gregory Waller has recently observed that movie theaters often functioned, in the 1910s, as nontheatrical venues when screenings were sponsored, the venue rented out, and screenings open only to invited groups. It should be noted that the theatrical screenings I've identified were advertised in local papers and were open to the public. See Gregory A. Waller, "Locating Early Non-Theatrical Audiences," 92.

101 The acceptance of the two-step flow model follows the publication of Katz and Lazarsfeld's *Personal Influence*. But even there, the authors' discussion of motion pictures considers what other media lead to the selection of entertainment films and not film itself—whether designed for entertainment or to influence—as a form of mass media that might shape opinions. See Elihu Katz and Paul Felix Lazarsfeld, *Personal Influence, the Part Played by People in the Flow of Mass Communications* (Glencoe, IL: Free Press, 1955).

support—including, ironically, the limited penetration of electrification—that prevented cinema from being an omnipresent technology; and the uncertain status of motion pictures as an informational tool. That cinema has, as Wasson and Acland put it, been crafted "into a tool that is useful, a tool that makes, persuades, instructs, demonstrates, and *does* something" is not a polemical assertion but a proposition that can be tested—qualified, refined, and made more precise—through further research.[102] Despite its modernity and the appeal it held for progressive educators and other reformers, theorists of employee training, and those seeking to create appropriate subjects for industrial and postindustrial democracy, cinema did not easily find a use for all institutions, for all of their communications functions, in all times and in all places. In the growing field of "useful cinema," cases such as the utility industry's should help film and media historians to identify which necessary conditions needed to be met for an organization to find cinema more or less useful and which determinants might condition the use to which the medium was then put. As a result, we will continue to refine our understanding of how moving-image culture can be "integrated into a fuller spectrum of historical analysis" and how it participated in "the intricate relations among films, institutions, and exhibition locations."[103]   ✳

I thank the numerous readers who provided valuable insights and questions when reading earlier versions of this essay, in particular Caroline Frick, Vinzenz Hediger, Bruce J. Hunt, Gregory Waller, Haidee Wasson, and the editors of Cinema Journal. *For their encouragement and helpful comments on early drafts of this article, I thank my supervisors Thomas Schatz and Janet Staiger. For her patience and incisive editorial suggestions on successive drafts of this article, particular thanks are due to Colleen Montgomery.*

102   Wasson and Acland, "Introduction," 6.
103   Ibid., 13.

New Hollywood in the Rust Belt: Urban Decline and Downtown Renaissance in *The King of Marvin Gardens* and *Rocky*

by Lawrence Webb

Abstract: This article reviews the geographical dynamics of New Hollywood, arguing that the industrial crisis of 1969–1971 catalyzed further decentralization of location shooting beyond Los Angeles, bringing new types of urban space into view. It examines the parallel crisis and restructuring of the film industry and the inner city via two films, *The King of Marvin Gardens* (Bob Rafelson, 1972) and *Rocky* (John G. Avildsen, 1976), which are emblematic of distinct phases in the development of New Hollywood. Through their aesthetic strategies, narrative structure, and mapping of cinematic space, these films produced allegories of urban decline and renewal that closely engaged with the transformation of the American city, from the urban crisis of the late 1960s to neoliberal programs of renewal in the late 1970s.

At the end of the 1960s, the Hollywood studios and the American inner city faced historic crises that seemed to threaten their very existence. While the studios recorded substantial losses, estimated at a combined figure of $600 million between 1969 and 1971, the formerly prosperous centers of American cities were mired in an urban social crisis that was fast transforming into a widespread economic crisis.[1] Although both situations were products of complex and distinctive historical factors, there are nevertheless important ways in which the two crises not only occurred in parallel but also were necessarily intertwined. This article explores the simultaneous crisis and restructuring of the motion picture industry and the American inner city, arguing that taking an explicitly spatial perspective opens up new avenues for conceptualizing an apparently well-understood period of Hollywood history.[2]

---

1   David A. Cook, *Lost Illusions: American Cinema in the Shadow of Watergate and Vietnam, 1970–1979* (Berkeley: University of California Press, 2000), 9.

2   Despite the large volume of work on New Hollywood, much of the existing literature privileges the cultural impact of Watergate and the Vietnam War, displacing other important concerns such as deindustrialization, globalization, and urban decline.

Lawrence Webb is lecturer in film studies at the University of Sussex.

© 2015 by the University of Texas Press

The crisis and reorganization of the Hollywood film industry at the end of the 1960s had important, and as yet underexamined, geographical dynamics. While the industrial crisis accelerated the long-term shift toward package deals and independent production, it also had a significant impact on the volume and geographical pattern of location shooting. This opened up new cinematic terrain for Hollywood, expanding location shooting beyond its established coordinates—for example, Manhattan or parts of the American West—into new locales, from small towns and rural landscapes to the (post)industrial cities of the so-called Rust Belt. In this piece, I focus in detail on two films that are emblematic of two phases of New Hollywood and that illuminate different aspects of this historic transition. The first, Bob Rafelson's melancholy, autumnal *The King of Marvin Gardens* (1972), made in Atlantic City and produced on a low budget for BBS Productions, epitomizes the small-scale, personal cinema that emerged from the industrial crisis of 1969–1971. In contrast, *Rocky* (John G Avildsen, 1976), shot on location in Philadelphia, stands at a key transition point in the late 1970s, when a second wave of New Hollywood, best exemplified by the more commercially oriented and accessible work of the so-called movie brats, was radically departing from (and for many critics, vanquishing) the artistic and political possibilities of the first wave.[3] Through close analysis of the films' locations and construction of cinematic space, I propose to reframe our understanding of their political meanings within the specific context of urban crisis and neoliberal paradigms of redevelopment that emerged in the 1970s.

My aim here is to combine an industrial and economic perspective with a fine-grained analysis of the spatial and textual dynamics of seventies cinema. In doing so, I draw on Fredric Jameson's notion of cognitive mapping and its lineage in the work of the American urbanist Kevin Lynch, whose classic book *The Image of the City* compared the mental cityscapes recalled by citizens of Boston, Jersey City, and Los Angeles.[4] Analyzing drawings made by local residents, Lynch contrasted the "image-ability" of dense, historically layered cityscapes such as Boston with the formlessness and fluidity of the built environment in cities such as Jersey City and especially Los Angeles, where few iconic landmarks were available to orient users in their surroundings.[5] For Jameson, this relationship of the individual subject to a wider social structure provided a compelling spatial figure for the problematic of contemporary capitalism, in which a new set of global relationships essentially displaced older forms of political thought and representation.[6] This was developed in one of Jameson's earlier pieces on film, an essay on *Dog Day Afternoon* (Sidney Lumet, 1975) that appeared seven years before his seminal piece on postmodernism.[7] The geographical focus of this piece was later underscored by Jameson's call for a "spatial analysis of culture," in which a close

---

3 On the two phases of New Hollywood, see Derek Nystrom, "The New Hollywood," in *The Wiley-Blackwell History of American Film*, ed. Cynthia Lucia, Roy Grundmann, and Art Simon (Chichester, UK: Blackwell, 2012), 3:409–434.

4 Kevin Lynch, *The Image of the City* (Cambridge, MA: MIT Press, 1960).

5 Ibid.

6 Fredric Jameson, *Postmodernism, or, The Cultural Logic of Late Capitalism* (London: Verso, 1992).

7 Fredric Jameson, "Class and Allegory in Contemporary Mass Culture: *Dog Day Afternoon* as a Political Film," *College English* 38, no. 8 (1977): 843–859.

attention to space was vital in moving beyond the impasses of Marxist aesthetics and the seemingly irresolvable split between realism and modernism (terms, of course, beginning to lose purchase in the media-saturated world of the late twentieth century). Films produce cognitive maps through both their formal articulation and engagement with space and the relationship developed between the protagonist(s) and their diegetic world. Importantly, *cognitive* here is not understood to exclude embodied spectatorship; it also encompasses a range of affective responses to cinematic space. In this piece, I adapt elements of both Lynch's and Jameson's notions of cognitive mapping to establish ways in which a film's spatial form produces relations of visibility, mobility, and affectivity within the urban environment, and I examine how these produce political meanings in a specific geographical and historical context.

New Hollywood: A Geographical Perspective. Hollywood and the American city were both deeply affected in the mid-twentieth century by large-scale demographic, geographical, and cultural shifts. Foremost among these was the historic migration of young, prosperous couples and families from the city to the rapidly expanding suburbs. Suburbanization therefore played a central role in the fate of the inner city and the crisis of Hollywood's mass audience: as urban centers declined, so did their entertainment districts and the first-run theaters that had generated the lion's share of studio profits in the era of vertical integration. Yet even more than this was at stake: no less than a wholesale reorganization of patterns of urban life, of consumption and leisure, and the use and meaning of public and private space. By the late 1960s, the most visible manifestation of the burgeoning crisis in the inner city was the series of urban uprisings, or "ghetto riots," that ripped across African American neighborhoods from coast to coast, most famously in Watts, Los Angeles (1965), Detroit (1967), and Newark (1967). Yet the riots were not a cause but a symptom of a wider malaise.[8] The "urban crisis" of the mid- to late 1960s, closely associated with the ghetto riots and largely understood in the United States as grounded in issues of poverty, racial discrimination, and civil rights, developed into a broader, more fundamental second phase in the 1970s. As an editorial for the *Wall Street Journal* outlined in 1975, this "new urban crisis" compounded the familiar symptoms of urban blight and social unrest with mushrooming deficits, decaying infrastructure, faltering public services, and fiscal crises that pushed municipal governments to the brink of bankruptcy.[9] New York City was an exemplary case, narrowly avoiding default in 1975 despite the Ford administration's famous refusal to extend federal aid and later "rescued" and restructured by an emergency coalition of investment banks and other corporate interests. Likewise, major cities across the Rust Belt, such as Philadelphia, Detroit, and Cleveland, were pushed close to insolvency by the double whammy of eroding tax bases and spiraling welfare commitments.

From the mid-1970s, a new paradigm began to emerge from the ashes of the urban crisis. The perceived failure of both Keynesian economics and liberal social policy

8 On the urban crisis, see Robert Beauregard, *Voices of Decline: The Postwar Fate of US Cities* (New York: Routledge, 2002).

9 "The New Urban Crisis," *Wall Street Journal*, June 23, 1975, 10.

paved the way for a set of neoliberal political strategies at urban and national scales. Building on the economic theories of Milton Friedman and the Chicago School, and reinforced by an ideological commitment to the free market and entrepreneurialism, neoliberal policies advocated fiscal deregulation and retrenchment in social spending and placed a new emphasis on finance capitalism as the motor of economic growth. Cities were therefore not merely passive subjects of neoliberalism; rather, they were often at the cutting edge, operating as testing grounds for national economic policy. Deregulation, public-private partnerships, and property speculation became established, if contested, protocols for downtown and neighborhood redevelopment.[10] By the late 1970s, *Time* magazine heralded a "downtown renaissance." Conveniently bracketing the deep social problems of American cities, the editorial championed a new skyscraper boom that was transforming central business districts from Cleveland and St. Louis to Atlanta and Los Angeles.[11]

Of course, the same time span, from roughly 1967 to 1977, also witnessed the first iteration of New Hollywood, during which the so-called Hollywood Renaissance or New American Cinema exploded onto movie screens. Accounts of this celebrated period of American cinema emphasize, in varying degrees, different aspects of the narrative, whether industrial or institutional (package production, corporate takeovers, the demise of the Production Code), aesthetic (the influence of European cinema, television, and exploitation film), auteurist (a new "film school generation"), or sociocultural (the New Left and the counterculture).[12] Nevertheless, most commentators agree that the preconditions for a "new" Hollywood were generated by industrial instability, opening up a relatively brief period of innovation and experimentation that would be foreclosed by the emergence and triumph of the blockbuster logic in the second half of the decade.

The origins of the crisis can be traced back to the late 1940s, when post–Paramount Decree Hollywood sought resolutions to its various problems, whether through production differentiation, technological innovation, or accommodation with (and expansion into) the new medium of television. At the same time, geographical expansion provided a vital lifeline in the struggle to maintain profitability and market dominance. While distribution and marketing further saturated Hollywood's international market coverage, increasing amounts of runaway production capitalized on cheap European studios, locations, and labor. But runaways became less attractive in the face of an emerging global recession, industrial unrest in Europe, and Nixon's devaluation of the dollar in 1971. In contrast, the industry's "spatial fix" of the 1970s would involve the reorganization of production in the United States, with the increased

---

10 Neil Brenner and Nik Theodore, eds., *Spaces of Neoliberalism: Urban Restructuring in North America and Western Europe* (Oxford, UK: Wiley-Blackwell, 2002), ix.

11 "Downtown Is Looking Up," *Time*, July 5, 1976.

12 The critical literature is extensive. See, for example, Cook, *Lost Illusions*; Thomas Elsaesser, Alexander Horvath, and Noel King, eds., *The Last Great American Picture Show: New Hollywood Cinema in the 1970s* (Amsterdam: University of Amsterdam Press, 2004); Jon Lewis, ed., *The New American Cinema* (Durham, NC: Duke University Press, 1999); and Geoff King, *New Hollywood Cinema: An Introduction* (New York: Columbia University Press, 2002).

mobility and territorial flexibility offered by location shooting becoming central to the new business structure.[13]

The breakup of the studio system and its movement toward a flexible and characteristically post-Fordist model had been developing throughout the 1950s and 1960s but accelerated during the intensive period of change between 1969 and 1971.[14] At the end of the 1960s, the structural flaws in the industry's business model were brought to the surface by a series of expensive flops, largely studio-based musicals such as *Doctor Doolittle* (Richard Fleischer, 1967) and *Hello, Dolly!* (Gene Kelly, 1969). The studios fell deep into the red: in 1969, the Hollywood majors recorded combined losses of $200 million, while over the following two years, the industry suffered total losses of some $600 million.[15] In the aftermath of the financial crisis, the studios (and their new corporate owners) responded with efforts to restructure and reorganize the business.[16] At Fox, often viewed as the bellwether of the film industry, August 1970 saw the studio in what *Variety* described as the "throes of economic uncertainty," with Darryl Zanuck and his son Richard initiating "a restructuring program of perhaps unprecedented proportions" to "redesign the make-up of Twentieth to bring it in tune with today's film business and national economy."[17] Streamlining of payroll and the production slate was combined with further exploitation of real estate assets, especially continuing development at Century City (which had been under way since the early 1960s).[18] The other studios made broadly similar cost-cutting moves, cutting headcount, shaking up creative and management structures, placing limits on production budgets, and making further divestitures of land and other fixed assets.[19] MGM was perhaps the most extreme case. A year after posting losses of $35 million in 1969, new owner Kirk Kerkorian sold the entirety of MGM's soundstages to real estate developers for $7.3 million, saved a further $8.3 million by shifting the head office from New York to Culver City, and closed twenty-two of the studio's thirty-two sales offices.[20] By early 1971, MGM's withdrawal from Los Angeles was complete, with the small slate of forthcoming MGM features shooting either in New York City or overseas.[21]

---

13   Here I am adapting "spatial fix" from the work of geographer David Harvey. See Harvey, *The Urban Experience* (Oxford, UK: Basil Blackwell, 1989).

14   Michael Storper, "The Transition to Flexible Specialization in the US Film Industry: External Economies, the Division of Labour, and the Crossing of Industrial Divides," *Cambridge Journal of Economics* 13, no. 2 (1989): 273–305.

15   Cook, *Lost Illusions*, 9; see also "Red Sunset on Writedowns," *Variety*, November 26, 1969, 3.

16   See, for example, Gene Arneel, "Radical Knife on Fox Costs," *Variety*, August 5, 1970, 3, 23; "United Artists Pares Payroll," *Variety*, January 20, 1971, 4.

17   Arneel, "Radical Knife on Fox Costs," 3.

18   Ibid.

19   For example, Columbia and Warner Bros. merged studio facilities at Burbank, a move announced in 1971 and accomplished in 1972. See Robert E. Wood, "Warner's, Columbia to Merge Studio Facilities: Films Will Still Operate Separately at Site in Burbank," *Los Angeles Times*, June 4, 1971, e13; and "Columbia Moves to Burbank Building," *Box Office*, August 28, 1972, 4.

20   Earl C. Gottschalk Jr., "The Hatchet Man: How Aubrey Is Reviving MGM by Cutting Out the Fat and Nostalgia," *Wall Street Journal*, October 23, 1970, 1.

21   "Another 50 out at MGM Studio: Dead until May; Shun 'Staff' in Future," *Variety*, January 20, 1971, 4.

Stanley R. Jaffe, chief operating officer at Paramount, described its restructuring strategy to *Life* magazine in 1970:

> We intend to cut down this company until we have an organization that can support twelve to fifteen pictures a year. In a small building in Beverly Hills our whole feature production staff will be just twenty-five people including secretaries. As for the studio, we're going to get rid of it. That delights me personally. Without that tremendous overhead we will finally have flexibility. It's like the army. A general can move ten men more easily than a thousand. In the future we can be more receptive to changes in the marketplace without the studio hanging around our necks.[22]

Although Paramount did not go quite as far as Jaffe suggests, his comments give a sense of the prevailing corporate attitude in Hollywood at the time. The picture painted here indicates a new ideal conception of the "studio" as a streamlined operation, outsourcing everything but core financial and managerial functions to remain flexible and receptive to changes in the audience. From this point on, the Hollywood majors became primarily financiers and distributors, with the greater share of production subcontracted to independent companies that could operate more efficiently, flexibly, and innovatively than the studios. With neither in-house production space nor the economies of scale involved in serial production, independent production companies increasingly used nonstudio locations for most exterior and interior scenes. This was made possible by technological innovation in more sensitive film stocks, lightweight cameras such as the Arriflex 35BL and the Panaflex, faster lenses, and other mobile filming equipment such as the Cinemobile, a portable, self-contained film studio in a van.[23]

Between the mid-1960s and the early 1970s, location shooting shifted from being an important component part of what was essentially still a studio-based production process to become the dominant production technique in Hollywood filmmaking.[24] If the Hollywood sound stages were often empty at the end of the 1960s, it was in part because of a new generation of filmmakers for whom the authenticity and directness of location shooting was fundamental to their artistic vision. However, it might have remained a minority technique without the economic pressures of the 1969–1971 crisis; following the restructuring of the studios, location shooting became a necessity rather than a choice. The benefits of location shooting meshed neatly with the cost-cutting imperatives of the studios' corporate management. According to Don Haggerty, president of the AFL-CIO Film Council, the incentives of location work might include "avoidance of studio overhead, avoidance of state corporate taxes on production, free or cheap city and state licensing, the ability to dodge payment on

---

22 "The Day the Dream Factory Woke Up," *Life*, February 27, 1970, 38–41, 41.

23 "Said's Cinemobile," *Variety Daily*, July 25, 1967.

24 An article in the *Wall Street Journal* provides a sense of the discourse around this shift, although we should be skeptical about the statistic (which can be only a rough estimate at best): "Today 95% of all films made by US producers are shot principally on locations far from the sound stages of Hollywood, as compared with only 49% as recently as 1968." Earl C. Gottschalk, "Goodbye Hollywood: More Movie Makers Do Filming in Sticks for Realism, Savings," *Wall Street Journal*, July 25, 1972, 1.

fringe benefits, cheaper extras, and loose or non-existent union regulations that allow production savings."[25] The increased mobility of production also allowed the studios to evade direct confrontation with labor. If disputes flared up, shooting could be relocated with little difficulty, as Paramount had done with the Woody Allen project *Play It Again, Sam* (Herbert Ross, 1972), one of three films pulled from production in Manhattan as a result of what Paramount president Frank Yablans deemed "intransigence" on the part of local unions.[26]

During the 1970s, the turn to flexible specialization developed in what Michael Storper and Susan Christopherson describe as a "split-locational pattern."[27] While corporate headquarters and the majority of the new independent pre- and postproduction facilities remained in Southern California, shooting itself became widely dispersed across the United States. Although this is necessarily difficult to quantify, contemporary estimates suggested that around 70 percent of production was being filmed on location outside Los Angeles by 1974.[28] If this was due in part to Hollywood's search for cheap and novel locations, there were also forces pulling from the other direction. In the face of industrial decline and eroding tax bases, cash-starved municipal governments were beginning to turn away from publicly funded construction projects in favor of public-private partnerships and new policies of culture-led regeneration that would become widespread in the decades to come. As a result, from the late 1960s, cities and states began to compete at a new level of intensity for the expanding location-shooting dollar, luring production companies with tax breaks, minimal regulation, and non-unionized workforces. Such incentives were increasingly coordinated by city and state film commissions, leading to what the *Hollywood Reporter* called a "scramble for the now fragmented lodes of movie gold" and the *New York Times* referred to as "an ever spreading though undeclared war for location shooting."[29] New York City was a trendsetter in this respect. The Mayor's Office of Motion Pictures and Television, established in 1966 by Mayor John V. Lindsay, effectively provided a blueprint for city and state film commissions across the world in terms of coordinating permits, streamlining procedures, and promoting the city as a destination for Hollywood productions.[30] By 1976, when the first convention of film commissions, or "Cineposium," was held in Denver, thirty city and state governments had departments or associated organizations dedicated to promoting location shooting.[31]

25   Ibid.

26   Mel Gussow, "Third Movie May Be Shifted from Production Here," *New York Times*, September 2, 1971, 40.

27   Susan Christopherson and Michael Storper, "The City as Studio; the World as Back Lot: The Impact of Vertical Disintegration on the Location of the Motion Picture Industry," *Environment and Planning D: Society and Space* 4, no. 3 (1986): 305–320.

28   Gene Siskel, "Filmed in Chicago," *Chicago Tribune*, October 14, 1973, e3.

29   Phyllis Funke, "How You Gonna Keep 'Em Down in Hollywood Once You've Seen the Sticks?," *New York Times*, September 22, 1974, 135; *Hollywood Reporter*, October 6, 1971.

30   The development of the Mayor's Office of Film and Television was widely covered in the media. See, for example, Felix Kessler, "New York City Gets Rave Notices for Bid to Lure Filmmakers," *Wall Street Journal*, March 10, 1967; McCandlish Phillips, "City Is Successful as It Courts Moviemakers," *New York Times*, August 15, 1968, 39.

31   Charles Schreger, "States' Right to a Hunk of Hollywood," *Los Angeles Times*, March 21, 1980, G1. See also "26 State Film Groups' Colo. Meet," *Back Stage*, February 2, 1976, 1, 27.

This decentralization of production was widely reported in the trade press and in local newspapers, often mixed with a shot of civic boosterism. For example, in 1976, *Chicago Tribune* film critic Gene Siskel summed up the benefits of location filming for the Windy City: "To put it simply, this moviemaking boomlet is one very nice development. Nice, because our town and state are benefitting financially. Nice, because our town's talented film crews are getting work. And nice, because a variety of public and private citizens are working together to freshen our city and state images by exposing them to display on wide and small screens throughout the world."[32] While in the first instance the promotion of urban location shooting was motivated by economic imperatives, as Siskel's comments suggest, the cultural representation of the city was also becoming an increasingly important commodity itself during the 1970s. In this way, the rise in location filming during the period was also congruent with the strategic aspiration of city governments to manage and project an image of their city for a global marketplace. As cities adapted to a predominantly service-sector economy, they began to position themselves as global financial centers and tourist destinations, hubs of leisure and consumerism. This reflects David Harvey's assertion that modes of urban governance had begun to shift during the 1970s from what he terms a "managerial" to an "entrepreneurial" paradigm, whereby cities and regions have been increasingly compelled to compete on the open market for mobile flows of capital and labor.[33] The cinematic representation of the city thus developed alongside and in tandem with new schemes for city branding during this period.[34] Film commissions were therefore one of a number of quasi-public bodies at the municipal level, such as redevelopment agencies and convention and visitors bureaus, that sought to promote the city and its revitalized downtown as a safe place for tourists and an attractive location for company headquarters. In this way, two simultaneous processes—the terminal crisis of the studio system and the rise of cultural strategies for redeveloping and rebranding the postindustrial city—provided the institutional and economic framework for the decentralization and dispersal of Hollywood location shooting.

The postindustrial city therefore emerged not only as an artistic inspiration for New Hollywood but also as a production resource and visual commodity. As a result, American cinema of the 1970s displayed a new authenticity or verisimilitude in its images of the urban landscape; not since the heyday of film noir in the late 1940s had Hollywood film engaged so closely with the American city.[35] The most prominent production centers were undoubtedly New York and San Francisco, both of which experienced a film industry boom in the early to mid-1970s.[36] Both cities

32 Gene Siskel, "Roll 'Em! Chicago Sets the Scene for Today's Film Action," *Chicago Tribune*, December 5, 1976, c4.

33 David Harvey, "From Managerialism to Entrepreneurialism: The Transformation in Urban Governance in Late Capitalism," *Geografiska Annaler*, series B, *Human Geography* 71, no. 1 (1989): 3–17.

34 Miriam Greenberg, *Branding New York: How a City in Crisis Was Sold to the World* (New York: Routledge, 2008); Stephanie Hemelryk Donald, Eleonore Kofman, and Catherine Kevin, eds., *Branding Cities: Cosmopolitanism, Parochialism, and Social Change* (New York: Routledge, 2009).

35 On the American city in film noir, see Edward Dimendberg, *Film Noir and the Spaces of Modernity* (Cambridge, MA: Harvard University Press, 2004).

36 On San Francisco, see Joseph Robert, "Tapping S.F. film potential," *Los Angeles Times*, April 30, 1967, c16; Mel

could capitalize on distinctive, instantly recognizable, and often beautiful cityscapes, were long-standing cultural hubs, and had proactive local government support for filmmaking. But equally important, Hollywood location shooting moved beyond these established cinematic cities. In the late 1960s and 1970s, films were shot in cities—and importantly, specific *areas* of cities—that had been rarely, if ever, seen in mainstream feature films before. Previously peripheral or marginal spaces came into view. Cinematic New York extended beyond its traditional Manhattan base into unexplored parts of the Bronx, Brooklyn, and Queens. Hollywood made new forays into Brooklyn, taking in gentrifying areas such as Park Slope in *The Landlord* (Hal Ashby, 1970) and Brooklyn Heights in *Desperate Characters* (Frank Gilroy, 1971), as well as working-class districts such as Bay Ridge in *Saturday Night Fever* (John Badham, 1977). African American filmmaking and the so-called blaxploitation genre capitalized on authentic locations in Harlem, in films such as *Cotton Comes to Harlem* (Ossie Davis, 1970) and *Super Fly* (Gordon Parks Jr., 1972). Further afield than New York, the streets, buildings, and neighborhoods of declining industrial cities began to assume a new prominence on screen: for example, Philadelphia in *Rocky*, Chicago in *Medium Cool* (Haskell Wexler, 1968), blue-collar Boston in *The Friends of Eddie Coyle* (Peter Yates, 1973) and *The Last Detail* (Hal Ashby, 1973), Detroit in *Scarecrow* (Jerry Schatzberg, 1973) and *Blue Collar* (Paul Schrader, 1978), and the steel town of Clairton, Pennsylvania, in *The Deer Hunter* (Michael Cimino, 1978). In the remainder of this article, I analyze two of these films in detail and consider the ways in which their cinematic mapping of urban space engaged with contemporary political concerns, generating what I define as allegories of urban decline and renaissance.

The King of Marvin Gardens: **Urban Crisis on the Monopoly Board.** *The King of Marvin Gardens* was produced by BBS Productions and financed by Columbia as part of a six-picture deal.[37] Alongside films such as *Five Easy Pieces* (Bob Rafelson, 1970), *The Last Picture Show* (Peter Bogdanovich, 1971), and *A Safe Place* (Henry Jaglom, 1971), *Marvin Gardens* exemplified a new trend toward small-scale, auteur filmmaking and flexible production strategies within Hollywood. Budgeted at less than $1 million apiece, the productions were able to take advantage of International Alliance of Theatrical Stage Employees (IATSE) concessions that allowed location filming with smaller crews.[38] As Andrew Schaefer argues, the filmmakers and writers clustered around BBS were the most closely associated with the counterculture and the New Left of all the New Hollywood generation.[39] Bob Rafelson has since described how part of the political outlook and realist ethos of BBS was to explore the hidden corners of the American

Gussow, "Movies Leaving Hollywood Behind," *New York Times*, May 27, 1970, 36; Gerald Nachmans, "Coast's Bay Area Is Lure for Filmmakers," *New York Times*, August 12, 1971, 28; Philip Hager, "City Helps Out: Background for Films? Often It's San Francisco," *Los Angeles Times*, December 9, 1973, f1.

37 Cook, *Lost Illusions*, 108–109.

38 On IATSE concessions, see Derek Nystrom, "Hard Hats and Movie Brats: Auteurism and the Class Politics of the New Hollywood," *Cinema Journal* 43, no. 3 (2004): 18–41, 21.

39 Andrew Schaefer, "The Movement Inside: BBS Films and the Cultural Left in the New Hollywood," in *The World the Sixties Made: Politics and Culture in Recent America*, ed. Van Gosse and Richard Moser (Philadelphia: Temple University Press, 2003), 114–137.

urban landscape, focusing on what he refers to as "backwater cities," such as Taft, Bakersfield, and Birmingham, Alabama.[40] *Marvin Gardens* was shot entirely on location, predominantly in Atlantic City, New Jersey, where the screenwriter, Jacob Brackman, had grown up, with some material filmed in nearby Philadelphia. Although neither city had opened an official film bureau at that stage, permission to film in Atlantic City, including interior scenes at the jail and the convention hall, was directly granted by Mayor William T. Somers, who had reviewed the script and deemed (perhaps somewhat optimistically) that the film would generate "good publicity" for the city.[41] As the inspiration for the original Monopoly board layout and home of the Miss America pageant, Atlantic City has a symbolic presence and an especially representational quality that Brackman and Rafelson explored, allowing the film to work both as the documentation of a specific city in decline as well as a self-reflexive, allegorical piece about the fortunes of America (and Hollywood) at the turn of the 1970s.

Atlantic City was established by real estate speculators in the 1880s and first rose to prominence as a holiday resort in the 1900s. It remained a successful, even affluent seaside town throughout the 1920s and 1930s; its Prohibition-era heyday has, of course, recently been carefully recreated on-screen in *Boardwalk Empire* (HBO, 2010–2014). But its glamour had already begun to fade in the 1950s, with the rise of international tourism, jet travel, and new domestic destinations such as Disneyland. By the 1960s, it had become an exemplar of urban decay. From this perspective, the rise and fall of Atlantic City, a booming resort town from the early 1900s until the late 1940s, roughly paralleled the fortunes of the Hollywood studio system itself. As products of American industrial and economic expansion, both capitalized on the emergence of a new urban consumer to produce new kinds of entertainment and leisure. Similarly, the relative decline of both Atlantic City and the Hollywood studios from the 1950s on was to a large extent caused by similar factors: suburbanization, white flight, and the rise of new forms of leisure and consumption, be it television, out-of-town malls, or theme parks. Indeed, as Bryant Simon has documented, Atlantic City itself had no fewer than fifteen movie theaters in the mid-1950s, the majority of which had closed their doors only a decade later, a microcosm of the wider decline in inner-city exhibition that was so influential in the demise of the studio system.[42]

The King of Marvin Gardens captures Atlantic City in the grip of an economic downturn that had left it permanently out of season. In a *New Yorker* article from 1972, John McPhee captured the extent of its decay, making striking connections between the American urban crisis and the ruins of postwar Europe:

> The physical profile of streets perpendicular to the shore is something like a playground slide. It begins in the high skyline of Boardwalk hotels, plummets into warrens of "side-avenue" motels, crosses Pacific, slopes through church missions, convalescent homes, burlesque houses, rooming houses, and liquor

---

40 Bob Rafelson, DVD commentary for *The King of Marvin Gardens* (Criterion Collection DVD, 2010).

41 "Atlantic City 'Loans' Public Edifices," *Variety*, December 15, 1971, 7.

42 Bryant Simon, "Segregated Fantasies: Race, Public Space, and the Life and Death of the Movie Business in Atlantic City, New Jersey, 1945–2000," in *Beyond the Ruins: The Meanings of Deindustrialization*, ed. Jefferson Cowie and Joseph Heathcott (Ithaca, NY: Cornell University Press, 2003), 64–87.

stores, crosses Atlantic, and runs level through the bombed-out ghettos as far—Baltic, Mediterranean—as the eye can see. . . . Then beyond Atlantic Avenue, North Carolina moves on into the vast ghetto, the bulk of the city, and it looks like Metz in 1919, Cologne in 1944. Nothing has actually exploded. It is not bomb damage. It is deep and complex decay. Roofs are off. Bricks are scattered in the street. People sit on porches, six deep, at nine on a Monday morning.[43]

However, the film commences not in Atlantic City but in Philadelphia, where bespectacled, bookish radio DJ David Staebler (Jack Nicholson) is delivering one of his trademark semifictionalized autobiographical monologues. Leaving the radio station at 3 a.m., he walks back through anonymous streets, taking the deserted subway back to his grandfather's house. The next morning, David receives a call from his brother summoning him to Atlantic City. Jason Staebler (Bruce Dern) is a small-time hustler with outsized entrepreneurial ambitions; on his arrival, David finds Jason temporarily jailed on a trumped-up automobile offence. Jason lives with two women in a suite at the Marlborough Blenheim Hotel: Sally, "a middle-aged Kewpie doll" (Ellen Burstyn), and her stepdaughter, Jessica (Julia Ann Robinson). David soon becomes drawn into Jason's latest scheme: a flawed real estate venture to develop a casino resort on a tiny Pacific island, Tiki. Meanwhile, the two women are obsessed with the Miss America pageant and rehearse their routines in empty club venues on the boardwalk. The fruitless entrepreneurial schemes of Jason and David unravel against a drama of family psychology that operates on two intersecting levels: the resentment and reconciliation between the Staebler brothers on the one hand and the growing rivalry and antipathy between mother and daughter on the other.

The film ends with a climactic yet pointless act of violence that resolves nothing; ultimately, it reads as a satire on the American dream, entrepreneurship, and individual success. As such, the film is emblematic of a particular strand of early 1970s American cinema in which a mood of inertia, disillusionment, and regret predominates. In his landmark 1975 piece on New Hollywood, Thomas Elsaesser memorably describes this tendency as "the pathos of failure."[44] These were films that rejected the affirmative, goal-oriented narrative causality of the classical cinema, its action-hero protagonists and their implicit ideological functions.[45] Instead, this broadly left-oriented cinema crystallized this moment of cultural and political aporia through the figure of the "unmotivated hero," whose trajectory was followed either through unresolved, meandering journeys—in road movies such as *Two Lane Blacktop* (Monte Hellman, 1971)—or else, as in *Marvin Gardens*, through recourse to "dramatic situations that have a kind of negative, self-demolishing dynamic."[46] While the Staebler brothers are not, strictly speaking, "unmotivated"—Jason in particular is propelled by the manic

43   John McPhee, "The Search for Marvin Gardens," *New Yorker*, September 9, 1972, 45–62, 48.

44   Thomas Elsaesser, "The Pathos of Failure: American Films in the 70s; Notes on the Unmotivated Hero," *The Last Great American Picture Show*, Elsaesser, Horvath, and King, 279–292.

45   Ibid.

46   Ibid., 282.

entrepreneurial zeal of the con artist—the film is nevertheless marked by various failures, from the brothers' doomed real estate venture to the more personal and psychological blockages that lead to the film's tragic conclusion.

The "Marvin Gardens" of the title is, of course, a direct allusion to the Monopoly board, which took the names of Atlantic City's streets when it was first mass-manufactured by Parker Brothers during the 1930s.[47] This provides a symbolic map—one closely associated with a specific period of American capitalism—which Rafelson juxtaposes to the real geography of the city to explore his themes of crisis and failure. As the director confirmed, "Monopoly and Atlantic City are very clear metaphors for the American Dream."[48] Each block of the original Monopoly board corresponded to a genuine location in Atlantic City, with the exception of Marvin Gardens. This property is a misspelling of a real suburb just outside the city, Marven Gardens, its name a composite of two neighboring areas, Margate and Ventnor. The film's use of the Monopoly spelling therefore opens up a split or opposition between Marven and Marvin—the symbiotic relationship between a "real" place and its representation—while at the same time setting up the Monopoly board as an organizing metaphor for the film as a whole. In this way, the title also makes an allusion to a particular phase of American capitalism—"monopoly capitalism"—then entering into a period of crisis.[49] The film's Monopoly-board metaphor therefore offers a useful way to frame some of the relationships between the crisis of classical Hollywood narrative and the spatial reorganization of American cities in the 1970s.

The Monopoly board is not only an implicit narrative form—Horatio Alger reformatted as financial bildungsroman—but also a diagram of the American city. Significantly, it schematizes the urban basis of capital accumulation: making a fortune is directly related to the player's ability to invest in real estate, build housing, and speculate on hotel construction. The central irony of *Marvin Gardens* is, of course, that the blighted urban landscape of Atlantic City seems to offer no possibility of success for those "playing" the game. Indeed, by the 1970s, the Monopoly diagram of the city was looking increasingly anachronistic as global market forces reconfigured the relative relationship between cities and regions at national and international scales. In short, the symbolic space of the Monopoly board had become fundamentally estranged by the influence of places and processes not visible on the board—that is to say, beyond the city or the macro economy of the nation-state.

As Franco Moretti has argued, narrative forms have often been strongly influenced by their geographical context. For example, Moretti maps connections between narrative conventions in the nineteenth-century realist novel (e.g., Dickens, Balzac) and the geography, complexity, and class structure of the rapidly expanding cities of London

47   Philip E. Orbanes, *Monopoly: The World's Most Famous Game—and How It Got That Way* (Philadelphia: Da Capo Press, 2006); Calvin Trillin, "Monopoly and History," *New Yorker*, February 13, 1978, 90–96.

48   Bob Rafelson, "Le Monopoly ést une métaphore trés évidente du rêve américain . . . ," *Cinéma 73* (1973): 116–119. Translation is mine.

49   See, for example, Julie Graham, Katherine Gibson, Ronald Horvath, and Don M. Shakow, "Restructuring in US Manufacturing: The Decline of Monopoly Capitalism," *Annals of the Association of American Geographers* 78, no. 3 (1988): 473–490.

and Paris.[50] Similarly, Fredric Jameson has argued that the modernist breakdown of realist narrative in the early twentieth century crystallized a schism between the lived experience of the individual and the increasingly complex and abstract structures that defined and organized that experience.[51] Postmodernism stages this same problematic at a higher order, for the global financial and technological networks of advanced capitalism have developed a hitherto-unimaginable level of complexity, scale, and abstraction such that traditional narrative forms have been faced with incommensurable representational crises.[52] As Jameson succinctly put it in an interview: "Narrative seems supremely able to deal with the way in which the truth of individual life was constructed by smaller environments. In the nineteenth-century novel, the narrative apparatus became much more complex in order to deal with the truth of individual experience in a national setting, and of course even more so in imperial settings. But in the global perspective of late capitalism, there's a real crisis in this older narrative machinery."[53] This crisis of the "narrative machinery" of classical Hollywood is, of course, one of the key characteristics of 1970s cinema, in which we often find narratives that are episodic, dedramatized, and essentially unresolved.[54] In these terms, Elsaesser's "pathos of failure" can be closely linked to a crisis of cognitive mapping, of space and political subjectivity. As films such as *The King of Marvin Gardens* demonstrate, this problematic relationship between the individual and his or her cognitive mapping of social space is not only evident in overtly postmodernist "hyperspaces" such as Portman's Bonaventure Hotel but is also applicable to the decaying cities of the Rust Belt.[55]

This inability to effectively map the global and the local is articulated in the film through the disparity between the protagonists' point of view and the spatial or cartographic imagery offered to the spectator. While the film's locations document the effects of disinvestment in the urban environment, the narrative provides little means of historical contextualization. The Staebler brothers' plan to open a holiday resort on a Pacific island gestures at the new global realities of the 1970s, as do the now-dated scenes with the Japanese businessmen. Their attempts at offshore expansion inevitably fall flat, and the narrative remains largely contained within the boundaries of the seaside town. Two specific moments in the film underscore the Staeblers' attempts at "cognitive mapping." In an extended scene in the hotel suite, they spread out maps of the Pacific on the floor, projecting their dreams for success beyond the city and into global space (Figure 1). Later, they survey their surroundings from the panoramic viewpoint of a fairground ride, which offers a broader view of the cityscape uncharacteristic of the film's largely contained mise-en-scène. Jason's dialogue here also acknowledges the lamentable decline of Atlantic City itself, which

50   Franco Moretti, *The Atlas of the European Novel, 1800–1900* (London: Verso, 1999).

51   Jameson, *Postmodernism*.

52   Jameson, "Cognitive Mapping."

53   Fredric Jameson, *Jameson on Jameson: Conversations on Cultural Marxism*, ed. Ian Buchanan (Durham, NC: Duke University Press, 2007), 159.

54   On narrative structure in New Hollywood, see Todd Berliner, *Hollywood Incoherent: Narration in Seventies Cinema* (Austin: University of Texas Press, 2010).

55   Jameson, *Postmodernism*, 38–45.

Figure 1. The Staebler brothers attempt to map their offshore casino development, in *The King of Marvin Gardens* (Columbia Pictures, 1972).

he promises will not be allowed to happen on Tiki: "This could have been a fantastic island right here. It was full-out class until about 1930—until you could hop a plane out to Bermuda for the weekend. . . . Let that be a lesson to us. I promise you—strict controls on Tiki. We can't ever let it go downhill. That's why I won't let anyone build on anything less than ten acres. No Pokerino, no frozen custard, no salt water taffy." Beyond Atlantic City, the film is bookended with scenes of Nicholson in Philadelphia, which is chiefly figured outside the family home through two carefully framed shots of the neon-lit curtain wall of the Industrial Valley Bank. These brief, silent images hint at another architectural and social world—of global finance, downtown redevelopment, International Style modernism—visual signifiers of the wider economic and urban processes in which Atlantic City is implicated.

While linear narrative arguably became less central to Hollywood film in the early 1970s, this was frequently counterbalanced by the heightened importance of location and place. In *Marvin Gardens*, Rafelson and cinematographer Laszlo Kovacs used a series of specific aesthetic strategies to depict the urban environment. Shots linger on the empty space of the windswept boardwalk, a starkly depopulated locale in which the teeming crowd of the modern city has disappeared (Figure 2). Kovacs's deep-focus cinematography makes subtle use of the affective properties of winter light to give the deserted cityscape a melancholy quality that Rafelson likened to the work of painter Maurice Utrillo.[56] Throughout, the material presence of the built environment takes precedence over the classical Hollywood emphasis on narrative. This sense of de-dramatized narrative is accentuated by Rafelson's decision to keep the camera entirely still in all the exterior shots, a technique he borrowed from the films of Yasujiro Ozu.[57]

56 Bob Rafelson, DVD commentary for *The King of Marvin Gardens* (Criterion Collection, 2010), DVD.

57 John Russell Taylor, "Staying Vulnerable: An Interview with Bob Rafelson," *Sight and Sound* 45, no. 4 (1976): 203–204.

Figure 2. The Atlantic City boardwalk in *The King of Marvin Gardens* (Columbia Pictures, 1972).

This languid temporality and sense of stillness or stasis is further emphasized by insistent long takes and the complete absence of nondiegetic music. Such nonclassical stylistic patterns were noticed by contemporary critics, who found strong echoes of European cinematic modernism in *Marvin Gardens*. For example, Foster Hirsch in the *New York Times* drew a comparison between the desolate backdrop of Atlantic City and the empty landscapes of Antonioni's *L'avventura* (1960). Hirsch also noted other formal motifs with European resonances: "There are Antonioni shadows, as well, in the languorous and rhythmic pacing, and in the device of allowing the camera to remain, fleetingly, on the scene after the action proper has been completed."[58]

Rafelson has recently described how the properties of Atlantic City inspired this stylistic approach, recalling how he had fallen in love with "the geometry of the place." The Monopoly-board metaphor also influenced his construction of cinematic space, leading him to place the camera at an unusually diagonal or perpendicular angle to the actors as if they were pieces in the board game itself: "The way the board is organized fascinates me: it's very linear, very geometric. The pieces can only move in straight lines and right angles. . . . I thought this peculiar way of moving the pieces could be used as a style of movement for the film images."[59] This style is perhaps most clearly articulated in a sustained two-shot where the Staebler brothers talk to each other while mounted on horseback at ninety degrees to the camera (Figure 3). This slightly mannered and self-conscious construction of space also operates through what Rafelson has referred to as "creative geography" in exterior scenes: a set of framing and editing strategies for emphasizing and amplifying certain elements of the profilmic space in relation to the characters, so that shots would alternately frame the protagonists against the boundless, open natural space of the beach and the ocean, and the decaying hotel facades.[60]

A further element of the Monopoly-board metaphor needs to be illuminated. When considering how geographical locations operate within the spatial system of a film, we must always also ask, which spaces are not represented, remaining invisible and implicitly marginalized, and what logic of exclusion might govern such choices or render them possible? Such missing spaces can be seen to operate as structuring

58   Foster Hirsch, "I Know I Shouldn't Like It, but . . . ," *New York Times*, November 5, 1972, d13.

59   Rafelson, "Le Monopoly," 118; Anna Maria Tatò, "Entretien avec Bob Rafelson," *Positif* 206 (1978): 30.

60   Ibid., 203.

absences, implicitly framing, stabilizing, or destabilizing the meaning of the visible screen space. In the case of Rafelson's film, the Marvin (Marven) Gardens of the title is such a missing location, neither referred to nor physically present in the film. As Jay Boyer puts it in his study of Bob Rafelson, "Much of the board game Monopoly

Figure 3. Geometrical framing replicates board-game pieces, in *The King of Marvin Gardens* (Columbia Pictures, 1972).

has a basis in the actual geography and street system of Atlantic City; not so Marvin Gardens. This most valuable piece of property is purely fictitious, and for Jason to be its monarch is to be an emperor of air."[61] Although technically this is true—Marvin Gardens, following the Monopoly-board spelling, is indeed a fabrication—the real location and meaning of Marven Gardens has a further resonance that is worth some consideration.

In his *New Yorker* piece "The Search for Marven Gardens," John McPhee develops a running joke: nobody in Atlantic City appears to have heard of this elusive area or knows of its whereabouts. Finally, he discovers its location: a couple of miles south of the city, it lies between the suburbs of Margate and Ventnor. The area "consists of solid buildings of stucco, brick, and wood, with slate roofs, tile roofs, multi-mullioned porches, Giraldic towers, and Spanish grilles." Marven Gardens, we are told, is "the ultimate outwash of Monopoly . . . a citadel and sanctuary of the middle class." Interviewing a local resident, he elicits a clear expression of suburban fear: "We're heavily patrolled by police here. We don't take no chances."[62] An exclusive suburban development, Marven Gardens is emblematic of one of the crucial factors behind the urban crisis: that the mass disinvestment from inner-city areas was predicated on the migration of the white middle classes away from the increasingly plural, democratic public spaces of the city toward secluded and implicitly segregated private spaces that could be safely monitored and controlled. As Bryant Simon explains, the historical development and decline of Atlantic City can be elucidated through an understanding of the role of the white middle class and its attitudes to race and public space:

> Beginning in the 1960s, Atlantic City stopped being a place where people lived their lives on the streets and on their porches. Many families retreated inside behind lace curtains, barred windows, and double-locked doors, and then out to the suburbs. Foregoing sidewalks, parks, corner stores, and movie houses, they looked inwards, and in so doing, they exchanged the close quarters and intense daily interactions of the neighborhood for the more controlled, easily

61 Jay Boyer, *Bob Rafelson: Hollywood Maverick* (New York: Twayne, 1996), 55.

62 McPhee, "Search for Marvin Gardens," 62.

protected, yet less stimulating life of private homes in segregated, middle-class sanctuaries like Marven Gardens.[63]

As Simon demonstrates, the type of public space represented by Atlantic City was "never about democracy; it was about exclusion. . . . During its heyday, Atlantic City was a Jim Crow town."[64] The decline of Atlantic City as a holiday destination was determined to a large extent by two external factors. First, the advent of cheap intercontinental jet travel had made foreign holidays accessible to many for the first time, against which traditional resorts such as Atlantic City seemed pedestrian and outdated; and second, the development of two new holiday resorts: Disneyland (opened in Anaheim, California, in 1955) and Las Vegas, both of which represented new forms of proto-postmodern consumer space, selling differing sorts of fantasies to holidaymakers. As Simon observes, Disneyland capitalized on a desire for "long-lost, safe public places," precisely that type of public experience that had once been provided by the boardwalk itself: "Behind its thick fortress walls, Disney created a public sphere, much like the Boardwalk, the shopping mall, and the casino, based on the economically viable principles of exclusion mixed with the illusion of equal access and democracy."[65]

Tellingly, the issue of race was little discussed in the US reception of the film, though the French critic Michel Grisolia went so far as to suggest to Rafelson that *Marvin Gardens* might be seen as "a political film about the rise of black power."[66] While the director remained equivocal on this point, he nevertheless recognized elements of truth to the critic's overstatement. Although it is relatively submerged, *Marvin Gardens* does suggest that a certain kind of white middle-class space has been displaced or decentered. The real center of power in the Staeblers' world is, in fact, the sharply attired mob boss Lewis (Scatman Crothers), who appears to have the power to keep Jason in or out of prison. Beginning with David's initial meeting with Lewis, during which a heated argument is taking place in the adjacent room, we are left with the sensation that a more exciting and conventional crime film is unfolding off-screen. This notion is redoubled by the sudden appearance of two of Lewis's associates in the hotel, who appear to have stepped straight out of a blaxploitation movie (a genre then in its first flush of success) and in the representation of Lewis's nightclub, the only public space represented as having any vitality in the entire city (Figure 4).[67]

While the Staebler brothers' casino development and real estate speculation remained a pipe dream in the film, it was shortly to take on a new topicality. Following a referendum in November 1976, the state of New Jersey passed an amendment to legalize gambling within the boundaries of Atlantic City. This rapid change was

63   Bryant Simon, *Boardwalk of Dreams: Atlantic City and the Fate of Urban America* (Oxford: Oxford University Press, 2004), 82.

64   Ibid., 13–14.

65   Simon, *Boardwalk of Dreams*, 16.

66   Rafelson, "Le Monopoly," 116–119. My translation.

67   On blaxploitation, see Ed Guerrero, *Framing Blackness: The African-American Image in Film* (Philadelphia: Temple University Press, 1993), 69–111.

Figure 4. David is threatened by one of Lewis's associates, in *The King of Marvin Gardens* (Columbia Pictures, 1972).

captured on film by Louis Malle, in his 1979 film *Atlantic City*. The opening and closing credits of Malle's film show documentary footage of the empty hotels that dominated the mise-en-scène of *The King of Marvin Gardens* being dynamited to make way for new casino-hotel developments. Intended as a "magic bullet," the legislation aimed to revitalize the flagging resort town by stimulating economic growth, creating employment, and driving urban redevelopment. Described by the architectural historian Thomas Hines as "radical therapy for a dying city," the gambling experiment in Atlantic City stands not only as a prototypical neoliberal restructuring strategy but also as a microcosm of the wider transition of the American economy toward "casino capitalism."[68]

***Rocky:* Steadicam Aesthetics and Downtown Renaissance.** While *The King of Marvin Gardens* and *Atlantic City* both contained brief scenes filmed in Philadelphia, these presented the city relatively anonymously, a generic big city in contrast to the seaside town of Atlantic City. Indeed, despite the historical and cultural importance of Philadelphia to the United States, the city's rich architectural heritage was relatively rarely seen on-screen throughout the classical period, a situation perhaps best exemplified by the fact that *The Philadelphia Story* (George Cukor, 1940) was not shot in the city but entirely at the MGM studios in Culver City. However, from the late 1970s, increasing numbers of location shoots were drawn to the city. This trend built on the runaway success of *Rocky*, which played a vital role in bringing Hollywood productions to the city; despite being shot without municipal permits, *Rocky* is now feted by the Greater Philadelphia Film Office as the inaugural picture in a sequence

---

68 Thomas S. Hines, "Atlantic City: What Happens When Gambling Is Used as a Tool for Urban Renewal," *Journal of the American Institute of Architects*, November 1982, 34.

of films that would use Philadelphia as a back lot during the 1980s and beyond.[69] The character's transformation and triumph was, of course, also paralleled by the film's own extraordinary box-office success—returning $117 million in domestic rentals against production costs of less than $1 million—and the rise of Sylvester Stallone as a self-made Hollywood entrepreneur.[70]

Although *Rocky* is arguably one of the key films in which American cinema regained its confidence in linear, goal-oriented narrative, it remains fundamentally split between the urban realist tendencies that characterized certain strands of early 1970s cinema and an individualist, rise-to-success plot that would become commonplace in 1980s Hollywood. In this regard, *Rocky* reworks the boxing genre's social realist traditions: while its use of the authentic urban locations of Philadelphia's working-class districts suggests a critical and potentially progressive stance on the urban crisis, this is countered by a narrative paradigm that allows collective renewal only on individualist terms through self-help and free enterprise. Further, *Rocky* was one of several films of the mid-1970s that developed new relationships to screen space through their then-innovative use of the Steadicam, and it is precisely this new spatial mobility in *Rocky* that provides not only a compelling figure for social mobility but also an enduring symbol for the fiscal "disciplining" and revitalization of the city itself at the end of the decade.

Like other Rust Belt cities, Philadelphia had entered into a state of precipitous decline by the late 1960s. Rapid suburbanization led to extensive population loss from the central city, with processes of deindustrialization, suburbanization, and containerization producing devastating effects on the city's economic well-being. Though New York's famous fiscal crisis and near default of 1975 is more widely remembered, former industrial hubs such as Philadelphia, Detroit, and Cleveland were also in dire financial straits by the mid-1970s. A substantial decline in industrial output, the erosion of the city's tax base through population outflow, and the increased spending commitments concomitant with high unemployment were compounded both by the worldwide economic downturn of 1973–1974 and the retrenchment in urban welfare programs enacted by the Nixon administration.[71] In the year that *Rocky* was released, the city recorded municipal debts of $86 million, and the city's credit status was subsequently downgraded by rating agencies Moody's and Standard & Poor's. Cuts ensued in public services, jobs, and public-sector wages, alongside a punitive 30 percent rise in local tax rates, leading the *New York Times* to reflect on the disparity between the state of the city and its newfound cinematic icon: "In the movie, Rocky lost the championship fight, but it didn't matter. In Philadelphia, there are plenty of real life losers. Some of the problems here are a school fund crisis, dilapidated housing, a federal

69 Desmond Ryan, "New Film Office Brings to Region a Bonanza and a Milestone," *Philadelphia Inquirer*, October 20, 1992. See also Paul Swann, "From Workshop to Backlot: The Greater Philadelphia Film Office," in *Cinema and the City: Film and Urban Societies in a Global Context*, ed. Mark Shiel and Tony Fitzmaurice (Oxford, UK: Blackwell, 2001), 88–98.

70 *Rocky* grossed more than $117 million in the United States and $225 million worldwide. Sheldon Hall and Steve Neale, *Epics, Spectacles and Blockbusters: A Hollywood History* (Detroit: Wayne State University Press, 2010), 214.

71 Robert P. Inman, "Anatomy of a Fiscal Crisis," *Business Review* (Federal Reserve Bank of Philadelphia), September–October 1983, 15–22; "Now Philadelphia's Broke," *Economist*, May 29, 1976, 42.

investigation of the police department for alleged brutality and friction between the one third of the population that is black and the two thirds that is white."[72] Yet 1976 was also the year that America celebrated the bicentennial anniversary of its founding, an occasion that offered its oldest city an opportunity to reposition itself on the global stage as a revitalized center of tourism, entertainment, and commerce. As Andrew Feffer explains, "The staging of the Bicentennial underscored the spectacular nature of redevelopment, in which the visual makeover of private and public spaces served efforts to improve the city's 'symbolic economy'—to reshape the urban landscape as a marketable commodity and to advertise the downtown as an attractive destination for tourism, consumerism, and resettlement."[73] Indeed, city officials of all stripes were quick to seize on *Rocky* as a local icon and symbol for the city's renewed vitality and projected renaissance.[74] In this sense, *Rocky* engages with the city at a distinctive watershed moment when a neoliberal paradigm of redevelopment was emerging from the ashes of the urban crisis. As I explore further through an analysis of two key moments in the film, *Rocky* allegorizes the city's crisis and revitalization through its central narrative of individual discipline and achievement and its construction of cinematic space.

The first half of the film develops a strong sense of containment within the Italian neighborhood through a series of distinctive locations: the boxing gym and the pet shop, the docks and peripheral industrial spaces, the characteristic Philadelphia row houses and street corners. The financial opportunities of such an environment are limited and on the edge of legality: as a small-time boxer, Rocky's physical labor is unrewarding (he wins just forty dollars for a fight in the opening sequence); as a debt collector for the Mafia, he hassles hard-up dock workers, themselves struggling against inflation and wage freezes. The exterior street scenes in Rocky's neighborhood were filmed in Kensington, one of the city's declining inner-ring areas, which contemporary accounts described as a desolate landscape of empty factories, derelict stores, and rubble-strewn lots.[75] The earlier sections of the film focus closely on the decay of the Italian neighborhood and the industrial zone surrounding the docks—still operating but, it is suggested, affected by containerization—which, unlike the busy New Jersey docks portrayed in *On the Waterfront* (Elia Kazan, 1954), are almost empty of workers. Camera viewpoints are on the whole pedestrian and largely static; the only cars belong to Rocky's Mafia employers. Wide shots predominate, situating Rocky as an isolated figure in the industrial landscape. In one particularly notable sequence, Stallone walks into the distance along a railway siding, the camera remaining fixed. The railings and sidewalk bisect the frame diagonally, converging toward the vanishing point in a geometrical composition, a muted, wintry palette of grays, browns, and blacks (Figure 5). Elsewhere, the camera lingers on wasteland and the decaying infrastructure of the industrial city, paying close attention to the material decline of the built environment.

72   James F. Clarity, "In Philadelphia, Pride in the City Grows," *New York Times*, July 4, 1977, 32.

73   Andrew Feffer, "Show Down in Center City: Staging Redevelopment and Citizenship in Bicentennial Philadelphia, 1974–1977," *Journal of Urban History* 30, no. 6 (2004): 791–825, 792.

74   Clarity, "In Philadelphia," 32.

75   Paul R. Levy and Roman A. Cybriwsky, "The Hidden Dimensions of Culture and Class: Philadelphia," in *Back to the City: Issues in Neighborhood Renovation*, ed. Shirley Bradway Laska and Daphne Spain (New York: Pergamon Press, 1980), 138–155, 140.

Figure 5. Images of stasis and decay in the first half of *Rocky* (United Artists, 1976).

While the first half of the film is characterized by a sense of stasis and immobility, drawing on the "pathos of failure" of early 1970s Hollywood and its evocation of postindustrial masculinity in crisis, it is in the later sections, as Rocky Balboa begins his training, that the film's relationship to space is transformed by the introduction of the Steadicam through which the film finds a new mobility around the city. The famous rise-to-success montage is, crucially, constructed as a journey through Philadelphia, linking Rocky's physical and psychological transformation directly to the urban environment and, as I argue, producing an allegory or spatial metaphor for urban renaissance.

As the Steadicam is central to producing the speed, fluidity, and mobility of Rocky's training sequences, it is worth briefly considering the development of the technology itself and its relationship to this specific historical conjuncture. Though the first feature to use the Steadicam was Hal Ashby's decidedly nonurban Woodie Guthrie biopic *Bound for Glory* (1976), it came to prominence in two films from the same year, *Rocky* and *Marathon Man* (John Schlesinger, 1976), both of which memorably focused on the motif of running and movement through urban space. Developed by the cameraman and inventor Garrett Brown in the early 1970s and first marketed by Cinema Products Corporation in 1975, the Steadicam was one of a number of technological innovations that helped develop new practices in location shooting during the decade. A camera-stabilizing device that attaches to the operator's body, enabling fluid, mobile shots without the unevenness and bumpiness of handheld camerawork, the Steadicam opened up new possibilities for location filming and the presentation of screen space, allowing for lengthy sequence shots without laying dolly track, and novel camera movements such as 360-degree pans.[76]

As John Belton has argued with respect to the introduction of CinemaScope and color processes, technological innovation in Hollywood is not necessarily the primary driver of change; rather, new technologies have tended to be adopted only when they also fulfill economic and ideological functions for the industry.[77] The economic and logistical benefits of the Steadicam were clearly articulated across a series of promotional features in the trade press at the time, which emphasized its ability to reduce costs, cut down on crew, and enable shooting in difficult locations, especially

---

76 On the development of the Steadicam, see Serena Ferrara, *Steadicam: Techniques and Aesthetics* (Oxford, UK: Focal Press, 2000).

77 On the introduction of CinemaScope and the historiographical questions around film technology, see John Belton, "CinemaScope and Historical Methodology," *Cinema Journal* 28, no. 1 (1988): 22–44.

city streets. Writing in *American Cinematographer*, experienced Steadicam operator Ted Churchill described the usefulness of Steadicam for working in urban locations, allowing film crews to operate relatively unobtrusively among city crowds and respond to the contingencies of such situations. As he put it, "It's indispensable when it becomes impossible to 'own' the territory in which one is shooting."[78] Avildsen exploited this territorial flexibility on the production of *Rocky*, which minimized costs by shooting rapidly in Philadelphia with a non-union crew and without city permits.[79] The director explained how he would use the neighborhood as a kind of filmmaking resource: "We went in low profile and did it like the old days, operating in the poor section of town and getting people into the spirit of things."[80] Avildsen's reference here to the "old days" refers to his early days making low-budget exploitation films for Lloyd Kaufman's Troma Entertainment, an experience that informed the style and production values of *Rocky*.[81] Kaufman assisted on the shoot and later recalled himself and Avildsen "zipping around the city in eight days making sure his non-union crew wasn't spotted by union representatives. At a Los Angeles screening of *Rocky*, Kaufman said, '[U]nion guys were trying to remember when they shot that footage.'"[82] Philadelphia was also central to the development of the training sequence, which drew direct inspiration from Garrett Brown's original test film for the Steadicam prototype, in which he filmed his partner running up and down the steps of the Museum of Art.[83]

While Steadicam therefore fit the new mobile and flexible production regime of New Hollywood, its aesthetic properties also fulfilled what we might describe as ideological functions for the industry. At a time when Hollywood's continuity codes and conventions of screen space had been seriously challenged and destabilized, Steadicam provided a way of absorbing and smoothing out some of the more disruptive elements of the first wave of New Hollywood. On the one hand, it enabled freedom of movement, spatial dynamism, and the kind of restless, excessive visuality now associated with postclassical style. Yet at the same time, it ensured stability, smoothness, continuity, and—as was argued at the time—an enhanced realism. As Churchill explained, "Steadicam was designed to solve a persistent problem which had plagued cinematographers for quite a few years: how to make the camera as mobile and versatile as a human being while rendering a stable and accurate frame competitive with traditional, but more complicated, techniques."[84] While freeing up radical new possibilities, the Steadicam and its aesthetics were also consonant with essentially classical

78 Ted Churchill, "Steadicam: An Operator's Perspective," *American Cinematographer* 64, no. 4 (1983): 36–39, 113–120, 115.

79 The boxing scenes were filmed later in Los Angeles. James Crabe, "The Photography of 'Rocky,'" *American Cinematographer* (1977): 184–185, 205, 221.

80 John M. Wilson, "Location Hunters Seek Sites for Sore Eyes," *Los Angeles Times*, November 28, 1976, o50.

81 On Troma, see Bill Landis, "Tromatized," *Film Comment* 22, no. 4 (1986): 77–80.

82 G. Michael Dobbs, "Inside Troma Films: Thirty Years in Low Budget Movies," *Journal Bravo*, May 29, 2003, http://www.troma.com/tromapress/journalbravo/2003-05-29/index.html.

83 Brown discusses the development of the Steadicam and his Philadelphia test films in Bryan Bierman, "Q&A: Steadicam Inventor and Rocky Cinematographer Garrett Brown," *Philadelphia Citypaper*, http://citypaper.net/article.php?Q-A-Steadicam-inventor-and-Rocky-cinematographer-Garrett-Brown-12242.

84 Churchill, "Steadicam," 37.

values, such as the stability of the frame and the accentuation of a human subjectivity allied to the camera's viewpoint or embodiment of space. Ed DiGiulio, president of Cinema Products Corporation, also argued that it increased realism by eliminating the shaky footage associated with handheld shooting; as he put it, "The human eye does not rock-and-roll and bump the way the hand-held camera of Cinéma Verité was wont to do."[85] The Steadicam therefore operated both literally and figuratively as a "shock absorber," allowing postclassical cinema to incorporate a new fluidity and complexity of movement within the shot while eliminating the more disruptive, imperfect, and essentially modernist properties associated with films of the late 1960s and early 1970s.[86]

In *Rocky*, Steadicam is central in producing the formal and affective properties of the training sequences and in their engagement with the city. Rocky's physical transformation, the self-discipline of the body—symbolically, the self-discipline of the body politic of the city—is mapped out as a journey across urban space. Starting in the industrial wasteland surrounding the docks (Figure 6), we are reminded of Gilles Deleuze's "any-space-whatever": spaces that are "deserted but inhabited, disused warehouses, waste ground, cities in the course of demolition or reconstruction."[87] Moving fluidly through the litter-strewn streets of the Ninth Street Market, the camera follows Rocky in smooth, uninterrupted takes through the park, along the waterfront, and then, famously and triumphantly, up the steps toward the monumental neoclassical edifice of the Philadelphia Museum of Art, looking out across the Benjamin Franklin Parkway and downtown Philadelphia (Figures 7 and 8). Here, we are presented with a set of spatial oppositions to the confinement and stasis of the docks and the Italian neighborhood: this is open, classical, public space, highly iconic and elevated above the city. The architecture associated with Rocky's transformation—the Greek-revival museum, designed by Horace Trumbauer (1919–

Figure 6. Rocky's mobility through urban space as symbol of urban regeneration, beginning in industrial wasteland, in *Rocky* (United Artists, 1976).

1928)—is pointedly not the International Style modernism of Philadelphia's central business district but rather leaps further back to draw on the city's status as the birthplace of American democracy. Through identification with this monumental space and its elevated position, the

85 Ed DiGiulio, "Steadicam-35: A Revolutionary New Concept in Camera Stabilization," *American Cinematographer* 57, no. 7 (1976): 786–787, 802, 786.

86 The term *postclassical* is, of course, contested. For elaboration on the classical-postclassical debate, see Barry Langford, *Post-Classical Hollywood: Film Industry, Style and Ideology since 1945* (Edinburgh: Edinburgh University Press, 2012); Murray Smith, "Theses on the Philosophy of Hollywood History," in *Contemporary Hollywood Cinema*, ed. Steve Neale and Murray Smith (Abingdon, UK: Routledge, 2006), 3–20.

87 Gilles Deleuze, *Cinema 2: The Time Image*, trans. Hugh Tomlinson and Robert Galeta (Minneapolis: University of Minnesota Press, 1997), xi.

viewpoint suggests a newly acquired ability to produce a cognitive map of the spatial and social surroundings of Philadelphia.

Through his paradigmatic movement from the old neighborhood to the monumental space of American democracy, Rocky's "urban voyage" becomes a figure for upward social mobility and the revitalization and renewal of the city more generally. Through this celebratory, highly influential rise-to-success montage sequence, Hollywood film can be seen as having regained its "action image," which is here aligned with individual enterprise and entrepreneurship.

Figure 7. Rocky moves through the traditional community space of the Italian Market, in *Rocky* (United Artists, 1976).

Figure 8. Rocky's triumphal moment on the steps of the Philadelphia Museum of Art, in *Rocky* (United Artists, 1976).

Steadicam not only enables this new mobility through urban space but also is central in producing the affective charge and euphoric rush of Rocky's transformation for the spectator. This moment marks an implicit move away from the "pathos of failure" associated with American cinema in the first half of the 1970s—and away from the crisis both in Hollywood and in the American inner city—and points forward to the renewed dominance of the blockbuster and the neoliberal downtown renaissance of the 1980s and beyond.

The film's politics are broadly populist, reflecting Avildsen's notion of the film as a "classic, Frank Capra type story."[88] Indeed, Capra himself is known to have admired the picture, and its relationship to Capra's Depression-era populism is clear at the level of ideology as well as narrative form.[89] Yet the values that constituted the ideological backbone of Capra's work—individualism, enterprise, and "self-help" in the economic sphere, alongside a distrust of both corporate power and federal government—take on different resonances in the context of neoliberal economic policy and urban redevelopment in the 1970s. As Leger Grindon argues, the revitalized boxing movies of the late 1970s constructed "the boxer as a white-working class hero no longer

---

88   Cited in inlay card for *Rocky* (MGM, 2004), DVD.

89   See Jeffrey Richards, "Frank Capra and the Cinema of Populism," in *Movies and Methods: An Anthology*, ed. Bill Nichols (Berkeley: University of California Press, 1976), 65–77.

under allegiance to New Deal liberalism but as spokesman for the 'silent majority.'"[90] Rocky's chance at the title is explicitly associated with American individualist ideology. As Rocky's adversary Apollo Creed (Carl Weathers) puts it, "American history proves that everybody's got a chance to win." This viewpoint resonates with emerging right-wing positions on the urban and economic crisis, exemplified by influential studies such as Edward Banfield's *The Unheavenly City* (1970).[91] For Banfield and other neoconservative thinkers such as Irving Kristol and George Gilder, urban renewal programs, and social welfare policies more generally, were not only misguided but also damaging and ideologically suspect. It was to become a totemic belief for the right that renewal policies and social welfare had not only failed to solve the urban crisis; they had, it was argued, helped cause the crisis through fostering a sense of dependency and a ghetto mentality that worked against their ideal, equality of opportunity—an equality best offered by a deregulated free-market consumer society.[92]

The film's submerged anticorporate sentiments are implicitly mobilized against Apollo Creed, who is consistently identified with big business: sharp suits, downtown office space, and an immaculately managed media profile. In contrast, Rocky is a self-styled "ham-and-egger." As Peter Biskind and Barbara Ehrenreich have argued, Rocky symbolized a beleaguered, white working-class masculinity under siege from the advances of feminism and civil rights.[93] *Rocky* is also notably based around a white protagonist in a period in which both boxing and the inner city had become to a large extent African American. The film imagines African Americans gaining political and economic ascendancy, be it the up-and-coming black fighter displacing Rocky in the gym or through the figure of Apollo Creed himself. Yet despite the obvious racial significance of the confrontation between Balboa and Creed, the film skirts around the issue of racial politics, arguably concealing or seeking to downplay the real extent of racial tensions within the city. Since World War II, Philadelphia had undergone a substantive demographic shift that reordered its racial profile: while ethnic minorities made up 18.3 percent of the total in 1950, African Americans alone constituted 37.8 percent of the city's population by 1980.[94] The race riots that exploded in 1964 were one of the first signals of a widespread escalation of the urban crisis during the 1960s, reflecting the fact that urban disinvestment and destructive renewal policies had made a disproportionate impact on black neighborhoods in central and north Philadelphia. Racial tension in the city was further escalated by the election of so-called supercop Mayor Frank Rizzo (chief of police from 1967 to 1971 and mayor from 1972 to 1980). Indeed, *Rocky*'s celebration of "white ethnic" working-class identity tallies with the rise to power of Rizzo, whose law-and-order rhetoric, reputation for brutality, and racist policing tactics frayed race relations in the city throughout the 1970s.

90 Leger Grindon, "Body and Soul: The Structure of Meaning in the Boxing Film," *Cinema Journal* 35, no. 4 (1996): 54–69, 66.

91 Edward C. Banfield, *The Unheavenly City: The Nature and Future of Our Urban Crisis* (Boston: Little, Brown, 1970).

92 See Barry Bluestone and Bennett Harrison, *The Deindustrialization of America* (New York: Basic Books, 1982), 13; Irving Kristol, "Sense and Nonsense in Urban Policy," *Wall Street Journal*, December 21, 1977, 12.

93 Peter Biskind and Barbara Ehrenreich, "Machismo and Hollywood's Working Class," in *Gods and Monsters* (London: Bloomsbury, 2004), 53–74.

94 Robert A. Beauregard, "City Profile: Philadelphia," *Cities* 6 (1989): 300.

Conclusion. Across these two films, I have traced the ways in which substantial re-alignments in Hollywood's spatial and affective landscape—from the sensations of stasis, failure, and immobility evoked by much of the lower-budget output of the early 1970s to mobility, flexibility, and euphoria in the later part of the decade—can be linked to the wider economic-industrial shifts both in Hollywood and the American city. As Hollywood's new production practices and developments in urban public policy catalyzed a new engagement with urban space, New Hollywood cinema established what Thomas Elsaesser has referred to as "a new iconography of place alongside a new emotional topography."[95] However, the first phase of New Hollywood was only a brief interregnum, and the dominating legacy of the 1970s is, of course, the second phase and the revitalized blockbuster format. Yet the mobile and flexible production strategies developed in the 1960s and 1970s, alongside the series of tax breaks and incentives that lured filmmakers to location shooting, remain central to the political economy of contemporary Hollywood. Indeed, since a new global economic crisis emerged in 2008, following a collapse in property markets and "subprime" lending in the United States, the streets of the postindustrial Rust Belt city have become, perhaps paradoxically, ever more visible on-screen and increasingly popular as location shooting destinations. The municipal advocacy for location shooting that developed in the 1970s, though recently tested by fiscal restraint, is still strong, with aggressive tax breaks providing persuasive financial incentives for Hollywood while the paradigm of the cultural or "creative" city remains an enduring ideology for city governments. In particular, there has been a sharp increase in location shooting in recent years in so-called second-tier cities such as Philadelphia in *Baby Mama* (Michael McCullers, 2008), *How Do You Know* (James L. Brooks, 2010), and *Silver Linings Playbook* (David O. Russell, 2012); Pittsburgh in *Adventureland* (Greg Mottola, 2009), *The Perks of Being a Wallflower* (Stephen Chbosky, 2012), and *The Next Three Days* (Paul Haggis, 2010); Detroit in *Gran Torino* (Clint Eastwood, 2008); and Boston in *The Company Men* (John Wells, 2010) and *The Town* (Ben Affleck, 2010). The streets of the postindustrial city therefore remain a vital artistic inspiration and production resource for the motion picture industry: whether gentrified and redeveloped (Brooklyn) or seemingly stuck in 1970s-era crisis (Detroit), Rust Belt cities have since become firmly established features of the landscape and iconography of Hollywood cinema.   *

---

95 Thomas Elsaesser, *The Persistence of Hollywood* (New York: Routledge, 2012), 232.

IN FOCUS: *Homeland*

Analyzing *Homeland*: Introduction

by DIANE NEGRA and JORIE LAGERWEY, editors

I n the summer of 2014, Showtime's hit espionage thriller *Homeland* (2011–) was just beginning to promote its fourth season, in which star CIA agent Carrie Mathison (Claire Danes) leaves behind her newborn child to return to vital fieldwork that will protect the titular American homeland. The show's central romantic entanglement between Mathison and returned prisoner-of-war, terrorist sleeper agent, politician-hero Nicholas Brody (Damian Lewis) has concluded, Brody having sacrificed his life to redeem Mathison's love and his reputation as an American patriot at the end of the third season. In the trailers for this fourth season, Mathison insists she has no choice but to forgo motherhood and follow her assignment abroad. Despite her sister's claim that Carrie has engineered her mission to require her to leave her child behind, Mathison sees her public role as absolutely vital to national security and always prioritizes it over family life.

We explain these plot points in detail because they highlight many of the narrative, representational, and cultural elements that make *Homeland* a show worthy of an entire single-series In Focus. Upon its debut in 2011, *Homeland* quickly moved to a position of cultural prominence, becoming the kind of program that anchors middle-class taste formations and cultural literacies while earning numerous accolades and drawing record-setting audiences for the cable network. More significantly for our purposes, and as the following essays indicate, *Homeland* is a dense, polysemic text that provides rich grist for readings in relation to class, gender, and genre. Notably, the series has been analyzed as both a straightforward articulation of and a subversive critique of US foreign policy and the national security mind-set after the terrorist attacks of September 11, 2001. For some, it progressively interrogates the role of women in governmental and political regimes; for others, it works to hold in place conservative repressions regarding homeland security profiteering. The essays here reflect this complexity. Lindsay Steenberg and Yvonne Tasker set *Homeland* in the context of other American crime series, arguing that it articulates tropes of an unstable or unwell female investigator with those of the post-9/11 surveillance and security state. James Castonguay argues that the program's "quality television" status supports its function as propaganda for the Obama administration's foreign and domestic surveillance operations. Alex Bevan uses feminist geography to argue that Carrie Mathison's mental illness functions as a stand-in for the unrepresentable and unpalatable features of a twenty-first-century warfare and geopolitics that are deeply mediated, waged from a distance, and fought between the United States and nonstate actors. Finally, Stephen Shapiro argues that *Homeland* speaks directly to the uncertain positioning of the middle class that was accentuated by the financial crisis that began in 2008.

Underpinning all of these collected essays is a concern with the gender and class discourses of "quality television." It is our task here to set *Homeland* in relation to the female-centered network and basic-cable programs in the United States that have seemed to proliferate around and grow from the series' ratings success. As a dimension of this, we also investigate Mathison's emotionalism as expressed through Claire Danes's Emmy- and Golden Globe–winning performance and the popular parodies thereof, which we understand as part of a reaction formation to the series' female centrality.

Definitions of "quality television" and their significance to the industry, fans, and scholars have been debated for decades.[1] Recent articulations of this debate have often focused on the subscription-cable service HBO, its role as creator of high-budget, high-gloss, highbrow series like *The Sopranos* (1999–2007), *The Wire* (2002–2008), and *True Detective* (2014–), and the basic-cable series that borrowed their emphasis on style and complicated, male-centered narratives from these predecessors.[2] AMC's *Mad Men* (2007–2015) and *Breaking Bad* (2008–2013) and FX's *Sons of Anarchy* (2008–) and *Justified* (2010–2015) are just a few programs that have received critical attention for following HBO's example. Praise for this cycle of "quality" television often starts by positively comparing these series and others like them to higher-status cultural forms, calling their aesthetics "cinematic" and their complexity "novelistic," taking them out of the historically feminized (and feminist) discourses of television studies. Emily Nussbaum, pointing out the gendered generic hierarchies implicit in the way that a series like *Sex and the City* (HBO, 1998–2004) is reflexively excluded from this "quality" canon, notes, "*The Sopranos* deserves the hype. Yet there's something screwy about the

---

1 See, e.g., Charlotte Brunsdon, "Problems with Quality," *Screen* 31, no. 1 (1990): 67–90; Jane Feuer, Paul Kerr, and Tise Vahimagi, eds., *MTM: Quality Television* (London: BFI, 1984); Mark Jancovich and James Lyons, *Quality Popular Television: Cult TV, the Industry, and Fans* (London: BFI, 2003); Diane Negra, "Quality Postfeminism? Sex and the Single Girl on HBO," *Genders* 39 (2004): http://genders.org/g39/g39_negra.html.

2 See, e.g., Gary Edgerton and Jeffrey P. Jones, eds., *The Essential HBO Reader* (Lexington: University Press of Kentucky, 2009); Mark Leverette, Brian L. Ott, and Cara Louise Buckley, eds., *It's Not TV: Watching HBO in the Post-Television Era* (New York: Routledge, 2008).

way that the show and its cable-drama blood brothers have come to dominate the conversation, elbowing other forms of greatness out of the frame."[3]

In notable counterpoint to the centrality of masculinity in so much of the televisual fare that goes under the "quality" banner, recent television seasons have seen a proliferation of sharply drawn, sometimes idiosyncratic female leads in network sitcoms like *The Mindy Project*'s Mindy Lahiri (Mindy Kaling; Fox, 2012–), *Parks and Recreation*'s Leslie Knope (Amy Poehler; NBC, 2009–2015), and *30 Rock*'s Liz Lemon (Tina Fey; NBC, 2006–2013). The question of what female-centered television looks like in the period of *Homeland*'s success is a complex one, with evidence of exciting new prospects and possibilities (even while the depressing spectacle of Sofia Vergara on a turntable at the 2014 Emmys is evidence that there has hardly been wholesale industry transformation).

But where these masculine-centered shows have proliferated and received ample scholarly attention, less heed has been paid to *Homeland*'s female-centered influence and the spread of premium-cable production values not just to basic cable but also to US broadcast networks and to international formats and coproductions.[4] The troubled men at the center of those narratives are often understood to be acting out a "crisis" in masculinity that is sometimes construed as having been brought about by financial calamity and/or achievement by women and people of color. In contrast, the women at the center of shows like *Homeland* and those it has influenced appear to be vehicles for working through more public shifts in the relationships among government, politics, and private family life. In both instances, attributions of "quality" status often reinforce middle-class taste cultures and elevate certain types of television—often television that requires expensive subscriptions and/or intense time commitments—to high-culture status and relegate more accessible, more watched types of programming to the category of "trash," traditionally associated with the medium at large. *Homeland* participates in this formation and reinforcement of middle-class taste cultures, but its central female character has been influential on basic cable (less expensive, sometimes even free to air without a cable subscription) and broadcast (free to air) network programming in the United States as well.

We see *Homeland*'s influence in network dramas like *Scandal* (ABC 2012–), *The Blacklist* (NBC, 2013–), and *The Good Wife* (CBS 2009–), and the limited series *Hostages* (NBC, 2014) and *The Honourable Woman* (BBC and Sundance, 2014), which feature women as consummate problem solvers, not in the domestic spaces in which advertisers and sitcoms have consistently placed them but in the public arenas of politics and national security. This move from the domestic and comedic to the public and overtly

---

3 Emily Nussbaum, "Difficult Women: How *Sex and the City* Lost Its Good Name," *New Yorker*, July 29, 2013, 64.

4 Accounts of cable and premium channels' masculine-centered shows include Amanda D. Lotz, *Cable Guys: Television and Masculinities in the 21st Century* (New York: New York University Press, 2014); and Brett Martin, *Difficult Men: Behind the Scenes of a Creative Revolution from "The Sopranos" and "The Wire" to "Mad Men" and "Breaking Bad"* (New York: Penguin, 2013). The single series most subject to academic attention is *The Wire*. Scholarly treatment of it ranges from David Bzdak, Joanna Crosby, and Seth Vannatta, eds., "*The Wire*" and Philosophy: This America, Man (Chicago: Open Court, 2013); to Liam Kennedy and Stephen Shapiro, eds., "*The Wire*": Race, Class, and Genre (Ann Arbor: University of Michigan Press, 2012); C. W. Marshall and Tiffany Potter, eds., "*The Wire*": Urban Decay and American Television (New York: Bloomsbury Academic, 2009); and Linda Williams, On "*The Wire*" (Durham, NC: Duke University Press, 2014).

"serious" and political is part of what allows for the popular understanding of *Homeland* and its ilk as "quality" while *Sex and the City* and its offspring (despite their use of workplace settings) are not. Even with this move to the realm of national security, however, women's specifically sexed, reproductive bodies function in these narratives in ways that male bodies in espionage thrillers cannot. Women's bodies, as Alex Bevan argues here in relation to *Homeland*, work as a physical representation of the conflicts among aggressive US foreign policy, extensive domestic surveillance operations, and the rhetoric of civil liberties. In addition to their bodies being threatened with violence or overtaken by child bearing, these women also enact these conflicts in their own movements between the domestic and public spheres. Where Carrie Mathison conflates sex and work in her illicit romance with Brody, as Steenberg and Tasker maintain here, the FBI agent heroine of *The Blacklist*, for example, comes to realize that home life is just an extension of work life. She learns this lesson when she discovers that her husband, who has frequently criticized her lack of commitment to their adopting a child together, is in fact a criminal agent hired to monitor her both via their personal interactions and with video and audio surveillance of their home that closely mirrors Carrie Mathison's surveillance of Brody's home (discussed by Shapiro in his essay here). In the same vein, the surgeon-heroine of *Hostages* faces this conflation of work, public life, and national security with emotional and domestic life when she and her family are kidnapped in their own home, subject to release only when she agrees to murder the president while he is on her operating table. Olivia Pope, the proverbial white hat on *Scandal*, solves every possible political crisis (almost all of which involve sexual dalliances or the inappropriate mixing of the personal-sexual and professional) except her own, when she finds she simply can't quit her torrid love affair with the US president. *The Honourable Woman* offers the closest analogue to *Homeland*, with main character Nessa Stein (Maggie Gyllenhaal) attempting to sublimate her rape at the hands of Palestinian kidnappers and her motherhood of the resulting child for the good of her corporation's endeavors to foster peace between Israel and Palestine. For all of these women, and for Mathison on *Homeland*, the inability to extricate their personal, emotional, and sexual lives from national security seems to reflect a post-9/11 security state that insists that extensive domestic surveillance is necessary to protect the homeland.

It is no accident that women, and in particular mothers, are the characters who carry these story lines about government and security into the most private aspects of their personal and family lives. "Family values" television now includes and even prioritizes the (white, upper-middle-class) national family over the individual nuclear family. The overarching thematic across these series is the notion that the financialized and securitized mind-sets that now govern public life color all private relationships as well. Individuals and families can't hold themselves apart from the violence of the state and the violence of the market. This is TV well suited to address the economic and social conditions of the recession, TV that speaks to a culture of post–Edward Snowden revelations of domestic and international spying by the National Security Agency, and one still dealing with the detention and mistreatment of prisoners in Guantánamo Bay and remote-controlled drone attacks on US and foreign citizens abroad. As the wide array of interpretations of *Homeland* indicate, whether this phenomenon is a

Figure 1. Carrie Mathison's depiction as intense and obsessive at once reverses and sustains normative gender polarities (Teakwood Lane Productions).

critique or positive reinforcement of the movement of government surveillance and security apparatus into private and domestic spaces is a question largely of perspective. Nonetheless, these thematic questions seem open for conversation largely because of the program's status as "quality" television.

Perhaps to contain the significance of Carrie Mathison's role in national security, another dimension of her character is her mental illness and extreme emotionalism. Mathison is bipolar, and as Steenberg and Tasker point out, her prowess as an intelligence officer is often represented as contingent on her illness, her "special" brain. Such figuring of a female law enforcer as particularly successful because she is mentally ill also appeared in the Danish-Swedish original version of *The Bridge* (*Bron/Broen*; SVT1 and DR1, 2011–), as well as in the US version (FX, 2013–), and later in the very short-lived *Black Box* (NBC, 2014). In both *Homeland* and *The Bridge* the female main character's mental illness (in the US version of *The Bridge*, detective Sonya Cross, played by Diane Kruger, has an unnamed autism-spectrum disorder) stands in the way of romantic and familial relationships and helps her maintain focus on her job. In this sense, the series arguably participates in the contemporary habit of rewriting disability as specialness, which has given rise to representations linking the social limitations of autism-spectrum disorder to investigative brilliance, though more usually for a male character (as in the BBC's *Sherlock* [2010–] and CBS's *Elementary* [2012–]). For *Homeland*'s Mathison, her illness manifests in obsessive attention to detail, inappropriate sexual relationships, and frequent hysterical outbursts and crying. Danes's performance, which prominently features her ability to crumple her face and quiver her lip in intense distress, foregrounds this emotionalism with extremely wide-open eyes and gestures like raking her hand through messy hair that express frustration with her inability to fully protect the US homeland.

Danes's performance has won her prestigious awards, but it has also been the subject of several parody sketches that have spread virally across the Internet. *Saturday Night Live* (NBC, 1975–) parodied *Homeland* most famously in a skit featuring Anne Hathaway hyperbolically rendering Danes's emotional performance. In Hathaway's parody, Mathison defends her positions not with logic and evidence, but by repeatedly shouting "No!" while exhibiting the character's signature crumpled face and messy hair. Her stoic and skeptical male superiors—using vocal tones one might employ with an angry, insistent toddler—essentially put her in "time-out," cajoling her into exiting the conversation in favor of manically pinning pictures on a corkboard and connecting them with string. In keeping with the infantilization of Mathison's emotional responses, the other widely distributed *Homeland* parody came from *Sesame Street* (PBS, 1969–). In "Homelamb," Mathison and the rest of the CIA are sheep puppets searching for the Big Bad Wolf. Their biggest asset in this investigation is Baa-rody, who, sheep Mathison deduces, is actually a wolf in sheep's clothing. *Sesame Street*, a show for young children (and their parents), continues the emphasis on excessive emotion with Mathison bleating breathlessly, shaking her long blonde hair, quivering with suppressed feelings throughout, and giving in to her mindless interest in Baa-rody's handsome features despite knowing that he is in fact the dangerous criminal Big Bad Wolf.

These parodies bring us back to gendered debates about "quality" television dramas. While *Homeland*'s influence and acclaim put it in the "quality" category, its parodies emphasize the feminized elements of melodrama that link the show to "low" genres like soap opera and even to the broadcast dramas mentioned earlier, which still assume television's traditionally more feminine address. *Homeland* is, moreover, a consummate example of melodramatic political discourse in the sense that Elizabeth R. Anker has advanced the term in her far-reaching book *Orgies of Feeling*. Anker's depiction of post-9/11 melodrama describes *Homeland*'s ideological problematic well: "In legitimating violent and intrusive governing and corporate powers as a moral imperative for the practice of sovereign freedom, melodrama entrenches the disempowerment it is employed to overcome, and it abrogates the freedoms it promises to engender."[5] Indeed *Homeland*'s ongoing, doomed effort to mobilize state resources to alleviate vulnerability even requires it to stage (in the finale of season 2) a fuller culmination of 9/11's terrorist attack on the Pentagon, with greater loss of life, when a car bomb explodes at the CIA headquarters at Langley.

For us and for the contributors here, *Homeland*'s significance lies in its skillful rendering of affective and ideological economies apposite to ongoing debates about the securitization of American life. The series' emphatic female centrality rebuts the still-presumptive masculinity of quality crime TV, inspiring successors across the (narrowing?) network and cable divide. While popular parodies have sometimes trivialized and hyperemotionalized *Homeland*, negotiating the gendered anxieties that arise from its success, more significant to us is the series' break with the more masculine address that seems to go along with trends to compare TV favorably to cinema. *Homeland* is ultimately a trenchant political melodrama that does not seek to and never can quell the anxieties of the present moment with which it so forcefully engages.   *

---

5 Elizabeth R. Anker, *Orgies of Feeling: Melodrama and the Politics of Freedom* (Durham, NC: Duke University Press, 2014), 19.

"Pledge Allegiance": Gendered Surveillance, Crime Television, and *Homeland*

by LINDSAY STEENBERG and YVONNE TASKER

Although there are numerous intertexts for the series, here we situate *Homeland* (Showtime, 2011–) in the generic context of American crime television. *Homeland* draws on and develops two of this genre's most highly visible tropes: constant vigilance regarding national borders (for which the phrase "homeland security" comes to serve as cultural shorthand) and the vital yet precariously placed female investigator. In the immediate context of post-9/11 crime television (in programs such as *24* [Fox, 2001–2010] and *24: Live Another Day* [Fox, 2014]) the overarching message was that good people (i.e., trustworthy figures of authority) are watching. Thus, the surveillance of civil society was effectively legitimized as both responsibly managed and absolutely necessary. Moreover, the good people who both watch and respond are themselves suffering—whether conflicted over their actions and/or damaged through a personal history of violence and loss. These watchers' honorable trauma serves to assure audiences that surveillance is not undertaken lightly. Agents of homeland security suffer on behalf of average citizens, those who seemingly do not have the psychological or physical fortitude to bear the responsibility of surveillance.

Premiering ten years after the events of 2001, *Homeland* develops these themes in new directions, moving beyond the Manichaean opposition of right and wrong that characterized earlier representations. *Homeland* atypically dramatizes watchers who fail in their task and thus lack the absolute authority of earlier action-based intelligence thrillers. In a show that foregrounds multiple themes and resonances of fidelity, these failures take into account (and play with) the crime genre's established history of featuring damaged investigators who are doubted but ultimately triumph. (Fidelity here refers both to personal and professional loyalties within the fictional world and to the actual failures of intelligence agencies to which *Homeland* alludes).

A second key feature of American crime television, one that has been seamlessly absorbed by intelligence-focused programs like *Homeland*, is the centrality of a female investigator who is herself damaged and overinvested in her work.[1] Once again, *Homeland* acknowledges and develops this familiar construction of a professional woman whose personal trauma underpins her role as truth seeker and law enforcer. Particularly notable, we suggest, is the rich relationship explored in the show between these tropes of the female investigator and of legitimized surveillance.

The title *Homeland* of course refers to an America focused on the threat of terrorist activity at home as much as abroad and to the concessions in civil liberties that political violence is widely felt to require. From its initial broadcast, *Homeland* intervenes in a representational landscape in which the moral legitimacy of (political) violence is debated with intensity and regularity. Crime television has proved a fruitful site in which to rehearse ethical concerns over the extent of state surveillance, concerns of expediency over law, and the rights of suspected terrorists.

Unfolding in the aftermath of violence, crime television narrates processes of investigation and understanding, on the one hand, and pursuit and narrative resolution (if not always justice), on the other. The two are bound together, with the investigators seeking to understand a crime (scene), identify those responsible (and their motivations), and prevent further violence. The balance of investigation and pursuit in a crime show is one factor that determines its tone: Is it primarily a battle of wits, a chase, or a puzzle? Is the crime a pretext to explore the relationships within a work team (*Bones* [Fox, 2005–], *Numb3rs* [CBS, 2005–2010]), a character study (*Dexter* [Showtime, 2006–2013], *Elementary* [CBS, 2012–]), or a vehicle to elaborate concerns over contemporary politics (*The Wire* [HBO, 2002–2008], *24* [Fox, 2001–2010])? The narrative complexity deployed in *Homeland* is not novel in this larger generic context. Indeed, the plot twists of *24*, with its themes of loyalty and legitimacy, demonstrate the established character of these elements. Television narratives of homeland security in many ways require the shifts in allegiance, suspenseful revelations, and plot twists that the medium is particularly able to deliver.

As they have developed, the conventions of homeland security—at least on network television—have come to rely on particular models of heroism, as well as themes of terrorism, trauma, and violence. All of these elements are present in *Homeland*: Brody's status as damaged veteran, the traumatic explosion that provides the climax to season 2, Carrie's investment in her work, and Brody's conflicted commitment to home and homeland.

The interest of *Homeland* lies in part in its ability to renew and refresh what had become well-established conventions for representing the dangers of terrorism to Americans and the particular character—driven, intense, creative—of those who investigate and seek to prevent such violence. If narrative complexity (even at times incoherence) is a feature of many homeland security narratives, the psychological

---

1 For further studies of the female investigator, see Linda Mizejewski, "Dressed to Kill: Postfeminist Noir," *Cinema Journal* 44, no. 2 (2005): 121–127; Lindsay Steenberg, *Forensic Science in Contemporary American Popular Culture: Gender, Crime, Science* (New York: Routledge, 2013); Linda Mizejewski, *Hardboiled and High Heeled: The Woman Detective in Popular Culture* (London: Routledge, 2004); Yvonne Tasker, *Working Girls: Gender and Sexuality in Popular Cinema* (London: Routledge, 1998); Deborah Jermyn, *Prime Suspect* (London: BFI, 2010).

complexity evident in *Homeland*—not only Carrie's obsession with Brody but also the suggestion of an emotional and/or sexual tension between her and mentor Saul (Mandy Patinkin)—stretches the formulas it reproduces. In a way different from but related to the swearing and sexually explicit content so characteristic of "quality television," the psychological complexity marks the Showtime series as "adult" (both challenging and titillating) drama. Thus viewers understand relatively early that Carrie is right to be suspicious of Brody, but the show withholds diegetic recognition; indeed, her interest in and pursuit of Brody, which merges personal obsession and professional responsibility, begin to undermine her status as trustworthy cop protagonist.

Like other crime programs, *Homeland* centralizes surveillance as its key information-gathering tool, yet surveillance here does not yield knowledge, or rather, the knowledge it yields is partial. There are both literal and metaphorical blind spots in the CIA's surveillance apparatus. An example of the former is the Brodys' garage—the space where Brody goes to pray in secret and hides his Qur'an and his gun. The garage, traditionally a space for masculine retreat, is pivotal in revealing to the audience that Brody's national loyalties may have shifted with his religion. Themes of disguise and passing are explored with regularity in crime television shows concerned with political violence, encapsulated in the figure of an individual who passes as patriotic. Brody calls on the trope of the sleeper, a white American convert to Islam who is himself prepared to die in order to avenge Issa's (Rohan Chand) death and America's misdeeds abroad.[2] Venerated by the media and nation and encouraged to seek political office, Brody is readily able to penetrate the inner circles of US political power.

The literal blind spot of Brody's garage points to the metaphorical blind spots of surveillance that lie in Brody's motivation and his past. Because the show offers no reliable place or person, Brody's motivations, and the extent to which they are informed by his captivity, are hidden from all who watch him—on-screen and off. The more we, and Carrie, watch and become involved with Brody, the less certain we are as to the limits of his trauma and the possibility that what has been repressed (his military experiences, his love of Abu Nazir and Issa, his faith, his injuries) will violently return. In a conversation with his wife, Brody insists that not even he knows the extent of his trauma: "There was nothing anyone could have done. Even me. Because I tried too, to deal with everything that happened but that was beyond *me*. I was fucked the moment I left for Iraq. We all were." Thus, Brody himself cannot penetrate the blind spots in his own motivations or predict his own capacity for eruptive violence.

Michel Foucault has famously argued that "our society is one not of the spectacle, but of surveillance."[3] But it is a long-standing feature of crime television and cinema that surveillance provides a visual language for presenting violent spectacle, from *Rear Window* (Alfred Hitchcock, 1954) to reality crime programming. In the third episode of the series, Carrie expresses frustration with the blind spots in the Brody surveillance footage: "I have three weeks left and we're sitting around watching this . . . whatever

2 Yvonne Tasker, "Television Crime Drama and Homeland Security: From *Law & Order* to 'Terror TV,'" *Cinema Journal* 51, no. 4 (2012): 44–65.

3 Michel Foucault, *Discipline and Punish: The Birth of the Prison*, trans. Alan Sheridan (London: Penguin Books, 1991), 217.

this is . . . this reality show." This moment expresses both the feminizing of surveillance and the acknowledgment of surveillance as voyeurism; after all, the Brody footage reveals no useful intelligence data, only spectacles of dysfunctional sexuality and enactments of deep trauma.

Homeland's surveillance spectacles are both high and low tech—coupling well-worn crime techniques, such as the stakeout or going undercover, with the hypermodern multiscreen aesthetic inspired by video games and other crime shows, such as the *CSI* (CBS, 2000–) franchise. This allows the series to exploit both the authenticity associated with older models of detection and the sophistication and (transnational) mobility of newer information technologies. Surveillance-based visuals are all filtered through the bodies and emotions of the CIA watchers, who themselves are core to the series' spectacle. If crime television typically seeks to reassure audiences that good people are watching, *Homeland*'s spectacles question the morality as well as the efficacy of the watchers. Here the show reinforces the centrality of Carrie Mathison as the linchpin of the series' spectacles, morality, and expertise.

Homeland couples its refinement of thematics of homeland security with an equally ambiguous development of another televisual trope, the postfeminist female investigator. Like the female investigators who predate her (from Dana Scully to Temperance Brennan), Carrie Mathison is brilliant, dedicated, and deeply troubled. She is also characterized by a post-*CSI* fascination with, and generic dependence on, investigative expertise: "As with [Dana] Scully and [Clarice] Starling, this scientific expertise goes against traditional views of women as intuitive and emotive rather than logical and deductive. Simultaneously, however, the expertise of the female investigator incorporates more traditionally feminine forms of knowledge, such as intuition, to form a hybrid forensic intuition."[4] Perhaps even more than earlier female investigators, Carrie embodies a hybrid investigative expertise. She couples her proficiency as a CIA intelligence analyst with emotionally based interpretations of information (e.g., she knows that Brody has seen through her charade to get close to him because she sees it in his eyes). What marks Carrie as different from Scully, Brennan, or even a character like *CSI*'s Catherine Willows is her repeated performance of overwhelming emotion. Unlike the stoic and implacable women of crime television, Carrie frequently cries, swears, and becomes angry.

Mental Illness. Carrie's characterization as both acknowledged expert and perpetually at the brink of breakdown acknowledges and simultaneously complicates the female investigator's typical (even clichéd) coupling of professional toughness and emotional vulnerability. The most significant of these variations lies in Carrie's depiction as mentally ill. Established conventions see the female expert unable to maintain a healthy work-life balance because she is intensely dedicated to her job—calling into question the emotional stability of professional women more widely. Carrie's situation is, of course, different. Her bipolar disorder is not a generalized feature of postfeminist culture (like the discourse of work-life balance) but a specific condition: one that informs her actions and contributes to her persona. Initially, the program uses

4 Steenberg, *Forensic Science*, 63.

Carrie's illness to question her reliability—to her family, her profession, and even to herself, as she explains to Saul in the opening of the show's second season: "It fucked me up, Saul. Being wrong about Brody. It really fucked me up because I have never been so sure and so wrong. . . . [T]he way I am now, I wouldn't trust me either." The combination of being certain and then "proven" wrong is what drives Carrie to seek electroshock therapy, as the closing sequence of season 1 dramatizes. In a compelling exercise in restricted narration, the audience knows the truth: Carrie is not wrong. Thus, the device of using mental illness to question her reliability is ultimately revealed to be false.

In many ways the program frames Carrie's abilities as an analyst as contingent on her mental illness. In this fashion it taps into the crime genre trope of the tortured investigative genius, the questionable emotional intelligence of literary detective Sherlock Holmes being a primary example. Her obsession with Brody thus becomes a symptom of her mental ill health and a sign of her professional expertise and/or intuitive understanding. In several instances she exploits her own trauma and illness to forge a connection with Brody over their shared status as veterans and victims (at the veteran support group in the first season and again to turn him in season 2). As is characteristic of the conflicted nature of Carrie's character and the complexity of the series as a whole, sexual and emotional involvement with Brody is presented as both a job well done and a failure of duty.

It is certainly problematic to frame mental illness as a professional asset. Yet it does reveal larger patterns within *Homeland*—re-presenting familiar post-9/11 crime television conventions in such a way as to draw attention to them, and in this case recalibrating the pathological dedication to work that defined so many earlier female investigators.

Carrie's characterization hybridizes the troubled female investigator with the moral ambiguity and irreverent toughness of the hard-boiled *noir* hero. Like the hard-boiled hero, hard-drinking jazz aficionado Carrie must move through multiple social sites—from the back alleys of Beirut to the back rooms of political corruption. Infinitely quotable author Raymond Chandler describes the seasoned hero as the "the best man in his world."[5] Carrie Mathison is likewise the outsider (even from *inside* the CIA) who stands against all others to pursue threats to America.

This hard-boiled aspect of her professional persona is a strong feature of her character's setup in the first few episodes of the series and frames, from the outset, her relationship with her primary terror suspect, Sergeant Nicholas Brody. That relationship is presented as paranoid and erotically charged, in keeping with the traditional pairing between hard-boiled hero and femme fatale. Brody is thus introduced as a kind of *homme fatal*—dangerous, alluring, and mysterious. Like Carrie and her *noir* antecedents, Brody is a damaged veteran attempting to reintegrate. But where the *noir* hero struggled to place himself within a peaceful society, Brody layers this with shifting allegiances to Abu Nazir's (Navid Negahban) cause, with his affection for Nazir's lost son Issa tempering loyalties to his own family. *Homeland*, as we have

---

5 Raymond Chandler, "The Simple Art of Murder," in *The Second Chandler Omnibus* (London: Book Club Associates, 1979), 14.

established, transforms this archetypal partnership, rendering opaque or unreadable the emotional loyalties behind the central performances. Carrie's feelings are always on display, just as Brody's are always seen simmering just below the surface. Neither character's motivation is certain, whether to other characters or to the audience.

As elsewhere in crime television, Carrie and other female characters in *Homeland* conflate sex and work. This conflation, often in the service of the nation, recalls the enduring Mata Hari archetype of espionage stories. Sex as a patriotic duty is a device associated specifically with female spies and investigators, one drawn on in Carrie's pursuit of a sexual relationship with Brody and echoed in the first-season subplot involving CIA asset Lynne Reed (Brianna Brown), paid girlfriend to Prince Farid Bin Abbud (Amir Arison). Reed uses her position as sexual partner to obtain information for Carrie and is killed in the process. A woman who has placed herself at risk to serve her country, Reed comes to operate as a cautionary figure for Carrie, who is racked with guilt over her inability to protect an asset. The weaponization of sex in the service of country is thus both lucrative and dangerous in *Homeland*.

Despite her sexualized fascination with Brody, Carrie remains unswerving in her willingness to risk everything to do her job—and that job is founded on an intense patriotism, a commitment to protect the homeland of the program's title. Publicity posters for the show include a tagline that questions or demands "Pledge Allegiance." It is not surprising, then, that the show's thematics and characters circulate around one

Figure 1. This promotional image, with its prescriptive tagline "Pledge Allegiance," highlights the centrality of fidelity to the show (Teakwood Lane Productions).

structuring concept: fidelity. While this is the preoccupation of many crime shows, particularly those with homeland and terror themes (e.g., *24*, *Person of Interest* [CBS, 2011–]), *Homeland* depends on singularly intense concerns over fidelity—to one's spouse, employer, mentor, family, and country—teasing out the questionable fidelity of surveillance footage with its blind spots and lacunae.

Fidelity in *Homeland* is seemingly impossible. A few, of many, examples include Jessica Brody's (Morena Baccarin) affair with Major Mike Faber (Diego Klattenhoff), Carrie's complex relationship with Brody, Brody's commitment to Abu Nazir, and CIA Counterterrorism Director David Estes's (David Harewood) alliance with Vice President Walden (Jamey Sheridan). Carrie's relationship to Saul seems to be the only space in which consistent fidelity might be sustained. This type of mentoring relationship is the foundation of many crime stories, many of which feature an older man inducting a younger woman into the procedures of criminal investigation. Yet unlike other paternal role models of the genre, Saul Berenson is in many ways as broken as Carrie; a prime example of this is the disintegration of his marriage. *Homeland* also transgresses the conventions of the trusting paternal relationship, with Carrie exploiting her sexual appeal to ensure that Saul authorizes her initial surveillance of the Brody family. Thus, from the outset, the quasi-incestuous Saul-Carrie relationship resists being read as unshakable or fundamentally trusting.

Fidelity is foregrounded not only because of the narrative complexity of the show and its serial formatting, borrowed from television genres like the soap opera, but also because it is at the heart of how the show sells itself as unique—based as it is on faithful, authentic performances of complex emotional and psychological states such as Carrie's illness, Brody's trauma, and Saul's outrage.

Homeland's popular reception frequently implies a symbolic dichotomy between the Bush administration's *24* and Obama's *Homeland*.[6] This juxtaposition, one that values the complexity of *Homeland*'s narrative and the force of its performances, also acknowledges the profound changes in crime television since 9/11. *Homeland*, however, as we have argued, revivifies and reinterprets many long-established aspects of the crime genre, including the effective yet vulnerable female investigator and a complex form of narration that obscures motive and delays resolution. While *Homeland* atypically acknowledges a political landscape in which the use of surveillance technology, for example, is widely questioned, it works within (rather than against) the broader context of crime and espionage drama. After all, such generic retrofitting—looking backward to move forward—is a firmly established aspect of popular culture. In its blending of familiar and unexpected narrative and thematic elements, *Homeland* draws on and also troubles the conventions of American crime television, particularly in its post-9/11 form. *

---

6   Leslie Goffe, "The Homeland Phenomenon," *Middle East Magazine* 440 (2013): 54–56.

Fictions of Terror: Complexity, Complicity and Insecurity in *Homeland*

by James Castonguay

At the 2012 Society for Cinema and Media Studies conference, I seemed to be almost alone in my negative criticisms of *Homeland*'s (Showtime, 2011–) first season. Although the critical enthusiasm for the program from many of my colleagues was a welcome corrective to the relative absence of sustained scholarly discussions of entertainment television and ongoing US wars, I was surprised by what I saw as an emphasis on the putatively positive and progressive aspects of the program at the expense of *Homeland*'s more regressive ideologies and repressive politics.[1] To be sure, *Homeland* intensifies the "many meanings, or polysemy, that television [already] offers" through its complex narrative and complicated characters to produce a level of enigmatic ambiguity that provides ample interpretive space for the overwhelming laudatory critical reception it has received.[2] Yet these positive evaluations require a highly selective critical reading that problematically ignores or downplays the more salient and dominant meanings produced by the series. In what follows I elaborate on some of these meanings to argue that *Homeland* successfully exploits post-9/11 insecurities, psychological trauma, and narrative complexity to produce "quality" television propaganda for the Obama administration's "overseas contingency operations" and its unprecedented domestic surveillance on the home front under the umbrella of an $80 billion US security state.[3]

1   For two notable exceptions to this scholarly neglect, see Stacey Takacs, *Terrorism TV: Popular Entertainment in Post-9/11 America* (Lawrence: University Press of Kansas, 2012); Yvonne Tasker, "Television Crime Drama and Homeland Security: From *Law & Order* to 'Terror TV,'" *Cinema Journal* 51, no. 4 (2012): 44–65.

2   Jeremy Butler, *Television: Critical Methods and Applications*, 4th ed. (New York: Routledge), 7.

3   See Scott Wilson and Al Kamen, "'Global War on Terror' Is Given New Name," *Washington Post*, March 25, 2009, http://www.washingtonpost.com/wp-dyn/content/article/2009/03/24/AR200 9032402818.html. As Timothy Melley sums it up, "[T]he US National Security State . . . consumes 42 percent of world military spending [through] 16 intelligence agencies[,] . . . 29 other federal agencies, 1,200 government bureaus, and 2,000 private companies, all operating in 10,000 locations within the United States and many more abroad." Timothy Melley, "Covert Spectacles and the Contradictions of the Democratic Security State," *Storyworlds: A Journal of Narrative Studies* 6, no. 1 (2014): 63. See also Dana Priest and William Arkin, *Top Secret America: The Rise of the New American Security State* (Hachette Digital, 2011).

There is no question that *Homeland* stands out in important ways from other examples of "terror TV" for, among other reasons, "its central premise that the trauma of war does not disappear," for "calling attention to the covert and largely unreported drone wars," and for its representation of the "psychic turmoil and bipolar extremes that have characterized . . . America's collective response to the [2001] terrorist attacks."[4] I would argue, however, that *Homeland* is a complicit validation of these post-9/11 insecurities that in turn contributes to the public acceptance of arguments in favor of increasing homeland security at the expense of individual rights. In addition, agent Carrie Mathison's gender, bipolar disorder, unorthodox counterterrorism methods (including illegal wiretapping and "sleeping with the enemy"), fierce independence, and "nearly pathological . . . devot[ion] to her job . . . [all] challenge the conventions of the male-oriented espionage thriller."[5] It is significant in this context, however, that Mathison's obsessive work is being done for the CIA, which makes her character another example of television's broader recruitment of fictional women to support the war on terror or to assist in covert operations at home in programs like *The Unit* (CBS, 2006–2009), *Army Wives* (Lifetime, 2007–2013), and *Covert Affairs* (USA, 2010–).

Similar to the Cold War logic of deterrence through arms escalation, according to *Homeland*, covert operations are necessary to prevent terrorist attacks while also having the inescapable consequence of creating more terrorist enemies. This is one of the many contradictions of the current US "democratic security state" that leads to increased support of military operations abroad and increased surveillance and counterterrorism operations at home.[6] *Homeland* thus represents what we might call, following Richard Hofstadter's classic Cold War thesis, a paranoid style in American television in which "the imitation of the enemy [is the] . . . fundamental paradox."[7] As Susan Buck-Morss notes in *Thinking Past Terror*, the result is that "terror produces terror . . . [as] we [are] subjected to the common paranoid vision of violence and counter-violence, and prohibited from engaging each other in a common public sphere."[8] *Homeland*'s paranoid style is biologically wired into Mathison, whose highly emotional and manic episodes provide her with a "superpower disorder" (as Danes and *Homeland*'s producers describe it) through which she is able to gather, interpret, and intuit intelligence in

4   Patrice Petro, "Globalization and the Humanities: Cosmopolitanism, Cities, Security" (paper presented at the Amsterdam Centre for Globalization Studies at the University of Amsterdam, May 24, 2012), 14. Writing shortly after the conclusion of season 1, Petro already expressed significant reservations about *Homeland* for "not offer[ing] an especially critical examination of . . . citizenship in our post-9/11 world," and in light of Carrie's "desperate effort to gain the normalcy . . . of marriage, family, and children, which are the only factors that motivate actors in this drama to turn against their allies, governments, and ideological ideals." Ibid., 17; Matt Delmont, "Introduction: Visual Culture and the War on Terror," *American Quarterly* 65, no. 1 (2013): 158; Gary R. Edgerton and Katherine C. Edgerton, "Pathologizing Post-9/11 America in *Homeland*: Private Paranoia, Public Psychosis," *Critical Studies in Television* 7, no. 1 (2012): 92.

5   Petro, "Globalization," 14.

6   Melley, "Covert Spectacles," 63.

7   Richard Hofstadter, *The Paranoid Style in American Politics and Other Essays* (New York: Alfred A. Knopf, 1965), 32, quoted in Susan Buck-Morss, *Thinking Past Terror: Islamism and Critical Theory on the Left* (New York: Verso, 2003), 27.

8   Buck-Morss, *Thinking Past Terror*, 28.

ways that her rational male superiors cannot.[9] When combined with her willingness to become emotionally connected to "assets" and terrorist suspects, Mathison becomes a uniquely effective and affective weapon in the "war against terror," as the paranoid bipolar CIA agent off her antipsychotic medication is the one person who is able to see the post-9/11 world objectively enough to find the terrorists in our midst.[10]

Descriptions in the popular media of the president binge-watching *Homeland* (reportedly his favorite program)—including, I assume, an episode portraying the US drone strike ordered by Vice President Walden (Jamey Sheridan) that kills Abu Nazir's (Navid Negahban) young son, Issa (Rohan Chand)—become more sinister in the context of the Obama administration's actual global war on terror, which *Wired* has summed up, following CIA director Michael Hayden, as being "the same as Bush's, only with more killing."[11] As Obama explained to *Rolling Stone*, "[T]here's a lot of overdramatization [in *Homeland*] of how our national security apparatus works . . . but it's a terrific psychological study, and that's what I enjoy about it."[12] Reports of White House weekly "kill lists" and the confirmed deaths of thousands of civilians and hundreds of children as a result of Obama's escalated drone warfare program might explain why Obama privileges *Homeland*'s representation of the psychology of terrorism over US security operations and policies.[13] Although *Homeland* does suggest that US policy and actions are partly to blame for the terrorists' reprisals, and the series explores in detail the personal psychological toll of US politics and aggression, it does so to reinforce the need for increased homeland security and the use of force in counterterrorism operations. Just as *Homeland* producers Alex Gansa and Howard Gordon's previous series *24* (Fox 2001–2010; *24: Live Another Day*, Fox, 2014) was effective PR for the Bush administration's "enhanced interrogation techniques" and even served as an actual model for interrogation for the US military, *Homeland* functions as a "quality" propaganda arm for the Obama administration's continued waging of "dirty wars" around the globe, including the CIA-led assassination of US citizens.[14]

9   Vanessa Thorpe, "*Homeland*: Destructive, Dynamic, Distinctive—Carrie and Brody Are Back on Screen," *Guardian*, October 6, 2013, http://www.theguardian.com/tv-and-radio/2013/oct/06/carrie-brody-back-homeland.

10 In addition to the well-known parody of emotionalism discussed by the editors in their introduction here, Danes's over-the-top affect has also led to the creation of a Tumblr page, "The Claire Danes Cry Face Project," *Tumblr*, October 2012–April 2014, http://clairedanescryface.tumblr.com.

11 David Kravets, "Former CIA Chief: Obama's War on Terror Same as Bush's, but with More Killing," *Wired*, September 10, 2012, http://www.wired.com/2012/09/bush-obama-war-on-terror. See also Jack Serle, "More than 2,400 Dead as Obama's Drone Campaign Marks Five Years," *Bureau of Investigative Journalism*, January 23, 2014, http://www.thebureauinvestigates.com/2014/01/23/more-than-2400-dead-as-obamas-drone-campaign-marks-five-years.

12 Jann S. Wenner, "Ready for the Fight: *Rolling Stone* Interview with Barack Obama," *Rolling Stone*, April 25, 2012, http://www.rollingstone.com/politics/news/ready-for-the-fight-rolling-stone-interview-with-barack-obama-20120425.

13 Jo Becker and Scott Shane, "Secret 'Kill List' Proves a Test of Obama's Principles and Will," *New York Times*, May 29, 2012, http://www.nytimes.com/2012/05/29/world/obamas-leadership-in-war-on-al-qaeda.html. See also Mark Mazetti, "Use of Drones for Killings Risks a War without End, Panel Concludes in Report," *New York Times*, June 26, 2014, http://www.nytimes.com/2014/06/26/world/use-of-drones-for-killings-risks-a-war-without-end-panel-concludes-in-report.html.

14 See Glenn Greenwald, "Confirmed: Obama Authorizes Assassination of US Citizen," *Salon*, April 7, 2010, http://www.salon.com/2010/04/07/assassinations_2; Nasser al-Awlaki, "The Drone That Killed My Grandson," *New York Times*, July 18, 2013, http://www.nytimes.com/2013/07/18/opinion/the-drone-that-killed-my-grandson.html; and *Dirty Wars* (Rick Rowley, 2013).

In addition to being endorsed by the commander in chief, *Homeland* works in close collaboration with an actual CIA liaison, running story lines by the agency "to help with . . . verisimilitude," and has military families and former special ops members on its production team, including in executive producer roles.[15] Maureen Dowd has reported in the *New York Times* that Claire Danes "was welcomed with open arms at the real [CIA]" and that CIA director John Brennan "even ushered his fictional counterpart, Mandy Patinkin, into his office [where they] talked about keeping America's relentless extremist enemies at bay." Dowd quotes Danes's claim that "there must be some urge to have their victories on positive display even in a fictional context," and concludes that "the agency prefers PR about sometimes haywire yet dedicated fictional characters to fumbling real ones," adding that "Carrie and Saul . . . actually boost the agency's brand."[16] This positive branding effort for the CIA resonates with *Homeland*'s promotional campaign demanding that fans "pledge allegiance" to the program and reflects a post-9/11 nationalism that extends beyond "support the troops" rhetoric to include the government agents who are spying on the home front to keep us safe from terrorism.

Although the *New Yorker*, *Mother Jones*, and the *New York Times* lauded *Homeland* for providing the "antidote to [Fox's] *24*" that finally "exorcis[ed] the ghosts" of Jack Bauer from our collective memories (despite being produced by the same creative team), Showtime shares *Homeland*'s profits with Fox 21 Productions and was singled out in financial reports as a major source of increased revenue for Rupert Murdoch's Twenty-First Century Fox.[17] In addition, *Homeland*'s success no doubt played a role in the much-delayed rebirth of Bauer in Howard Gordon's *24: Live Another Day* (Fox, 2014–), which has been updated for the WikiLeaks era by transforming Bauer's trusted colleague, Chloe O'Brian, into a "more radical, [Edward] Snowden-type" enemy of the United States.[18] In addition, although both *24* and *Homeland* frame their representations of Arabs and Muslims in the already-limited context of the espionage thriller and terrorism, *24* offered a significantly broader range of Muslim and Arab characters than *Homeland*, which problematically extends the familiar racial and national profile of the Muslim terrorist from a dark-skinned, Middle Eastern Muslim male to include white and African American Marines and white American

15 Gavin Edwards, "*Homeland*'s CIA Connection," *Men's Journal*, October 1, 2013, http://www.mensjournal.com/magazine/homelands-cia-connection-20121022.

16 Maureen Dowd, "My So-Called C.I.A. Life," *New York Times*, September 14, 2013, http://www.nytimes.com/2013/09/15/opinion/sunday/dowd-my-so-called-cia-life.html.

17 Emily Nussbaum, "'Homeland': The Antidote for '24,'" *New Yorker*, November 29, 2011, http://www.newyorker.com/online/blogs/culture/2011/11/homeland-the-antidote-for-24.html; See also Hamed Aleaziz, "Interrogating the Creators of 'Homeland,'" *Mother Jones*, November 4, 2011, http://www.motherjones.com/media/2011/10/homeland-season-2-claire-danes-howard-gordon-alex-gansa; Willa Paskin, "The Creators of 'Homeland' Exorcise the Ghost of '24,'" *New York Times*, September 26, 2012, http://www.nytimes.com/2012/09/30/magazine/the-creators-of-homeland-exorcise-the-ghost-of-24.html; "Twenty-First Century Fox Reports Second Quarter Total Revenue of $8.16 Billion," *Business Wire*, February 6, 2014, http://search.proquest.com/docview/1494781782?accountid=28645.

18 Jen Trolio, "*24: Live Another Day*: Yvonne Strahovski Joins the Cast to Hunt Jack, Chloe's an Edward Snowden Type, and More," *TV.com*, January 13, 2013, http://www.tv.com/shows/24/community/post/24-live-another-day-yvonne-strahovski-joins-the-cast-to-hunt-jack-chloes-an-edward-snowden-type-and-more--138963472768.

women.[19] Indeed, although not all of the Muslims in *Homeland* are terrorists, all of the terrorists are Muslims, including Sergeant Brody, whose Islamic "turn" is represented as a prerequisite to becoming a terrorist.[20] While Islam may provide Brody with therapeutic comfort, he is a Stockholm-syndrome convert coerced into his Islamic faith and its concomitant terrorist politics. *Homeland* thus exploits the viewer's initial surprise associated with seeing a white US Marine worshipping Allah in his garage by anticipating and refuting the stereotypical assumption that Brody's faith is evidence that he is a terrorist. Of course, we later learn that Brody is in fact a terrorist who assassinates the vice president and murders three other people (and were it not for a malfunctioning suicide bomb vest, he would have killed many more). Similar to the way homeland security is integrated into the broader genre of the procedural crime narratives discussed by Tasker, *Homeland* asks viewers to examine their prejudices only to reconfirm those stereotypical assumptions later, which Tasker has described as Showtime's "'quality TV' version" of the tropes present in procedural crime drama franchises like *CSI* (CBS, 2000–) and *Law & Order* (NBC, 1990–).[21] As Jason Mittell has also shown, following Stuart Hall's theory of articulation, the meaning of Brody's video testimonial takes a similar trajectory through *Homeland*'s complex narrative structure: "Brody first articulates a terrorist bombing to American patriotism, then *Homeland* rearticulates the video to anti-terrorist pursuits and eventually to condemn terrorism and frame Brody as wrongly-accused, solidifying the dominant notion that terrorists are Arab foreigners, not white Marines."[22] Like the earlier "reveal" that Brody is a devout Muslim, *Homeland* adds layers of narrative and psychological complexity but ultimately ends up in the same representational place. *Homeland* may open up possibilities for alternative and even subversive meanings in a US context of reception, but it closes them down by rearticulating, reinforcing, and ultimately amplifying the familiar representation of the militant Muslim terrorist.

If we move beyond the important but methodologically limited consideration of stereotypes and distortions to include the context of reception, one might also suggest, following Hall's influential encoding-decoding model, that these dominant notions are negotiated and resisted by *Homeland*'s audience, yet there is also evidence to suggest that these dominant meanings are communicated effectively and reinforced for a

---

19　See Evelyn Alsultany, *Arabs and Muslims in the Media: Race and Representation after 9/11* (New York: New York University Press, 2012).

20　Laila Al-Arian named *Homeland* "TV's most Islamophobic show . . . [for] warn[ing] that Muslims are a hidden danger to fellow Americans," and the Lebanese tourism minister was reportedly "so upset about the portrayal of Beirut that he [was] considering a lawsuit." See Laila Al-Arian, "TV's Most Islamophobic Show," *Salon*, December 15, 2013, http://www.salon.com/2012/12/15/tvs_most_islamophobic_show; Bassem Mroue and Elizabeth A. Kennedy, "'*Homeland*': Lebanon Considering Legal Action against Showtime Series," *Huffington Post*, October 18, 2012, http://www.huffingtonpost.com/2012/10/19/homeland-lebanon-lawsuit_n_1986086.html.

21　Michael Kackman, interview with Yvonne Tasker, *Aca-Media*, "Episode 2," podcast audio, February 28, 2013, http://www.aca-media.org/episode2.

22　Jason Mittell, "Ends," in *Complex TV: The Poetics of Contemporary Television Storytelling*, prepublication edition (MediaCommons Press, 2012–2013), http://mcpress.media-commons.org/complextelevision/ends/.

significant portion of the US audience.[23] During *Homeland*'s first season, for instance, Peter King, conservative chair of the House Committee on Homeland Security, who in 2004 told Sean Hannity that the "[Muslim] enemy is living amongst us" and was a vocal opponent of the "Ground Zero mosque," received media attention for organizing what he described as "a series of hearings dealing with the critical issue of radicalization in the American Muslim community."[24] The results of a national poll released shortly before *Homeland*'s premiere also found that 47 percent of Americans believed the values of Islam are at odds with American values, and Muslims were the only religious group to receive an overall unfavorable rating. Given that 60 percent of respondents claimed to not know any Arab Americans or Muslims, *Homeland*'s representations become especially important, since versions of the "real" or "truth" about these groups and individuals are not grounded in viewers' actual experiences.[25] To be sure, *Homeland* opens up the theoretical possibility for subversive meanings through its brief explicit criticisms of US politics and policies, yet these meanings are outweighed by these contexts of reception and *Homeland*'s representation of the ubiquitous Muslim enemy.

The comparisons made by news outlets between *Homeland* and the actual release in May 2014 of US Army Sergeant Bowe Bergdahl—including a CNN segment titled "'Brody' vs. Bergdahl"—bolstered the program's cultural legitimacy and the plausibility of its main premise, which, as John Carlos Rowe notes, adds a *Manchurian Candidate*–like "twist" to a traditional captivity narrative in order to "play . . . upon the broad paranoia within the general population of the US, [and trade] on the panoptical presence of 'Homeland Security' in Americans' daily lives."[26] The beginning of the post-Brody season 4 would seem to offer renewed possibilities for subversive political meanings, as Mathison quickly earns the nickname "drone queen" for the assassinations she has supervised as the CIA's Kabul station chief. Peter Quinn (Rupert Friend), the psychologically traumatized black ops agent, expresses his disgust for Carrie's callous blaming of "collateral damage" on the victims for associating with people on the CIA's "kill list," and the introduction of Aayan Ibrahim (Suraj Sharma), the sole survivor of Mathison's "botched attack" on a wedding party, establishes a Middle Eastern Muslim character who appears to be uninterested in jihad. It remains to be seen if *Homeland* is simply introducing these moral ambiguities and political realities to offer

---

23   See Ella Shohat and Robert Stam, *Unthinking Eurocentrism: Multiculturalism and the Media* (New York: Routledge, 1994); Stuart Hall, "Encoding/Decoding," in *Culture, Media, Language: Working Papers in Cultural Studies, 1972–79*, ed. Stuart Hall, Dorothy Hobson, Andrew Lowe, and Paul Willis (New York: Routledge, 1992), 128–138.

24   "NY Congressman Calls US Mosque Leaders 'An Enemy amongst Us,'" Council on American-Islamic Relations, February 11, 2004, http://cair.com/action-alerts/268-ny-congressman-calls-u-s-mosque-leaders-an-enemy-amongst-us .html; Committee on Homeland Security House of Representatives and Committee on Homeland Security and Governmental Affairs United States Senate, *Compilation of Hearings on Islamist Radicalization—Volume I*, 112th Congress, 1st sess., December 7, 2011 (Washington, DC: U.S. Government Printing Office, 2012), 2.

25   "What It Means to Be American: Attitudes towards Increasing Diversity in America Ten Years after 9/11," *Public Religion Research Institute*, September 6, 2011, http://publicreligion.org/research/2011/09/what-it-means-to-be-american.

26   Gideon Raff, who produced the Israeli series *Hatufim* [*Prisoners of War*] (Keshet, 2010–) on which *Homeland* is based, also appeared on CNN as an expert commentator after Bergdahl's release; John Carlos Rowe, "American Orientalism after Said," *Popular Culture in the Middle East and North Africa: A Postcolonial Outlook* (New York: Routledge, 2013), 183–196.

counterarguments and justifications in favor of US policies and the CIA's actions. Facilitated by a culture of fear and a context of reception that includes ubiquitous media coverage of the "ISIS threat to America," *Homeland*'s previous seasons suggest that its potentially progressive polysemy can be effectively contained, controlled, and rearticulated through a complex narrative structure that may continue to do its ideological work on behalf of the Obama administration's aggressive counterterrorism policies abroad and repressive security policies at home.   ✳

The National Body, Women, and Mental Health in *Homeland*

by Alex Bevan

The academic literature on postfeminism, pathology, and quality television observes the traditional commitment of quality television to stigmatizing the single professional woman, and at first glance, *Homeland* (HBO, 2011–) adheres to this convention.[1] This essay, however, explores the symbolic position of the single working woman in *Homeland* within larger discourses on national security, surveillance, and the relationship of the individual with the state. Drawing on work in feminist geography that analyzes women's symbolic operation in the war on terror, I argue that the mental and bodily health of Carrie Mathison become battlegrounds for the series' overarching questions about state surveillance and citizenship. Gender in *Homeland* is less concerned with the personal being political than it is with personhood and "geopoliticality," that is, the relationships between personal privacy and domestic security, and between a US-branded feminism and American imperialism. Carrie's mind and body territorialize geopolitical struggles that elude representability because of their very lack of national, spatial, and material boundaries. The post-9/11, "post"–Iraq War climate is characterized by a crisis of national representability: drone wars violate the integrity of national borders; war is declared on individuals rather than nations; perceived threats from the "outside" (terrorist attacks like 9/11) merge with those that come from within (the 2013 Boston Marathon bombings, the escalation of mass shootings in the United States), including violence that defies physicality and territory, like cyberterrorism. Carrie's mind and body humanize and literalize the war on terror,

---

1 Diane Negra, "'Quality Postfeminism'?: Sex and the Single Girl on HBO," *Genders* 39 (2004), http://www.genders.org/g39/g39_negra.html.

where traditional notions of territory and warfare are in crisis. Through institutions and decisions that govern her mind and body, the series manages and workshops larger national discourses on security. Carrie embodies the intersections of geopolitical struggles, gender, and American discourses around national identity, thereby redirecting scholarly attention toward television geographies of gender and feminism.

Carrie is a talented CIA operative with bipolar disorder. Her pathology is, however, a double-edged sword. At times, it undercuts her legitimacy when she must convince the agency of an imminent terrorist attack, and yet it also inspires her professional breakthroughs. Carrie's sanity is scrutinized in season 1 when the series' portrayal of her manic episode discredits her theory that the decorated US war hero, Brody, is secretly a terrorist. Only in that season's finale is it revealed that Carrie was, in fact, right and that her disorder did not dull her logic but enabled the case's breakthrough. In season 3, Carrie uses her bipolar disorder as a smoke screen in courting a high-priority Iranian informant; her boss, Saul, pretends to fire and institutionalize her as a security risk, and Carrie then acts as bait, appearing to be a disgruntled and possibly treasonous ex-operative. The true intention of this play comes to light only episodes later, at a stage when it appears that the CIA has institutionalized Carrie against her will.[2] At this point in the series, Carrie's mental illness, as the repeated focus of agency surveillance and censure, becomes repurposed as an effective gambit in reconnaissance missions.

Because Carrie's mental and physical health are under constant scrutiny, they are implicated in her struggles to assert power and authority in her workplace and her sex life. She offers Saul sex in return for his turning a blind eye to her illicit surveillance of the Brody household.[3] When Saul shuts down her operation after rejecting her, Carrie continues her surveillance of Brody by pursuing him sexually. Carrie also has multiple sexual encounters with strangers in the series.[4] *Homeland* repeatedly frames Carrie's promiscuity as pathological because her one-night stands narratively coincide with periods of psychological distress. Her method of pursuing men (she frequents bars wearing a fake engagement ring to ward off those interested in a relationship) and her failure to remember exactly who she slept with are also colored as deviant. Consistent with hackneyed associations among women, espionage, and trading sex for national secrets (à la Mata Hari), Carrie uses her body as currency for asserting control both at work and in her sex life. The symbolic value of Carrie's body culminates at the end of the third season with her discovery that she is pregnant with Brody's child and her decision to keep the baby and raise it as a single mother despite her reservations about balancing work with home life.[5]

Carrie's mental health and her reproductive and sexual body manifest the lines between selfhood and state power in key American ideological debates. The friction between self and state is apparent when she is hospitalized twice for manic episodes. During these institutionalizations, her body is literally placed under state control and surveillance, which poignantly contrasts with how the series begins when Carrie is

2   "Yoga Play," *Homeland* 3.05 (October 20, 2013).

3   "Pilot," *Homeland* 1.01 (October 2, 2011).

4   "Pilot"; "Tin Man Is Down," *Homeland* 3.01 (September 29, 2013).

5   "The Star," *Homeland* 3.12 (December 15, 2013).

in the position of surveilling Brody after she illegally bugs his family home. Carrie is in the position, then, either of analyzing terrorist threats or of being analyzed by US intelligence, military, and medical institutions. In this way, her pathological body materializes the binary between surveyors and the surveilled that the series constructs. However, the lines between watching and being watched become less clear once the audience learns that Carrie is complicit in being surveilled when the agency uses her mental illness as bait in the play for Iran. The uncertainty the narrative constructs around Carrie's mental stability and the blurred lines between the subject and object of state surveillance parallel the mixed sentiment and confusing messages that characterize the popular discourse on state surveillance during the American war on terror. The intensification of drone warfare in the Obama administration, the retrospective scrutinization of the Patriot Act, and the 2013 Edward Snowden leaks (which revealed that Homeland Security tracks the Internet activity and phone calls of private citizens) are all part of the growing public discourse on government surveillance and rights to personal privacy in a security state. Indeed, public knowledge about the security state raises significant questions about what exactly constitutes surveillance in a digital era, post-9/11 America, and to what extent submitting to surveillance is a fair compromise for possibly deterring a terrorist attack. News media continually report on the conflicting interests between individual rights to privacy and government responsibilities for national security. The tension between what some see as pernicious surveillance and others view as necessary vigilance also coincides with mixed public sentiment about government ownership of private information and corporate access to this potential wealth of marketing data. The public concern around how the security state safeguards and/or impinges on personal freedom is reflected in news headlines like "We Kill People Based on Metadata," "Orwell's Nightmare: The NSA and Google," and "That Lamp Is Spying on You."[6]

The tenebrousness of twenty-first-century security and privacy rights makes the symbolic legibility of bodies and territory all the more important. Alexander Murphy argues that physical territory remains important to political ideology:

> The role of the territorial state has changed in recent decades in the wake of: the communications revolution; the explosion of transnational social, political, and economic formations; accelerated mobility across international boundaries. . . . Yet in the rush to document and assess the networks, flows, and relational spaces that are part of this shift, it is important not to overlook the continuing hold of modernist territorial ideas on the geographical imagination.[7]

6   "We kill people based on metadata" is an infamous quote by General Michael Hayden, former director of the CIA and NSA. Michael Hayden (GA), Debate with Dr. David Cole, "The Price of Privacy: Re-Evaluating the NSA, a Debate," Johns Hopkins University Foreign Affairs Symposium, Baltimore, MD, April 1, 2014; John W. Whitehead, "Orwell's Nightmare: The NSA and Google—Big Brother Meets Big Business," Huffington Post, May 13, 2014, http://www.huffingtonpost.com/john-w-whitehead/orwells-nightmare-the-nsa_b_5310171.html; Johnny Duggan, "That Lamp Is Spying on You, and So Is Basically Everything Else," Ryot: News + Action, http://www.ryot.org/lamp-spying-pretty-much-everything-else/653945.

7   Alexander B. Murphy, "Territory's Continuing Allure," Annals of the Association of American Geographers 103, no. 5 (2013): 1212.

I would add that *media negotiations* of these "flows" and "relational spaces" reconstruct the sense of territory *and bodies* under surveillance to address topics like networks and security, which tend to elude representability. This is particularly true of digital-era warfare and surveillance, which defy spatial representability because they cannot be reduced to one event in a single time and place. The Pakistan drone attacks in season 3 of *Homeland* represent the Langley-based control center, action on the ground, and satellite images that mediate the two spaces and time zones. Thus, drone intelligence, which is rooted in abstract satellite images, must be narratively and visually translated by the series into images of violence on the ground and emotional response in the control room. *Homeland* applies a similar narrative and visual protocol of spatial fragmentation and permutation to representing surveillance more generally. Part of the difficulty of contemporary debates about drone warfare and surveillance is that they are difficult to perceive, bear witness to, or even conceive of. They rely on elusiveness, invisibility, and the porousness of national borders, where "the enemy" may be diffused across several countries and a string of bank accounts and e-mail addresses. The "hunt" for terrorists in *Homeland* often relies on the anticlimactic and monotonous tracking of e-mail, cell-phone activity, and international transfers of large sums of money. Depictions of graphic violence are therefore relatively rare in the series, as its "chase scenes" are primarily digital. Hence, the war on terror and consequences of government surveillance are made reassuringly visible (and violent) in the form of Carrie's hospitalization and treatment. The interaction between Carrie's pathology and the state imbues the elusive terms of twenty-first-century warfare and geopolitical power with representability and symbolic territorialization. The gendered reproductive and sexual currencies of Carrie's body are burdened with this symbolic work. Similarly, popular Western discourses on war in the Middle East and the security state mobilize women's bodies to address the unrepresentability of twenty-first-century warfare.

In addition to the spatial and geographic dislocatedness of the war on terror, there is also a temporal and cognitive ambiguity. Brian Massumi observes the affective (il)logic of preemptive attacks by the United States on potential terrorist threats, pointing out the "would-have/could-have" reasoning behind the American invasion of Iraq, which George W. Bush later justified with the claim that *had* Saddam Hussein had access to "weapons of mass destruction," then he *could* have posed a viable threat.[8] This same reasoning permeates the temporal affect of the war on terror and its definitions of security: "The security that preemption is explicitly meant to produce is predicated on its tacitly producing what it is meant to avoid: preemptive security is predicated on a production of insecurity to which it itself contributes."[9] In other words, "threat has no actual referent" in this paradigm.[10] The affective politics of the war on terror extend to *Homeland* and its spatiotemporal disjunctions that appear in the state's governance of Carrie's mind and body. Carrie is institutionalized based on her

8 Brian Massumi, "The Future Birth of the Affective Fact," in *The Affect Theory Reader*, ed. Melissa Gregg and Gregory J. Seigworth (Durham, NC: Duke University Press, 2010), 55.

9 Ibid., 58–59.

10 Ibid., 59.

suspicions of Brody, which her employers presume to be pathological. The agency and viewer discover she is right about Brody after she has already been committed. Carrie is institutionalized again in season 3 because of the threat she poses as a security liability to the CIA. Later on in that season, the series reveals this manic episode to be part of an agency operation. *Homeland*'s narrative logic is rooted in the same retrospective affect used for justifying preemptive attacks on terrorist targets. The circular logic and time-bending, Wonderland irrationalism of the war on terror are reflected in the agency's preemptive measures to quiet Carrie before she has even spoken, and this logic is played out upon her "disordered" body. The viewer is roped into this retrospective logic when the series reveals *after* her institutionalizations that the security liability she posed was unfounded. In the same way that the Cheshire Cat reasons that Alice is mad *because* she is in Wonderland, and living in a perpetual state of insecurity is a product of the security state, Carrie is institutionalized for mental illness because of the information she *could* release if she goes mad. The series' ongoing management of Carrie Mathison's pathology and the government's control over her body are also meta-interrogations of the logical fissures marking the temporality of national security.

Feminist geography provides a broader discursive context for the ways that the series uses Carrie's health to corporealize and rationalize the war on terror. Work of this kind challenges understandings of security as protection or as a fortification of inside-outside boundaries and seeks to "link together the feminist concerns with the body with the critical geopolitical global vision. This reconfigures the geopoliticians' concern with abstracted, state-based notions of security into a form that is embodied in the material figure of the civilian body."[11] Feminist geographers respond to previous geographic paradigms that focus on metadiscourses on surveillance and security by focusing on the immediate effects of these exercises in state power on the female body. As Lise Siger and Joni Nelson state, "Feminist geography, anchored in the body, moves across scale, linking the personal and quotidian to urban cultural landscapes, deforestation, ethno-nationalist struggles, and global political economies."[12] In the introduction to their anthology *W Stands for Women*, Michaele L. Ferguson and Lori Jo Marso connect the George W. Bush administration's co-optation of feminist rhetoric to its consolidation of a patriarchal security state, which claims to have women's best interests at heart. Thus, in popular discourses on US national security, private citizenship, and the war on terror, feminist rhetoric functions to literalize and justify US imperialism in the Middle East.[13] The Western liberation of Muslim women and Western feminism as a civilizer of the Muslim "Other" have been significant arbiters in the United States' Orientalist rationales for the wars in Iraq and Afghanistan. Sunaina Maira and Sherene Razack suggest that the war on terror's political rhetoric mobilizes the concerns of Western feminism to justify its interventions in the Middle East. By associating Islam with the abuse of women's rights in that region, US propaganda

11 Joanne Sharp, "Geography and Gender: Finding Feminist Political Geographies," *Progress in Human Geography* 31, no. 3 (2007): 383.

12 Lise Nelson and Joni Seager, "Introduction," in *A Companion to Feminist Geography*, ed. Lise Nelson and Joni Seager (Oxford, UK: Blackwell, 2005), 2.

13 Michaele L. Ferguson and Lori Jo Marso, eds., *W Stands for Women: How the George W. Bush Presidency Shaped a New Politics of Gender* (Durham, NC: Duke University Press, 2007).

returns to an age-old Orientalist tactic that pathologizes Islam and constructs it as something that needs "curing" or Western "enlightenment."[14] In *Homeland*, this more broadly gendered, Orientalist rhetoric for the war on terror is present in Carrie's intermediation between sources of information and the agency. Many of Carrie's sources of information are Arab, and in the series "the Muslim woman's body is constituted as simply a marker of a community's place in modernity."[15] Carrie's solicitation of information from "oppressed" female informants in return for their "liberation" in the form of American citizenship, along with her staunch independence and confidence in her work, advertise the progressivist influence of Western feminism (or American presence) in the Middle East. In this way, corporeal symbolism and its mediation of US discourses on surveillance applies to other women in *Homeland* as well as Carrie. In season 1, Carrie approaches Lynne (Brianna Brown), an old recruit who spies for the CIA while working as the primary escort of a Saudi prince and terrorist affiliate. Lynne copies the contents of the prince's phone, and this ultimately costs her her life.[16] The agency is as responsible for her murder as the prince's henchmen because it refuses to provide Lynne with adequate protection, and its cavalier assessment of the risks involved in her actions is rooted in explicitly voiced gender- and class-based factors. In this instance the agency ignores Carrie's advice and refuses to assign government protection to Lynne, implying that her occupation as a sex worker does not make her important enough to warrant the allocation of agency resources. Another female recruit and wife of a known terrorist also places her life in danger while providing the agency with the crucial information necessary to track down Nazir (Navid Negahban), the series' main villain.[17] Women, particularly in their sexual relationships with men, repeatedly mediate between terrorists and agency operations. Women supply information and comply with surveillance by both the agency and their terrorist partners. While Brody remains officially unsurveilled by the agency, women's bodies are frequently traded by institutions of power in return for valuable information. In this context, Carrie's body becomes a site for competing domestic and international interests that model national attitudes about the relationship between individual rights and state security.

Links between corporeality, pathology, women, and the relationship of the individual to the state are apparent in depictions of the single, professional women in contemporary "quality television" more generally. In *The Fall* (BBC, 2013–), Stella (Gillian Anderson) is the lead detective investigating a serial killer in Belfast. Her one-night stand comes under scrutiny in the police department when her (married) lover is murdered the night of the affair. Stella is pathologized when her sexual encounter, in which she is the clearly the aggressor, is disturbingly intercut with the serial murderer's contemporaneous attack on a female victim. She defends her right to privacy about

14 Sherene Razack, "Geopolitics, Culture Clash and Gender after September 11," *Social Justice* 32, no. 102 (2005): 11–31; Sunaina Maira, "'Good' and 'Bad' Muslim Citizens: Feminists, Terrorists, and US Orientalisms," *Feminist Studies* 35, no. 3 (2009): 631–656.

15 Razack, "Geopolitics," 12.

16 "Grace," *Homeland* 1.02 (October 9, 2011).

17 "The Smile," *Homeland* 2.01 (September 30, 2012).

her sex life, while the patriarchal institutions of Belfast law enforcement make her adulterous promiscuity the object of more scrutiny than the murder itself. In *Dexter* (Showtime, 2006–2013), Debra Morgan (Jennifer Carpenter) is the sister of a serial killer and also a police detective. Throughout the series she struggles between the demands of her profession, which would mean turning her brother in, and her loyalty to family, which would mean compromising her career and sense of morality. Debra's promiscuity and alcoholism are the primary outlets for this ongoing internal struggle. Last, in *House of Cards* (Netflix, 2013–), Claire (Robin Wright) reveals that she is a rape victim during an interview following her husband's appointment to the vice presidency. However, the series never explicitly states whether this is an authentic moment in front of the camera or a calculated move to win voter sympathy. Claire, Stella, and Debra are pathologized for their sexuality, as straight women who enjoy anonymous and, in Claire's case, group sex. In these series, female sexuality and mental health (insofar as popular discourse stigmatizes rape victims and sexually active women) are tied to a character's motivational opacity, which extends to the legal and political institutions operating around (and against) her. The internal struggles the female characters suffer revolve around their negotiating institutional patriarchy and the rights of the individual, where mental health and socially unsanctioned female sexualities offer opportunities for rebellion.

Since *The Mary Tyler Moore Show* (CBS, 1970–1977), "quality television" has maintained a tradition of challenging gender boundaries, especially through female-centered television programs. Post-9/11 "quality television" has continued in this vein, as well as addressing and problematizing contemporary anxieties about the costs of national security to Western individualism. The female body and mental health in millennial "quality television" vehicularize contemporary anxieties around definitions of citizenship in the war on terror. Such representational trends linking pathology, gender, and national security call for a more geopolitically sensitive framework for studying gender on television. In this sense, gender should not be treated as an isolated category of self-identity but as a nexus point for geopolitical discourses. Rather than thinking of gender in *Homeland* as performance or lived experience, we might think of it as diagramming the integrities and ruptures in geopolitical selfhood and statehood. ✳

Homeland's Crisis of Middle-Class Transformation

by STEPHEN SHAPIRO

omeland's first season has few economic, let alone specifically capitalist, elements within its frame. There are only a few money transfers and a fleeting third-party reference to the bad finances of Nicholas Brody's family in his absence. Character motivation is overwhelmingly presented as driven by personal feelings about status and identity. Yet *Homeland*'s handling of its spy and conspiracy genre both represents and helps constitute its ideal audience's realization and response to its own collective class emergency. This essay investigates the way *Homeland* uses a complex temporality to grapple with some essential contemporary questions: How does the American middle class in crisis engage with television to think about its mutable position within capitalist history? If a US bourgeoisie, loosely outlined as the target audience for subscription "quality" television, is experiencing a crisis of social reproduction, in which it can decreasingly afford the middle-class status markers of housing, education, and health care, what are the cultural forms it uses to respond to vanishing prosperity?

Economists Gérard Duménil and Dominique Lévy see the twentieth century and onward as consisting of alternating capitalist crises wherein the professional-managerial, broadly middle classes align either with the upper class of haute capitalists against the working classes or the other way round. They suggest that we are in the midst of an ongoing realignment of class alliances wherein the (Western) middle classes might be in the process of shifting their allegiance away from the high capitalist class in favor of solidarity with those below.[1] During profitability crises such as those that occurred in the 1890s and 1970s, Duménil and Lévy suggest, the middle class forms a rightward alliance with elites. The rise of neoliberalism from the 1970s, wherein profit is restored by unraveling New Deal social welfare programs, manifests this kind of shift rightward. Yet only so much value can be mined from this sort of reappropriation, and the middle class eventually find themselves the new targets for expropriation by haute capital as the costs of essential aspects of middle-class status rise beyond even their means. Consequently, a crisis of financial hegemony emerges as

---

1 Gérard Duménil and Dominique Lévy, *The Crisis of Neoliberalism* (Cambridge, MA: Harvard University Press, 2011).

the middle classes lose confidence in their leadership by elites and look for a leftward alliance with the working class, such as we've seen recently with Occupy and related movements. Such a transfer of allegiances requires the kind of cultural narrative and temporal perspective (more on that later) that *Homeland* provides.

Georg Lukács has argued that during periods of middle-class society's fragmentation, "a not inconsiderable portion of the bourgeoisie becomes 'educated' to the dehumanization of bourgeois society" and seeks out cultural works that emphasize themes of "disappointment and disillusionment," often preferring "catastrophe" tales that depend on the "adventures of shadowy characters" and their stratagems of detection, conspiracy, and surveillance.[2] His suggestion that doom-laden cultural forms are ways of thinking through crisis is a useful rejoinder to Mark Fisher's claim that apocalyptic or terror tales proliferate now because it is easier to imagine the end of the world than an alternative to capitalism.[3] Moreover, tales of nervy suspense, like *Homeland*'s, are not merely symptomatic of crisis, but are also the means through which its audiences formulate a tactical response to crisis as they gain knowledge both about the singular *events* of financial catastrophe (like the 2008 housing market crash) and about the repeating systemic features of long-wave accumulation cycles (like the overproduction of commodities, including credit ones) in which crises continually occur.

One exciting feature of contemporary "quality" televisual narrative has been its efforts to take up Ernst Bloch's suggestion that history is a "polyrhythmic and multispatial entity," and thus think about simultaneous and nested valences of time, about the periodizable moment *and* long duration periodicity.[4] The move to an investigation of periodicity is associated with the current wave of complex serial or long-form drama, the consumption of which is itself a marker of sophisticated middle-class taste. As bourgeois audiences hone their skills in recognizing the longer units of time implicit in the multiepisode or season arc, they begin to understand a season within a long-running show as both periodizing, marking the beginning or end to a narrative arc, and involving periodicity, when one dramatic conflict recalls past relationships, themes, or plot developments.

Homeland's title sequence highlights the importance of television as a whole for locating the singular or exceptional moment against a pattern of longer duration. Carrie Mathison's complaint that she "missed something once before," that is, the telltale signs of the planning of September 11, 2001, and wants to make "sure we don't get hit again," is balanced against a sequence of continual terror-warning transmissions that are shaping her paraconscious ecology from the 1980s onward. The image of child Carrie's head framed by the television set has her pigtails askew like radial antennae as if to suggest a cyborg fusion of her cerebral cortex and the broadcast signal. Did Carrie really *miss* something (as in forgetting to watch a single

---

2   Georg Lukács, "Narrate or Describe," in *Writer and Critic and Other Essays*, ed. and trans. Arthur D. Kahn (New York: Grosset & Dunlap, 1970), 145, 124.

3   Mark Fisher, *Capitalist Realism: Is There No Alternative?* (Ropley, UK: Zero Books, 2009).

4   Ernst Bloch, *Heritage of Our Times*, trans. Neville Plaice and Stephen Plaice (Berkeley: University of California Press, 1991), 62.

Figure 1. Young Carrie's mind transmissions in *Homeland*'s title sequence (Teakwood Lane Productions).

episode) or was her consciousness systematically wired by her dedicated viewing to feel this way from an early age?

Carrie's paradox is that she uses the opportunity of uncertainty as a means not only of ascertaining the right *periodization* of events, which she catalogs on a classic color-coded police investigation board with photographs and connecting strings on the wall of her apartment, but also their recurring *periodicity*. Conventional historiography highlights the need to periodize time and segment it, usually linearly (e.g., the Industrial Revolution, modernism, post-1945, the petroleum age), by choosing factors that differentiate one phase from another and fix certain cultural formations as defining each stage's exceptionality. Periodicity is the less developed approach, since it not only tends to handle longer periods of time but also insists on the comparison of analogous points within these long phases by considering time in terms of spiraling cycles.[5]

Homeland's title sequence thus contrasts Carrie's desire for periodization (the "end" of terror moments) against a longer unit of time. That unit, extending from Reagan to Obama, may itself be framed as the "shock doctrine" time of rising neoliberal governmentality, but *Homeland* repeatedly suggests that analogous features recur throughout American history.[6] The Muslim fabricator (Nasser Faris) of Brody's suicide vest has learned his tailoring skills in Gettysburg, where he makes Civil War replica costumes for those reenacting a prior clash of civilizations, and Brody chants

5 Karl Marx, *Capital I* (New York: Vintage, 1977), 786; Karl Marx, *Capital III* (London: Penguin, 1981), 418. Historical accounts of systemic crises appear with Fernand Braudel, *The Perspective of the World*, trans. Siân Reynolds (London: Collins, 1984); Giovanni Arrighi, *The Long Twentieth Century: Money, Power, and the Origins of Our Times* (London: Verso, 1994). See also Charles Kindleberger, *Manias, Panics, and Crashes: A History of Financial Crises* (New York: Basic Books, 1978); Carmen M. Reinhart and Kenneth S. Rogoff, *This Time Is Different: Eight Centuries of Financial Folly* (Princeton, NJ: Princeton University Press, 2009).

6 Naomi Klein, *Shock Doctrine: The Rise of Disaster Capitalism* (New York: Picador, 2007).

the marine chorus commemorating repeated American military interventions abroad over centuries.

One of Carrie's defining character traits is her mental illness, and her bipolar events represent (among other things) an attempt to think about simultaneous registers of history and to situate events as variations on a structuring theme (a truism about the kind of jazz that scores the title sequence in which we see Carrie practicing her Louis Armstrong cornet). This kind of cultural analysis is discouraged by her CIA superiors, and it receives something like the Hasidic warning that any approach to the divine's real name must end only in madness. Carrie's problem, though, is not that she wants to gaze directly into the eye of terror, or even survey the nightmare of history, but that her apprehension of manifold temporality challenges prevailing models of cultural influence, lineage, and adaption. The value of cutting through time is that it provides a compass for one moment's actors to follow the direction of those in similar moments in the past, even if these were so long ago that they are barely remembered today.

Homeland's achievement is not only that it broaches this question of multiple temporalities but also that it draws its viewers into the perception of multiple time valences while also situating us within the play of social movement by having Carrie perform our own behavior in ways that create a *mise en abyme* in which we recognize *Homeland*'s characters mirroring one another and us as well. Whatever the mundane tasks of her day job, which viewers never see, Carrie's "real" work life begins at home. After having set up a surveillance network of cameras at Brody's home, she dedicates herself to watching nonstop what she calls a "reality show," often ending up horizontally slumped on her sofa as she watches Brody horizontally slumped on his sofa watching television.

But we viewers are next in this sequence, likewise slumped as we watch her watch Brody watch television. This looping effect is different from what is referred to as metareflection, the cultural product's awareness of and commentary on the medium or tradition of its own production.

Figure 2. Adult home viewing: The audience, Carrie, Brody loop (Teakwood Lane Productions).

The consumer of a metareflexive cultural product receives a sort of ironic stage whisper, but in this kind of recursion, our practices become indistinguishable from those of the characters. *Homeland*'s immersion of the viewer by mirroring her or his own actions is something different from what previous critical models have described, as it models the process of social recomposition by bringing viewers into approximation with a heterogeneous group of characters in their own process of realignment.[7]

---

7 This process of realignment can also be seen in another narrative feature of the crisis of the middle class in transformation: the rising prominence of adolescent actors. When *Homeland* focalizes through Nicholas Brody's

When Carrie watches Brody, we usually see this through shots of her neck and face lit by the screen's glow, often with headphone wires snaking along her body and her torso covered by the back of the screen.

Figure 3. Carrie's viewing is like Brody's suicide vest (Teakwood Lane Productions).

The significance of these shots appears when Brody first puts on the suicide vest made for him at the Gettysburg tailor shop. He speaks about how its wired detonation will slice off the wearer's (his) head and leave it intact while the body is obliterated. Brody's message is not for the tailor, who doubtless already knows this fact. Instead, it draws a new grouping together, since the frame and apparatus of Carrie's surveillance of Brody has already rehearsed this same kind of disembodiment, as if Brody's terror had already been enacted in advance by Carrie's, and our, television habits. By having this comparison occur at Gettysburg, as a set scene of historical recall, *Homeland* suggests that changing group alignments recur in analogous moments of cyclical long-wave history.

These formal moves, which concatenate the viewer with the unlikely pair of Brody and Carrie, capture the substantive narrative differences between *Homeland* and Gideon Raff's Israeli predecessor show, *Hatufim* (also known as *Prisoners of War* [Keshet 2009–2012]). Both shows have similar plot elements, but the latter has a different project and lacks the visual techniques described here. *Hatufim* concerns two returned Israeli prisoners who spend season 1 helping each other with the difficulty of posttraumatic reintegration. Consequently, *Hatufim* belongs to the new genre that depicts the existential anxiety of the Israeli Defense Forces soldier (*Waltz with Bashir* [Ari Folman, 2003], *Beaufort* [Joseph Cedar, 2007], *Lebanon* [Samuel Moaz, 2009]) to

teenage daughter Dana (Morgan Saylor), as it did to a considerable extent in season 2, it crystallizes the collective self-doubt of its target audience about their ability to secure the intergenerational transfer of the American dream to their children. While contemporary adolescents might no longer be able to realize their parents' aspirations, this failure stands as a possible escape and solution to the problem. It is Dana, not Carrie, who finally stops Brody's act of terror. *Homeland* thus guardedly suggests that the next generation might be freed from the mesh of our historical doom.

avoid any structural critique of the military's enforcement of ethnic inequality in the Israeli state's domestic and foreign policy. If *Hatufim* was unusual for spending nearly all of its first season focused on the soldiers' emotional state after their liberation, *Homeland* quickly moves back into the familiar ground of geopolitical suspense. The reason for this difference might be partially explained by Joshua Clover's proposal that contemporary cinema's filming of "existential panic" in the new gothic and apocalyptic genres has to be understood as exploring "systemic breakdown and assembly."[8] Whereas *Hatufim* is committed to reiterating the stability of the Israeli state, *Homeland* highlights US institutional fragility. Clover sees the theoretical object of tales of moral breakdown as conveyed through metareflection. He suggests that "films that are explicitly about film must be understood in the first instance as meditations on the situation of the real global empire to which cinema belongs—*metacinematic* now means *about US hegemony*," so that "as a consequence, Hollywood's cinematic form is now compelled to be a study of imperial form."[9]

Yet Clover's insight does not push far enough to grasp the class relations that magnetize contemporary cultural productions. If cinema and television are concerned about their institutional stability, it is not clear that American viewers see the source of their social fragility as resulting from American military crimes in distant lands, or even the fading hegemony of America within an increasingly China-dominated capitalist world system. The viewer's ultimate concern is not geopolitics but the way geopolitics mediate concerns about domestic class status and security. To paraphrase Clover, metacinematic and metatelevisual products should be interpreted as the domestic middle class examining its own existential crisis. More concretely, the kind of viewer immersion within a circle of mirroring among characters that we see in *Homeland* produces a form that better conveys the middle classes' sense that they need to learn how to rethink history's multiple temporalities as a guide to helping realign class allegiances to arrest or cushion their status deflation.[10]

Recent cable television drama has helped enact this realignment of class alliances with shows focusing on "allegiance ambivalence" in which bourgeois-located characters slip from initial doubt about the organization of dominant civil society to enacting a belligerent refusal of its predicates. Beyond *Homeland*, shows like *Sons of Anarchy* (FX, 2008–2014) and *The Americans* (FX, 2013–) register deep dissatisfaction with the status quo. Brody's and Carrie's attraction for viewers lies ultimately less in their concluding positions than in their willingness to perform the act of shifting allegiances and alliances for their viewers to consider repeating, much like the aforementioned emulative scenes of diegetic television viewing.

Carrie might easily be construed to be indicative of neoliberal, antibureaucratic, entrepreneurial individualism and its association with game theory, the use of mathematic models to predict social behavior. Game theory holds that human

---

8 Joshua Clover, "Remarks on Method," *Film Quarterly* 63, no. 4 (2010): 7–9.

9 Ibid.

10 Robert B. Reich, *Beyond Outrage: What Has Gone Wrong with Our Economy and Our Democracy, and How to Fix It* (New York: Vintage, 2012); Timothy Noah, *The Great Divergence: America's Growing Inequality Crisis and What We Can Do about It* (New York: Bloomsbury, 2012); Christopher Newfield, *Unmaking the Public University: The Forty-Year Assault on the Middle Class* (Cambridge, MA: Harvard University Press, 2008).

interaction can be calculated in terms of variations of strategic choices in a world where betrayal is constant. (The prisoner's dilemma, a well-known game theory exercise about when to abandon cooperation in favor of self-interest, could be used as a titling theme for Brody's predicament as well).[11] Yet more is gained from reading *Homeland* as modeling a larger middle-class alliance shift from the elites to the working class. It is perhaps not insignificant that in nearly all the scenes of establishment figures, represented mainly by political party elites and CIA brass, these individuals are considered morally corrupt and beyond redemption. Meanwhile, the lower-middle-class figures who come from a culture of selfless Catholic service, like Brody and his marine friend Mike Faber (Diego Klattenhoff), rise in attraction. Carrie's mésalliance with Brody is not simply because he is her prey but also because he is not the kind of guy she normally goes home with. Much as Occupy Wall Street tested out a new collective formed by middle-class university graduates and labor unions, the relationship between analyst Carrie and the enlisted man–cum–noncommissioned officer Brody presents a model of different class alignments for a bourgeoisie in desperate search of new direction.   *

11 Philip Mirowski, *Never Let a Serious Crisis Go to Waste: How Neoliberalism Survived the Financial Meltdown* (London: Verso, 2013).

Contributors

Alex Bevan is a lecturer in media studies at Massey University. Her research is on national memory and industry histories, with a focus on television production design. She has published on the aesthetics of nostalgia in *Mad Men* and remakes of 1950s family sitcoms, and is currently working on a book titled *Designing Nostalgia: Memory for the Boomer Era in TV Production Design*.

James Castonguay is a professor of communication and media studies at Sacred Heart University. He has published on war and media in *American Quarterly*, *Cinema Journal*, *Velvet Light Trap*, *Bad Subjects*, *Discourse*, and *global-e*, and in the anthologies *Hollywood and War: The Film Reader*, *Rethinking Global Security*, and *Truth Claims*. Castonguay is a contributing writer for the human rights magazine *Witness*, and he collaborates with the nonprofit Vision Project on multimedia documentaries that focus on issues of social justice. He received the 2009 Service Award from the Society for Cinema and Media Studies.

Jorie Lagerwey is a lecturer in television studies at University College Dublin. Her primary research interests are representations of gender and religion on television, and television genre. She is currently writing a book titled *Brand Mom: "Real" Motherhood in Postfeminist TV and Digital Culture*, about mothers in "quality" reality and online brands. Her work has appeared in *Studies in Popular Culture*, *Spectator*, Flowtv.org, *In Media Res*, and *Antenna: Responses to Media and Culture*.

Diane Negra is professor of film studies and screen culture and head of Film Studies at University College Dublin. She is coeditor of *Extreme Weather and Global Media* (with Julia Leyda; Routledge, 2015), and her current project is *The Aesthetics and Affects of Cuteness*. She is coeditor of *Television and New Media*.

Stephen Shapiro teaches in the Department of English and Comparative Literary Studies at the University of Warwick. His publications include The Wire: *Race, Class, and Genre* (with Liam Kennedy); a translation of Françoise Guéry and Didier Deleule's *The Productive Body* (with Philip Barnard); *How to Read Foucault's* Discipline and Punish (with Anne Schwan); and the Warwick Research Collective's forthcoming *Combined and Uneven Development: Towards a New Theory of World-Literature*. Other work includes *The Culture and Commerce of the Early American Novel: Reading the Atlantic World-System* and editions of Charles Brockden Brown's novels and Wollstonecraft's *Vindication of the Rights of Woman*.

Lindsay Steenberg is senior lecturer in film studies at Oxford Brookes University. Her research focuses on violence and gender in postmodern and postfeminist media culture. She has published on the crime genre and reality television, and is the author of *Forensic Science in Contemporary American Popular Culture: Gender, Crime, and Science*.

Yvonne Tasker is professor of film and television studies at the University of East Anglia. She has published widely on gender and popular genres in film and television. Her most recent books are *Gendering the Recession: Media and Culture in an Age of Austerity* (edited with Diane Negra; Duke University Press, 2014) and *Hollywood Action and Adventure Cinema* (Wiley-Blackwell, 2015). She is currently working on issues of gender in US crime television.

Arab America: Gender, Cultural Politics, and Activism

by Nadine Naber. New York University Press.
2012. $79 hardcover; $25 paper. 320 pages.

reviewed by CHRISTINE BECKER

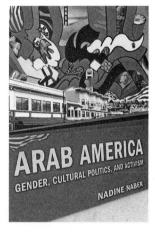

Nadine Naber's *Arab America* focuses on an Arab American community of young adult activists in the San Francisco Bay Area and explores the complex set of diasporic identities they grapple with. Many have grown up with immigrant parents insisting that they maintain allegiance to a conception of Arab culture set in direct opposition to American culture, which is associated with degeneracy, moral bankruptcy, and sexual deviance. Naber notes that this insistence puts particular pressure on Arab women to adhere to heterosexist norms of family duty and sexual responsibility. At the same time, Arabs are subject to Orientalist and imperialist attitudes in American culture, based on the impression that oppressed women need saving by American heroes, which serves as a justification for American military interventions in Arab lands. The Arab assumptions largely reverse the polarities of the Orientalist ones but still enable imperialist visions of Arab women as oppressed, thereby leaving that larger racist framework intact. What Naber aims to understand, then, is how individual young adults, especially women, navigate various "articulations of Arabness" related to family, religion, gender, and sexuality to maintain a sense of belonging in America without abandoning allegiance to the Arab community.

In researching this topic, Naber strove to utilize an academic methodology that would not replicate Orientalist and imperialist perspectives. So she turned to transnational feminist ethnography, participant observation, and autoethnography to capture "the specific and diverse narratives through which individuals who in one way or another affiliate with the Arab region and its diasporas make claims to, negotiate, live, reject, or transform" concepts of Arabness.[1] She immersed herself in the Bay Area Arab community in the late 1990s, the region where she herself lived; observed a range of cultural discussions, community meetings, and civic gatherings; and interviewed more than one hundred Arab men and women. Naber actually refers to her interview subjects as interlocutors because, she writes, "my interpretations of their stories were shaped as much by the analyses they shared as by my own."[2] This makes *Arab America* a particularly dynamic read as the historical and political contexts she describes come to life through the words of her interlocutors.

The first chapter is steeped in historical material providing the background context for cultural and political changes in the Bay Area that helped foster the conditions Naber observed. The author paints the 1950s and early 1960s as a period of assimilation in the Arab immigrant community in San Francisco, a time of relative calm when Arabs were accepted among whites as a "model minority," and a pan-Arab community identity prevailed. That shifted in the wake of the 1967 Arab-Israeli war, the 1970s oil crisis, and the 1979 Iranian revolution, and by the 1980s the US government and media had succeeded in characterizing Arabs as "the enemy," with images of rich, greedy sheiks and brutal religious fanatics prevailing. This left Arab Americans feeling immense tension in public, leading some to cloak their heritage and even change their names. The 1990s brought US imperialist interventions, such as the first Gulf War and sanctions against Iraq, which in turn spawned a commitment to political activism among young Arab American adults. A primary takeaway from this chapter is that articulations of Arab American identity cannot be understood without context or assumed to be timeless; they must be comprehended in terms of the specific historical and geographical conditions that help construct and transform them.

Naber's subsequent chapters accordingly explore in greater detail the diverse identity formations experienced in the late 1990s by Arab Americans in the Bay Area. Chapter 2 showcases the more conservative end of the spectrum of articulations, an identity concept that Naber dubs the politics of cultural authenticity. Immigrant parents see their traditional Arab culture as authentic and fear that their second-generation children will be corrupted by American individualism. Here, young women are constrained by idealized gender norms, much as they are in Orientalist conceptions, meaning that both schemas rely "on the symbolic presence of the idealized Arab woman to facilitate the belief that an essential, homogenous true Arab culture can be protected, maintained, and preserved in America."[3] Naber's discussions with women facing these pressures illustrate that no such homogenous culture exists, but some do find empowerment in the notion of an Arab identity distinct from an American one.

The next chapter looks at young adults who prioritize a Muslim identity over an Arab one. According to Naber, this emerged partly from a growing feminism among young Arabs who felt patriarchy ruled more strongly in their parents' Arab culture than in the Islamic religion and saw in Islam a broader range of ideologies, as well as greater

1   Nadine Naber, *Arab America: Gender, Cultural Politics, and Activism* (New York: New York University Press, 2012), 17.

2   Ibid., 21.

3   Ibid., 82.

gender and racial equality. Naber also looks at how the rise of this "Muslim First, Arab Second" mentality led youth toward activism when they were met with Islamophobia and saw deepening imperialism, especially via satellite television coverage of violence in Arab lands. Muslim college students in particular strove to provide counternarratives to US Islamophobic discourses. Naber writes, "Here, affiliating with a Muslim identity is just as much of a critique of capitalism, imperialism, militarism, racism, and war as it is a matter of ethics, morality, and religiosity."[4]

The final two chapters look at even more contested identities in Arab youth communities, in particular within the Leftist Arab Movement (LAM). These activists also rejected the politics of cultural authenticity and instead adopted a politics of diasporic anti-imperialism. But as Naber compellingly explores through extensive quotes from six female interlocutors, there were also complex tensions within the LAM. These women wanted to take command of traditional gendered narratives of Arabness and thus "generated a commitment to replacing representations of 'oppressed' Arab women with representations of 'powerful' Arab women."[5] However, changes in local migration patterns and the movement's makeup led to men taking on more leadership roles, leaving the women feeling increasingly marginalized by hetero-patriarchy. They even felt compelled to remain silent about this alienation, fearing that their charges of sexism would only reinforce negative images of Arabs and fuel more imperialist motivations. An interlocutor named Dahlia explains: "If I were to come out publicly and say this person is sexist . . . I can hear it now—even from other progressive activists. . . . 'Even progressive Arab women are oppressed by progressive Arab men!' That would just legitimate further violence, colonization, and oppression against us."[6]

The final chapter correspondingly showcases ways in which some women in the LAM tried to express a diasporic feminist anti-imperialism "that transcends the bifurcation of Arabness into an intra-communal and an external-political domain" and thus "expanded the possibilities for articulating anti-imperialist activism in feminist and queer terms."[7] There were two primary avenues for this, the first being grassroots work, which meant leaving the public speeches to men while women organized interpersonal gatherings that let Arab Americans share their own stories with each other. The second was artwork, which carried Arab counternarratives to broader crowds and expressed intersectional concerns.

By sharing personal chronicles amid the contextual cultural and geographic history, Naber declares that she "aimed to create an alternative model of Arab American identity, one that does not rely on the bifurcated and ultimately false options of the 'effeminate cultural self' and the 'masculinist political' self."[8] In this regard, one of the most evident lessons of the book is that reductive binaries and monolithic assumptions about Arab American culture can detrimentally affect everyday lives, whether they emerge from within Arab communities or are imposed externally. This idea resonated

4 Ibid., 146.

5 Ibid., 183.

6 Ibid., 194.

7 Ibid., 204.

8 Ibid., 249.

strongly with me in the wake of a conversation I recently had with my father. We were discussing recent events in the Middle East, and he expressed Islamophobic sentiments, insisting that Muslims bring nothing positive into global culture. I contested this, and he responded with surprise that I, an avowed feminist, would defend anything Islamic, "given how Muslims treat women." Although I should have challenged this troubling assumption on a number of accounts, especially the presumption of a monolithic Muslim culture, I was instead stunned into silence and retreated from the conversation. I now wish I could have handed him a copy of this book. Naber also successfully makes the case in *Arab America* that feminist ethnography is a vital tool for explicating identity formations while still tying them to broader cultural and political contexts. With respect to this, I wish the book had more to say about queer Arab American activism. Most of the chapters save discussions of queer subjectivities for near the end, lending an unfortunate impression that they are an afterthought. Conversely, I'm intrigued to know how conservative Arab American youth view the more liberal forms of activism that Naber explores. Of course, Naber acknowledges that she immersed herself in an activist community that she was already a part of. While this raises questions of objectivity, the intimate access she obtained across a number of years was invaluable for the depth of perspectives she shares. However, with San Francisco being a liberal region, one wonders how other Arab American communities would compare, such as Dearborn, Michigan. But this is more of a plea for another book rather than something problematic about this one. Indeed, more accounts like this should be written. Most fundamentally, *Arab America* humanizes complex people whose personal stories we rarely read, especially when, like my father and even myself, we rely only on the American media to inform us. ✻

Arabs and Muslims in the Media: Race and Representation after 9/11

by Evelyn Alsultany. New York University Press.
2012. $23.00 paper; $9.99 e-book. 240 pages.

reviewed by Tarik Ahmed Elseewi

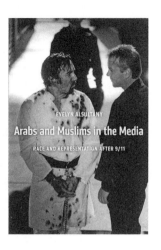

I n *Arabs and Muslims in the Media: Race and Representation after 9/11*, Evelyn Alsultany provides a useful resource for those who are interested in thinking through our "postracial" social moment generally and in the representational strategies deployed against Arabs and Muslims specifically.[1] An accessible yet theoretically sound work, this book was very well received by my students at Whitman College who were studying representations of the Middle East, and it provided substantial material examples, theoretical grounding, and room for productive discussion.

It is commonly held (at least among scholars) that the image of the Arab and/or Muslim has been rendered as distorted and monstrous in the affective wake of September 11, 2001. The most cursory of inquiries can confirm this belief. From the Islamic terrorists who stalk *Iron Man* (Jon Favreau, 2008) to the comparison of Ebola to Islamic terrorism on Fox News in October 2014, the association of Muslims and Arabs with social dysfunction, irrational violence, disease, and illogical political extremes is right there on the surface of everyday culture.[2] September 11, we've been repeatedly told, has changed *everything*.

However, for many scholars who work in fields that have been touched by the aftermath of this date (which very might well be *all* scholars), the notion that 9/11 was a transformative event is problematic. This "problem" is not that 9/11 *didn't* change culture but that 9/11 is used to *limit* discussion of historical transformation. Those who are interested in the Middle East or interested in race and representation in the American media (especially the representation of Arabs and Muslims) know well that the representations that dominate our contemporary public life have long taproots in the history of the American

1 Evelyn Alsultany, *Arabs and Muslims in the Media: Race and Representation after 9/11* (New York: New York University Press, 2012).

2 "RPT: ISIS Eyeing Ebola as Biological Weapon," *FOX News Insider*, November 16, 2014, http://insider.foxnews.com/2014/10/31/rpt-isis-eyeing-ebola-biological-weapon.

twentieth century. The political, social, diplomatic, cultural, and emotional problems that "9/11" is used to describe existed before September 11, 2001. An insistence on the primacy of 9/11 is also an insistence on a limited historical analysis, one that begins in 2001 and runs until the present: one that forgets a century of American involvement in the region and a century of negative stereotyping in our media, literature, and art.

If, in other words, 9/11 changed everything in terms of the representation of Arabs and Muslims, then what was Edward Said writing about in his (pre-9/11) *Orientalism*?[3] What kinds of problems was Jack Shaheen discussing in *Reel Bad Arabs: How Hollywood Vilifies a People*?, originally published in 2001 *before* 9/11.[4] It is this tradition of solid description and substantive, relevant theorizing of the troubled representational relationships between East and West that Evelyn Alsultany enters with her book *Arabs and Muslims in the Media*. Although Alsultany explores representations *after* 9/11, her critical nuance makes clear that, while 9/11 names a transformative moment in portrayals of Arabs and Muslims, it is neither the beginning nor the grounding cause of these portrayals.

While the reactionary, right-wing attacks against Arabs and Muslims by Fox News and its ilk—and the reactionary, liberal attacks on the same by figures such as Richard Dawkins and Bill Maher—are glaringly obvious and gather much of the scant public attention directed toward the representations of these groups, Alsultany chooses to begin in a different and much more interesting place: "positive" representations. Alsultany asks, in the face of a rising tide of overwhelmingly negative and stereotypical representations of Arabs and Muslims, in the face of a toxic cultural environment in which the simple existence of Muslims and Arabs in an American political context is problematized, how do we grapple with the seemingly positive representations that populate so much of our dramatic televisual output? The too-easy answer is to assume that these seemingly positive portrayals balance out the negative ones and ultimately leave our society in a position of equality and fairness.

In a similar way to how critical feminist theorists react toward (unfounded) claims of a "postfeminist" society in which feminism can be valorized only after it is pronounced dead, so too we recognize the frustration of critical race scholars who try to point out the injustice of representations in a "postracial" society where race can be discussed only in the context of its contemporary irrelevance.[5] This is the frustration born from trying to analyze a systemic demonization of Arabs and Muslims (or other racial, ethnic, and/or religious groups), only to be confronted with a handful of seemingly complex and robust "proper" representations.

In fact, as Alsultany convincingly shows, "the production and circulation of 'positive' representations of the (Arab and Muslim) 'enemy' has become essential to projecting the United States as benevolent, especially in its declaration of war and official support of racist policies. TV dramas have become essential, though often

3 Edward W. Said, *Orientalism* (London: Penguin Classics, 2003).

4 Jack Shaheen, *Reel Bad Arabs: How Hollywood Vilifies a People*, 3rd ed. (Northampton, MA: Olive Branch Press, 2014).

5 Angela McRobbie, "Post-Feminism and Popular Culture," *Feminist Media Studies* 4, no. 3 (2004): 255–264.

unwitting, collaborators in the forming of a new post-race racism."[6] She describes sympathetic images of Arabs and Muslims after 9/11 as working to give the impression that racism is not tolerated in the United States despite the numerous policies that have targeted and disproportionately affected Arabs and Muslims.[7] This, in turn, helps to support a new kind of racism that decries racism outwardly but produces the logic and facts necessary to legitimize racist policies and practices.

Theoretically, Alsultany assails these seemingly positive portrayals with her explanation of what she calls "simplified complex representations."[8] These are depictions that appear to challenge existing stereotypes and in doing so contribute to the multicultural, postracial moment we all supposedly inhabit. And yet, as she argues, most of these shows do this while maintaining representational strategies that legitimize racist policies and practices such as torture, incarceration, and accusation. She lists various modes of this "simplified complex representation": inserting patriotic Arab or Muslim Americans into the story; sympathizing with the plight of Arab and Muslim Americans after 9/11; challenging the Arab-Muslim conflation with diverse Muslim identities; flipping the enemy (i.e., pretending the enemy is Arab or Muslim until the final reveal, when it is shown to be someone from a mainstream group); humanizing the terrorist; projecting a multicultural US society; and fictionalizing the Middle Eastern or Muslim country.

For Alsultany, this new form of representing "terrorism" stems from a growing cultural sensitivity to the negative impact of stereotyping. Programs go out of their way to point out that not all Arabs are terrorists and not all terrorists are Muslims. Yet these programs maintain a context in which the representation of Arabs and Muslims is forever associated with terrorism. Even if, Alsultany argues, the individual characters represented are not themselves involved in terrorism, their existence is invoked in an exploration of terrorism.

A particularly salient example for Alsultany was the dramatic series *24* (Fox, 2001–2010). She argues that the show provided a platform through which to legitimize the efficacy of torture and helped paint Arabs and Muslims as associated with terrorism. By humanizing the terrorists or using patriotic Arab or Muslim characters, shows such as *24* co-opt multiculturalist discourse and produce an image of seeming social complexity. This represents the US government and military as anti-racist even though the very framing logic of such shows legitimizes torture and incarceration substantially on the basis of racial, ethnic, or religious affiliation. Above all, what shows like *24* and others that depict Arabs and Muslims in a troubled light do is articulate a nation in constant danger. This, in turn, helps to create a citizenry accustomed to war, fear of the ethnic or religious other, and ultimately willing to sacrifice democratic ideals to an ever more powerful surveillance state.

After introducing her argument and theoretical description, Alsultany goes into specific details. She does a wonderful job of grounding her potentially abstract arguments in the particulars of specific representations using a number of contemporary televisual examples. Of particular interest is her discussion of the Western penchant

6 Alsultany, *Arabs and Muslims in the Media*, 7.

7 Ibid., 15.

8 Ibid., 21.

for wanting to save Muslim women from Muslim men and the tendency in American representations to regulate and vent away sympathy for Arab men.

In short, Alsultany's book is of great value to those interested in contemporary cultural studies, politics, race and ethnic studies, or feminist representational analysis. It is straightforward and capable of supplying both the details and the larger principles to those interested in investigating our "postracial" social moment.   *

TV Milestones Series

Batman
by Matt Yockey. Wayne State University Press. 2014. $15.64 paper; $9.99 e-book. 160 pages.

Rowan & Martin's Laugh-In
by Ken Feil. Wayne State University Press. 2014. $15.99 paper; $9.99 e-book. 168 pages.

24
by John McCullough. Wayne State University Press. 2014. $15.99 paper; $9.99 e-book. 144 pages.

The L Word
By Margaret T. McFadden. Wayne State University Press. 2014. $15.99 paper; $9.99 e-book. 152 pages.

reviewed by DEREK KOMPARE

Short monographs based on single films, TV series, or video games have been a prominent format in media studies for the past decade or so. They're popular with publishers and scholars, though for different reasons. Publishers can build a potentially long-running series around a particular medium or genre, and scholars can carry out a relatively deep, multifaceted analysis on a single text. That said, as a form longer than an article but shorter than a traditional book, they also have their own potential pitfalls. While the singular focus has its advantages, the format certainly isn't boundless. The word count of thirty-five thousand provides enough room to develop multiple points but not enough to dig *too* deeply or *too* broadly. Similarly, the understandable remit from publishers to be widely accessible (to undergraduates as well as interested fans of the text) necessitates clearer writing, including the brief treatment of theoretical concepts that would otherwise be expanded in more advanced work. As someone who's written one of these, I appreciate how difficult it can be to balance the depth, breadth, accessibility, and brevity necessary to cover a long-running TV series in this format.

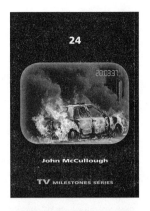

With twenty-eight titles published since 2004, the TV Milestones series from Wayne State University Press has been one of the most prolific and consistent of this type of series. It has covered a wide array of mostly US TV shows dating from the 1950s through the 2000s. Despite the great variety of genres and authors, the series editors, Barry Keith Grant and Jeannette Sloniowski, have effectively managed each volume's usual mix of historical, industrial, and cultural contexts, always coupled with extensive textual analysis. These books are effective introductions to key television series (particularly for the classroom) and provide intriguing analysis, even for those familiar with their subjects.

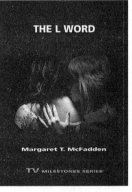

This review concerns four of the latest volumes, representing two distinct but, in retrospect, similar historical eras in American television. Matt Yockey's analysis of *Batman* (ABC, 1966–1968) and Ken Feil's investigation of *Rowan & Martin's Laugh-In* (NBC, 1968–1973) examine how the turbulent cultural changes of the late 1960s to early 1970s were managed at the peak of the classic network era by television producers and networks. Each of these series briefly dominated popular culture, and both were emblematic of television's political dance between appealing to a younger, more iconoclastic counterculture and retaining an older, more conservative mainstream. The other two books, John McCullough's study of *24* (Fox, 2001–2010, 2014) and Margaret T. McFadden's exploration of *The L Word* (Showtime, 2004–2009), focus on the more recent era of multichannel television, fragmenting audiences, and divergent industrial and cultural priorities. Appropriately, neither of these series aired on one of the traditional "big three" so dominant forty years earlier. However, as with the 1960s, the first decade of the twenty-first century was also a television era of shifting ranges of expression (in both form and content), as television producers and networks strategized to appeal not so much to a mainstream but to the extended loyalty of particular viewers. *The L Word* and *24* are radically different texts, yet both could have flourished only in the divided television ecosystem of the 2000s–2010s.

The TV adaptation of *Batman* blazed bright and faded quickly for just over two years, but Matt Yockey's long-needed volume rescues the iconic series from its usual footnoted treatment in television history as either a bold experimental failure or a sign of mid-1960s cultural vapidity. Yockey displays a thorough understanding of the ramifications of this particular comic book character, the status of television, and the issue of "mass" culture itself at that moment in American history. In particular, he explains how the series' much-noted camp aesthetic functioned with precise timing in the mid-1960s, channeling childhood nostalgia into a more skeptical adulthood and "exploit[ing] Pop art and camp strategies to authorize viewers to interrogate national values by way of a collective memory of the superhero."[1] Yockey's detailed analyses of how series episodes regarded criminality, civics, gender, and sexuality (all areas under particular scrutiny circa 1966–1968), as well as its wider appeal and legacy in popular culture, reveal how, "by making viewers complicit in the self-aware construction of national identity and consumer culture (a necessary component of its parody), *Batman* makes the utopian possibility of mass culture more transparent."[2]

Premiering early in 1968 as *Batman* wound down, *Rowan & Martin's Laugh-In* is another emblematic series of the era. While *Batman*'s camp sensibility was premised on the power of a single, extended joke, *Laugh-In*'s rapid-fire comedy-variety format, and more explicitly topical remit, allowed it to embrace a more direct, though also layered and ambivalent, style. Ken Feil locates *Laugh-In* alongside *Batman* as key examples of 1960s "mass camp," a new, malleable cultural form that "rendered subcultural affiliation a closeted, open secret whose partial presence safely ensured everyone's deniability, from the network and the producers to the spectators."[3] As Feil argues, this "deniability" is key to the series' evasive politics. Although the series deserves more credit than it usually garners for its presentation of "outsider" humor (primarily from African American and gay performers), its "distanciation, aestheticism, and ambivalence" (e.g., in the way it "put on" both establishment and countercultural figures) rendered it just palatable enough for mainstream, network tastes.[4] Along the way, Feil presents a particularly revealing analysis of a sequence in a 1969 episode that featured both a blackface gag (in which African American regular Chelsea Brown performed in whiteface) and a send-up of masculine homosociality in the military, typical examples of how the show could simultaneously mock conservative values yet still trade in archaic racist and homophobic tropes.[5]

Structurally, Feil's fascinating account is also an outstanding example of how the short monograph format should work, offering a probing yet relatively compact textual and contextual analysis of a pivotal show and a pivotal moment. Perhaps more could have been said in the conclusion about *Laugh-In*'s stylistic and cultural legacy (mentioned here in a note), but there was so much to cover about its actual run that this is a minor issue.

Both *Batman* and *Laugh-In* were representative of an era in which politics and representation had to be closeted (if with a wink) to meet conservative network standards. The other two series that these books address are indicative of a more recent era when politics and representation have been seemingly more direct yet are still, in many ways, as evasive and ambiguous as anything from the 1960s. The twenty-first century of both *24* and *The L Word* has been a time of media, technological,

1   Matt Yockey, *Batman*, TV Milestones Series (Detroit: Wayne State University Press, 2014), 8.

2   Ibid., 100.

3   Ken Feil, *Rowan & Martin's Laugh-In*, TV Milestones Series (Detroit: Wayne State University Press, 2014), 66.

4   Ibid., 83.

5   Ibid., 71–84.

economic, and social turmoil masked by dubious (or at best, deceptively triumphant) consumerist discourses of greater cultural freedom (e.g., on the new online social media platforms and on the prime-time schedules of the new, "sophisticated" cable networks). The two series may have engaged with the present from different angles, but, as the authors show, each also revealed the ambivalence and incoherence typical of much of contemporary culture.

John McCullough locates *24* firmly within the dominant American geopolitical perspective of the first decade of the twenty-first century: the war on terror. He writes that the series' "basic formal structure—the 'ticking bomb' scenario—[is] consistent with the culture of fear that emerged post-9/11."[6] While he acknowledges the power of the insistence and insecurity produced by its virtuosic real-time (and often split-screen) narrative and editing style, he argues that these techniques are ultimately in service of a "populist pastiche" of familiar and nostalgic tropes of danger and retribution from decades of film and television.[7] His investigation of the series is particularly thorough, illustrating many relevant textual examples from across its eight full seasons and drawing from an impressive array of media theory and contemporary accounts. Although the book occasionally shifts into deep formal descriptions that risk some clarity, its pace and depth are otherwise exemplary for this format.[8] The movement from "cultural forms" through "style" to "themes and meanings" is particularly effective. This study is one of the strongest accounts of 2000s US television I've yet read and culminates in a damning verdict for not only *24* but also much of the similar security-focused fare that has been a staple of American television in the Bush and Obama eras. The series' "postmodernism encouraged the full integration of terrorism with consumerism" such that it could not "reasonably engage with its historical moment or provide insight about that reality."[9]

In her multifaceted study of *The L Word*, Margaret T. McFadden is most concerned with how the series represented lesbian culture and how its representations were debated by the show's lesbian fans, who, she argues, were particularly "well equipped" critical viewers, given their long navigation through heterosexist media.[10] Accordingly, rather than looking at *The L Word* through the lens of bourgeois realist drama, McFadden argues that the series instead functions in the long line of critical lesbian and queer media that has played with and critiqued heteronormative representations of gender and sexuality, "[teaching] its viewers to see in new ways and to think hard about the relationship of representation to reality."[11] Given that most of the characters and plots in the LA-based narrative center around the industries and ideologies of various systems of media representation (including mainstream film, alternative documentary, straight porn, visual art, literature, poetry, and music), McFadden's emphasis on how the series constructs and critiques its representations of lesbian life

---

6 John McCullough, *24*, TV Milestones Series (Detroit: Wayne State University Press, 2014), 10.

7 Ibid., 88.

8 Ibid., 51–62.

9 Ibid., 100, 103–104.

10 Margaret T. McFadden, *The L Word*, TV Milestones Series (Detroit: Wayne State University Press, 2014), 4–7.

11 Ibid., 14.

is appropriate. In one chapter, she persuasively analyzes how the series knowingly engages with one of the core concepts of feminist film criticism—Laura Mulvey's critique of cinema's male gaze—to construct "a more complicated, alternative, lesbian spectating position."[12] While such a film-studies emphasis on cinematography and shot composition might otherwise be misplaced in an analysis of a long-running television narrative, McFadden makes it work here, given *The L Word*'s foregrounding of "lesbian looking" and its overarching question of lesbian identity itself. Similarly, in an entire chapter on the show's reflexivity, she argues that the series complicates its own system of representation by regularly "queering" established heteronormative stereotypes (e.g., from romantic comedies, melodramas, and women's prison films), instructing viewers "to think hard about representation and ideology, to cue us not to take what we are seeing at face value."[13]

Going outside the series itself to its fandom and role in a queer commodity culture, McFadden shows how the series' complex perspective on lesbian identity was hotly debated by fans and problematically marketed by Showtime and other corporate partners (e.g., to foreground the fashionable and comfortable upper-middle-class consumer lifestyle of its primarily white and normatively gendered characters rather than the more complex questions that the series often raised). McFadden sees the fan debates (in many online spaces) as a continuation of the series' questioning of representation, as fans tried to "control and shape . . . the discourse about what it means to be a lesbian."[14] The coverage of fan discourse in this study is particularly necessary given the nature of *The L Word*, which, unlike the other series covered in these books, explicitly sought to engage a particularly underserved viewing community. While this chapter is, by necessity, more of an overview of fan discussion than a deeper investigation of a more specific debate, McFadden effectively references many examples of fan and academic critique throughout.

As a format for scholarship, these short books may not be ideal for all tastes because of a focus that is potentially too narrow in some respects and potentially too deep in others. However, these four books, and the TV Milestones series in general, show how effective the short monograph can be in providing intriguing and insightful analyses of key past TV series that might otherwise get lost amid all the attention paid to recent critical favorites like *Breaking Bad* (AMC, 2008–2013), *Game of Thrones* (HBO, 2011–), *Mad Men* (AMC, 2007–2015), and *Orange Is the New Black* (Netflix, 2013–). They serve an important function in articulating and revisiting focused moments in television and cultural history, and that's reason enough this format should continue. ✳

---

12   Ibid., 29.

13   Ibid., 64.

14   Ibid., 116.

Wired TV: Laboring Over an Interactive Future

edited by Denise Mann. Rutgers University Press.
2014. $76.50 hardcover; $26.96 paper. 306 pages.

reviewed by ALLISON PERLMAN

T o read much of the scholarship of the past decade on television's transformations in the digital era is to be invited to see new possibilities—aesthetic, cultural, politi-cal, social—in the displacement of "old" tele-vision by "new." As Amanda Lotz has argued, for example, television "as we knew it"—as a mass medium, viewed in the home, addressing a broad and diverse audience—is being revolutionized through increased viewer control over the where, the when, and the what of viewing.[1] Technological changes, along with the remarkable expansion of media outlets, as Jason Mittell has demonstrated, have facilitated the growth of a new mode of narratively complex television programs.[2] Television in the digital era, according to Sharon Marie Ross, is premised on tele-par-ticipation, a reciprocal process in which viewers are hailed to interact with texts as television producers, writers, and executives increasingly incorporate an awareness of, and a desire to elicit, viewer engagement within them.[3] The mainstreaming of participatory culture that Henry Jenkins outlines in his *Convergence Culture* has expanded into "spread-able media," discussed in his recent book coauthored with Sam Ford and Joshua Green, which speaks to a mediascape in which the rigidi-ties of old media—of top-down distribution methods, of a one-to-many broadcast model, of presumedly passive audiences for media content—have given way to a more democratic and flexible environ-ment in which audiences create and circulate texts and in which hard

---

1 Amanda D. Lotz, *The Television Will Be Revolutionized* (New York: New York University Press, 2007).

2 Jason Mittell, "Narrative Complexity in Contemporary American Television," *Velvet Light Trap* 58 (2006): 29–40.

3 Sharon Marie Ross, *Beyond the Box: Television and the Internet* (Malden, MA: Blackwell, 2008).

distinctions between producer, marketer, and audience become blurred.[4] To think of media as spreadable, according to Jenkins, Ford, and Green, is not only to reimagine the flows and uses of content but also to see its "potential to dramatically reshape how central cultural and political institutions operate."[5]

To read Denise Mann's impressive new anthology *Wired TV: Laboring Over an Interactive Future* is to feel that the bloom is off the rose. In her introduction Mann acknowledges that her collection builds on insights from a number of the texts listed just above, yet the essays within it offer a more sobering look at the practices of television in the digital era. And though, as Mann suggests, the essays address "the myriad of new digital threats and the equal number of digital opportunities that have become part and parcel of today's post-network era," the threats loom a bit larger than the opportunities.[6] What emerges across the essays is a picture of contemporary industry practices defined not by freedom from restraints but by their reimposition, and a picture in which the blurring of boundaries and the leveling of distinctions yield not liberatory possibilities but practices that predominantly serve the interests of media companies.

As the subtitle indicates, the contributions in this volume focus on labor. Across the collection, the articles address the labor of fans, the division of labor across industry professionals, and the labor performed by media texts themselves. Four of the eleven contributions focus specifically on the imagined and actual labors of fans; the remaining seven interrogate labor and cultures of production within the contemporary television industry. And although in her introduction Mann suggests that what unites the collection is a shared methodological commitment to media industries study, what also emerges as one reads across the contributions is a recurring preoccupation with narratives of failure from which the contributors draw important lessons about the continued salience of cultural and institutional hierarchies for the way media are imagined, produced, promoted, and used.

The essays on fandom build on and expand what has been a central line of analysis in current media studies, namely the mainstreaming of fan practices as a defining characteristic of the convergent media era. In his contribution, Robert Kozinets analyzes marketing literature to map the increased acceptance of what he labels "fan creep," the notion that consumers should be courted as fans rather than as consumers. His analysis underlines that to bring consumers into brand fandom communities is not only to elicit feelings of belonging and identification but also to encourage fan production of additional texts, what marketing scholars refer to as "consumer co-creations."[7]

These consumer co-creations are at the center of Derek Johnson's, Will Brooker's, and Julie Levin Russo's essays. Although each of these contributions adds a unique

---

4 Henry Jenkins, *Convergence Culture: Where Old and New Media Collide* (New York: New York University Press, 2006); Henry Jenkins, Sam Ford, and Joshua Green, *Spreadable Media: Creating Value and Meaning in a Networked Culture* (New York: New York University Press, 2013). See also Louisa Stein, moderator, "Spreadable Media: Creating Value and Meaning in a Networked Culture," *Cinema Journal* 53, no. 3 (2014): 152–177.

5 Jenkins, Ford, and Green, *Spreadable Media*, 44.

6 Denise Mann, ed., *Wired TV: Laboring Over an Interactive Future* (New Brunswick, NJ: Rutgers University Press, 2014), 26.

7 Robert V. Kozinets, "Fan Creep: Why Brands Suddenly Need 'Fans,'" in Mann, *Wired TV*, 172.

perspective to assessing fan labor, they all tacitly mourn the incorporation of fan practices into corporate strategies and logics. Johnson's piece examines the process by which fans operate as de facto licensees of media franchises and the implications of that process. He specifically examines the *Battlestar Galactica* (Sci-Fi, 2004–2009) franchise and notes how fan-produced content ultimately operates as nodes within it. His analysis points not only to how fans' free labor has been absorbed into the existing model of licensed production but also to the continued authority exerted by intellectual property rights holders over the forms of expression and uses of licensed content in an open, networked environment.

Brooker examines an ascendant shift in the relationship between fan communities and media corporations. He distinguishes between an "old school" model of fandom, exemplified by female fan-fiction writers, which intentionally operates outside industry channels and within a gift economy of exchange and collaboration, and an increasingly dominant model of fans "going pro," in which fans' creative labor is "colonized" by a "system of shiny corporate worlds" in exchange for the potential for public and official recognition.[8] The labor of fans also figures centrally in Levin Russo's discussion of the Showtime series *The L Word* (Showtime, 2004–2009), in which she demonstrates how within the show's diegesis the characters work to produce a lesbian identity as a lucrative economic category; through engagement with website tie-ins, the show's fans perform the labor of authenticating the depictions and practices of the show's lesbian characters. For Levin Russo, as for Brooker, the problem of fan labor is one not only of its commodification and incorporation into official promotional strategies but also of its loss, in the process, of autonomy from the very ideological systems that in the past it has sought to resist.

Two tropes unite the contributions on labor within the contemporary television industry. First, those that narrate stories of failure implicitly argue that they result from the persistence of hierarchies within a mediascape paradoxically defined by the porousness and malleability of boundaries. Jonathan Gray's discussion of failed video-game adaptations of television series identifies how, in the act of translation from show to game, designers often ignore the experiential core of the show—its pace, tone, style, and timbre. As Gray indicates, game design frequently takes place under creative and temporal constraints that leave designers little space to innovate. Many of the resulting games fail because they neglect to replicate the temporal experience of the show for their players. Gray's analysis thus points not only to failures of translation but also to failures embedded in the circuit of transmedia storytelling that devalues video games as promotional afterthoughts.

Mann, in contrast, charts the trajectory of *The Lost Experience* (ABC, 2006), an alternate-reality game (ARG) that has been hailed as a groundbreaking, successful moment in transmedia storytelling. While *The Lost Experience* was to have been a turning point, in retrospect it was more of a flash in the pan. Despite the successful balance of fans, brand, and content in *The Lost Experience*, Mann details how networks increasingly have gained control over digital extensions of television shows

---

8 Will Brooker, "Going Pro: Gendered Responses to the Incorporation of Fan Labor as User-Generated Content," in Mann, *Wired TV*, 94.

via in-house digital promotion departments. Mann thus tells a declension narrative, one in which the labor struggles over digital rights, which reached an apotheosis in the Writers Guild of America strikes of 2007–2008, led networks to close ranks and foreclose future forms of collaboration by "taking a giant step backward toward their analog past."[9] Mann's analysis is echoed by Henry Jenkins's contribution, in which he highlights the pitfalls of what he labels the "mothership model" of transmedia production, one adopted by Hollywood that requires a core media property to which all other iterations are subordinate. In illustrating that transmedia production takes myriad shapes and responds to particularized production cultures, Jenkins models alternatives to the "mothership" and suggests that transmedia storytelling could yield far richer narratives and satisfy a wider range of functions than current industry practices in Hollywood permit.

Katynka Z. Martínez's narrative of failure focuses on MyNetwork TV, a short-lived initiative created after the WB/UPN merger into the CW in 2006 to provide programming to local Fox stations that had been affiliated with UPN. Part of its strategy was to adapt telenovelas for a US market. MyNetwork TV at once downplayed the Latin American origins of its programming to hail a wider audience and sought to access viewers in the "Latin pipeline" via appeals that often misjudged this audience's relationship to and affection for telenovelas. In addition, MyNetwork TV failed to attend to what made telenovelas so popular in its adaptation of the form, in particular the importance of their settings and anchoring in a recognizable geographical location. Although she does not state so explicitly, Martínez's analysis suggests that MyNetwork's problems emerged from its devaluation of Latin American formats and the Latina and Latino audience, expressed in its clumsy adaptation of telenovelas and its clumsy marketing strategies.

The second trope centers on industrial strategies, both institutional and textual, that navigate transformations in the labor practices of the television industry. John Caldwell's essay interrogates the ubiquity of textual and discursive practices of self-reference and self-reflexivity in the postnetwork era. Caldwell describes an environment defined both by the erosion of distinctions between job categories, facilitated by a production culture premised on multitasking, outsourcing, and downsizing, and by a marketplace saturated with products and promotions, in which distribution windows have shrunk and content is released on multiple platforms simultaneously. In this mediascape, both workers and corporations have developed strategies to reassert distinctions, though with very different aims. What Caldwell refers to as interpersonalized work reflexivity reasserts distinctions between different types of workers and between professionals and amateurs in the face of corporate practices and discourses that seek to erase those distinctions.[10] In contrast, institutionalized corporate reflexivity operates as a strategy to create a sense of distinctiveness among consumers who are hailed through these gestures of self-reflexivity and transparency.[11] M. J. Clarke similarly

9   Denise Mann, "The Labor behind the Lost ARG: WGA's Tentative Foothold in the Digital Age," in Mann, *Wired TV*, 136.

10 John Caldwell, "Post-Network Reflexivity: Viral Marketing and Labor Management," in Mann, *Wired TV*, 143.

11 Ibid.

explores how textual practices reflect on current business practices in his analysis of the US version of *The Office* (NBC, 2005–2013). The show both emerges from new ways of doing business in the television industry and is itself a self-conscious reflection on how US broadcast networks have adapted to transformations in the global media marketplace. *The Office* is a show about anachronism, rooted in an occupational culture unable to keep up with the rapid pace of change. But if the show itself represents a failed business culture, its own production process demonstrates US television's capacity to adapt and to resist outmoded practices; Dunder-Mifflin functions as a foil to its network home, its failures highlighting, by contrast, NBC's own success in adaptation.

In an article that initially reads as an outlier, Vincent Brooke analyzes the neo-platoon drama—shows with multiracial casts, interlocking narratives, serial storylines.[12] He situates its rise within a broader history of representational practices, against the backdrop of protests by civil rights groups in the late 1990s over the absence of people of color in programming, and amid network strategies of "convergent ethnicity" that were intended to appeal to broad, rather than "ghettoized," audiences. What sets the contemporary neo-platoon dramas apart from their predecessors is their egalitarianism, signaled not only by the characters' equivalent social and occupational standing, screen time, and position within the narrative, but also by the consistent inclusion of interracial romance in the series. Yet as these shows erase differences across ethno-racial groups, Brook argues that they also circulate a color-blind ethos that occludes, rather than interrogates, continued forms of inequity. Thematically, therefore, Brook's contribution fits well in a collection committed to interrogating the meanings, and political consequences, of the leveling of distinctions within our contemporary mediascape.

Wired TV, in summary, provides tremendously valuable insights by top scholars in television studies. The essays are grounded in strong, compelling research and collectively provide a rich snapshot of the tensions, anxieties, and especially failures of this particular moment in US television's development. (And, to be sure, US television is at the center of this collection; even the articles that gesture to other production cultures do so in the service of critiquing or explaining US network practices.) Its contributions raise important questions about television's "interactive future" and the degree to which it will replicate, expand, or exacerbate the aspects of television's past that the digital era was poised to upend.   ✻

---

12 Vincent Brook, "Converging Ethnicity and the Neo-Platoon Show: Recombining Difference in the Post-Network Era," in Mann, *Wired TV*, 197–198.

Terrorism TV: Popular Entertainment in Post-9/11 America

by Stacy Takacs. University Press of Kansas.
2012. $32.81 hardcover; $24.86 paper. 344 pages.

reviewed by STEPHEN PRINCE

W hen I wrote *Firestorm: American Film in the Age of Terrorism*, the topic of 9/11 and American film had been relatively unexplored.[1] Since the book's publication in 2009, however, numerous insightful works have taken up the subject. In *Firestorm*, I was mainly concerned with theatrical film and covered television but briefly in a single chapter that did not aim to be as comprehensive as those that explored feature film.

Stacy Takacs's *Terrorism TV: Popular Entertainment in Post-9/11 America* provides a wide-ranging and far more complete portrait of the influence of 9/11 and its aftermath on programming for television. She moves easily in her analysis from news to entertainment programming because she takes each category as containing elements of the other. She writes, "Rather than reimpose some false distinction between information and entertainment, nonfictional and fictional programming, my approach is to treat all program types as simultaneously entertaining and informative."[2] News, documentary, and entertainment programming, then, are seen to perform many of the same strategic tasks in proposing, constructing, and conveying the various meanings of 9/11 to viewers.

The comprehensiveness of *Terrorism TV* is one of its virtues. The chapters examine news programming, shows that valorize counterterrorist agencies, entertainment programs with a military focus, and various examples of resistant or counterhegemonic programming. News coverage of the 9/11 attacks, Takacs writes, drew on the tropes of melodrama to mobilize the public to support a war of vengeance, and she demonstrates the ways this operated. The melodramatic framing

---

1 Stephen Prince, *Firestorm: American Film in the Age of Terrorism* (New York: Columbia University Press, 2009).

2 Stacy Takacs, *Terrorism TV: Popular Entertainment in Post-9/11 America* (Lawrence: University Press of Kansas, 2012), 20.

functioned to make "militarism appear necessary and inevitable."[3] The ongoing efforts of counterterrorist agencies, depicted in heroic terms in shows like *Threat Matrix* (ABC, 2003–2004), *The Grid* (TNT, 2004), *The Agency* (CBS, 2001–2003), *Sleeper Cell* (Showtime, 2005), and *24* (Fox, 2001–2010), "helped normalize the state of emergency and promote the acceptance of policies of surveillance, detention and interrogation that were fundamentally antidemocratic."[4] "Militainment" formats—entertainment programs with strong military content—accompanied the invasions of Iraq and Afghanistan, according to Takacs. Shows like *JAG* (CBS, 1995–2005), *Over There* (FX, 2005–2006), and *Generation Kill* (HBO, 2008) helped turn viewers into "armchair imperialists."

While these categories of programming, according to Takacs, worked to manufacture popular consent for a new security regime and its affiliated policies, resistance to the new security order was voiced through shows like *The Daily Show* (Comedy Central, 1999–), *Whoopi* (NBC, 2003–2004), and *Battlestar Galactica* (Sci-Fi, 2004–2009). These "opened a space in the cultural terrain for dissent to be elaborated, explored and consolidated."[5]

The final chapter, titled "The Body of War," analyzes how the media sanitized the war by eliminating depictions of the scarred and maimed bodies of wounded survivor veterans and the corpses of those who did not survive. The topic has been written about by other scholars, but Takacs shows the myriad ways in which media worked to block honest depictions of war's human cost. On the occasion that viewers did see such images, as in the James Gandolfini documentary *Alive Day Memories* (2007), the encounter might produce a provocative form of witnessing. Takacs writes, "This may not have been the type of witnessing that required ethical response in the form of action, but it did require individuals to confront the experience of violence and duress unique to war and to analyze their own relationship to militarism."[6]

As this summary of the book's content suggests, Takacs undertakes two interpretive moves. The first is an explication of how television programming was affected by the 9/11 attacks. She provides an analysis of programming content that is valuable because it encompasses many salient content categories. The second interpretive move extends beyond the themes and tropes of TV programming. Takacs proffers a series of descriptions about how viewers allegedly react to television shows, how their minds are influenced by what they see on the small screen, and how they are influenced to think about terror-related events. While the first move works successfully within the province of cultural analysis, the second strikes me as more problematic.

Media influences are researchable. How is the influence manifest in viewers? In which viewers is it manifest? What is its outcome? How does the analyst reliably know that such an influence exists and is not merely a supposition on the part of the analyst? Takacs does not provide indicators that point toward the factual status of her claims about how terror-themed TV programming has affected viewers. As a result,

3   Ibid., 36.

4   Ibid., 26.

5   Ibid., 27.

6   Ibid., 209.

the claims sometimes seem to be deductions derived from the content of programming. Military-themed entertainment shows may persuade viewers to endorse a war on terror, but maybe not. It is clear that viewers can enjoy genres of programming without subscribing to the worldviews expressed in the films or shows. So while Takacs often seems to describe the ideological influence of terrorism TV as being very strong, its actual magnitude remains unclear.

According to Takacs's account, media content generally has fallen in line with the political imperatives of Washington administrations seeking to conduct what has come to be called a war on terror. I believe that this is a correct assumption regarding the aggregate universe of corporate-produced media content. Where I differ is in relation to the relative importance that is to be accorded to television in the shaping of public views. For Takacs, television is extremely influential and, indeed, seems to function as a necessary constituent of the administration's abilities to conduct its war on terror. She writes that the latter is not comprehensible without considering the former: "To understand how the War on Terrorism became possible, then, it is necessary to examine the regimes of knowledge and affect circulating in and through the popular media."[7]

Numerous statements throughout the book emphasize the success rate of television in shaping viewer conceptions of the politics of terror and its importance for Washington's ability to set policy. Special 9/11-themed episodes of *Third Watch* (NBC, 2001), *America's Most Wanted* (Fox, 2001), and *The West Wing* (NBC, 2001), she writes, "all helped prime the US public to support a war on terrorism."[8] "Militainment" programs like *JAG*, *Over There*, and *Generation Kill* "habituated viewers to the use of war as a strategy of peace and encouraged them to imagine themselves as virtual citizen-soldiers. Since the responsibility of soldiers is not to deliberate but to follow orders, this shift in the conception of citizenship explains, at least in part, why the US public was so willing to buy into the Bush administration's arguments for an unnecessary and unjust preventative war in Iraq."[9] These militainment programs produce viewers who are "fully invested in the system of military discipline and power projection."[10] By addressing viewers as citizen-soldiers, Takacs maintains, these programs contribute to the militarization of life in the United States: "*America's Most Wanted* prepares citizens of all sorts to accept, even embrace, surveillance as a social good, a tactical weapon in the 'fight for freedom.' Viewers are instructed to internalize the surveillance ethic as a condition of their inclusion in the community of 'Americans.'"[11]

Although the themes and tropes of these shows may well contain such values, the emergence of a surveillance society, a condition of perpetual war overseas, and the militarization of domestic life—developments that Takacs finds television to be a prime force in helping to carry out—may owe more to political decisions and sociological factors than to television scripts. The Bush and Obama administrations have been able to keep the United States continuously at war because there is no draft.

7 Ibid., 19.
8 Ibid., 52.
9 Ibid., 101.
10 Ibid., 145.
11 Ibid., 46.

This accomplishment doesn't depend on the airing of shows like *JAG* on television. If there were a draft targeting all Americans of serviceable age, the administration would find it far more difficult to prosecute long-range wars like that in Iraq. These wars are doable politically because most Americans never feel their effect—this is the calculus Washington has made since the Vietnam era, when the draft proved such a problem for the Johnson and Nixon administrations.

A most striking indicator of the militarization of domestic life, in real rather than metaphorical terms, is the transformation of local police into paramilitary forces, armed with sophisticated weaponry provided by the Pentagon. While this transformation gained a measure of public recognition because of the police response—with officers in military vehicles and combat gear—to the recent citizen protests in Ferguson, Missouri, the shift from police to soldiers has been under way for the past fifty years, since the Nixon administration, the development of SWAT teams, and the so-called war on drugs, with courts making Fourth Amendment exceptions for drug busts. There are now estimated to be fifty thousand to eighty thousand SWAT raids with combat-equipped agents in the United States every year. Since 2009, there have been, on average, four and a half SWAT raids every day in Maryland.[12] Most used forcible entry, and half were for the purpose of serving search warrants for nonviolent crimes, most often drug offenses. Takacs writes that TV programming hailed viewers as citizen-soldiers.[13] Far more worrisome is the transformation of police into soldiers, because for a militarized police force, as Ferguson demonstrated, the community may tend to become the enemy.

The militarization of law enforcement complements the rise of a surveillance society; and the public's acquiescence to ongoing surveillance, again, likely has less to do with television content than with the near impossibility of leading a modern life without the Internet and the electronic transactions that lubricate daily living. Smartphones, tablets, personal computers, and cloud storage have acclimated a younger generation to surveillance and made it seem inescapable and even strangely desirable. Produced in the Watergate era, Francis Ford Coppola's *The Conversation* (1974) sounds an alarm about intrusive government and corporate surveillance. But the movie did not anticipate how the public would collude in the invasion of its privacy and even welcome it when accompanied by consumer desirables like an iPhone and websites like Facebook.

Takacs's concept of the citizen-soldier hailed through popular media seems to miss the implications of these developments, namely, that the real soldiers are the security forces abroad and at home, while citizens increasingly have become a potential enemy to be subdued. This is where the politics of terror, pervasive surveillance, and endless war may tend to lead, and it raises questions about whether the kinds of polite media propaganda that Takacs studies remain efficacious as modes of social influence and control. She writes that 9/11-themed television shows demonstrate Washington's deliberate approach to using entertainment programming as a vehicle of social

---

12 Radley Balko, "Shedding Light on the Use of SWAT Teams," *Washington Post*, February 17, 2014, http://www.washingtonpost.com/news/the-watch/wp/2014/02/17/shedding-light-on-the-use-of-swat-teams/.

13 Takacs, *Terrorism TV*, 101.

influence, demonstrate, that is, "the importance of the domestic terrain—the winning of US hearts and minds—to the conduct of contemporary modes of war."[14]

Contemporary trends may be overtaking this notion. TV and cinema are blunt instruments to employ if the goal is to win hearts and minds. Why would a modern state continue to feel that the hearts-and-minds route is an imperative? Why the need to persuade in this way when modern society edges closer to conditions of total surveillance? Threats to privacy carry potent coercive force and may work far better as modes of social control than the old-line models of propagandizing through the media. When an electronic dossier can be compiled of every citizen's thoughts and actions, the need to win hearts and minds may grow less urgent. Digital coercion can compel conformity more effectively than the old-school blunderbuss approach of propagandizing via the media.

This points to an alteration in the cultural currency of the media. Do movies and television programs exert great force in defining the contours of public discourse and political belief? There are reasons to remain skeptical. Politics, economics, sociological factors, and access to technology carry much weight. Media scholars have important work to do in unpacking the ideologies expressed in film and television content, and Takacs ably covers a lot of ground in this respect. But the speed of technological and political change since 9/11 has cut the ground from under our traditional models of media influence and communication. These developments invite us to rethink the contours of contemporary popular culture within a surveillance society and the challenges the latter poses to our theories and work.   ✱

14   Ibid., 31.

Contributors

Christine Becker is associate professor in the Department of Film, Television, and Theatre at the University of Notre Dame, specializing in film and television history and critical analysis. Her book *It's the Pictures That Got Small: Hollywood Film Stars on 1950s Television* (Wesleyan University Press, 2009) won the 2011 Michael Nelson Prize of the International Association for Media and History for a Work in Media and History. She is currently working on a research project comparing contemporary American and British television production and programming.

Tarik Ahmed Elseewi received his PhD in 2010 in the Department of Radio, Television and Film at the University of Texas at Austin. His dissertation was on television and national identity in the new transnational broadcasting environment of the Arab Middle East. Elseewi's research and teaching interests include the cultural history of broadcasting in the United States, postcolonial and globalization theory in media, and media in the Arab world. After four years as a Mellon Postdoctoral Fellow and visiting professor at Vassar College, he now teaches at Whitman College. He has published articles on the Danish cartoon controversy and the Arab uprisings in *Global Media Journal* and *International Journal of Communication*.

Derek Kompare is an associate professor in the Division of Film and Media Arts at the Meadows School of the Arts at Southern Methodist University. In addition to many articles in journals and anthologies, he is the author of *Rerun Nation: How Repeats Invented American Television* (Routledge, 2005) and *CSI* (Wiley-Blackwell, 2010), and is coeditor (with Derek Johnson and Avi Santo) of *Making Media Work: Cultures of Management in the Entertainment Industries* (New York University Press, 2014).

Allison Perlman is an assistant professor in the Department of Film and Media Studies and the Department of History at the University of California–Irvine. She is coeditor of *Flow TV: Essays on a Convergent Medium* (Routledge, 2010); other published works include articles in *Feminist Media Studies, Television and New Media, Journal of Popular Film and Television*, and *Communication, Culture, and Critique*. She currently is completing a manuscript on the history of media advocacy in the United States.

Stephen Prince is a professor of cinema at Virginia Tech and a former president of the Society for Cinema and Media Studies. He is the author of numerous books on film history and theory that include *Digital Visual Effects in Cinema: The Seduction of Reality, Firestorm: American Film in the Age of Terrorism*, and *The Warrior's Camera: The Cinema of Akira Kurosawa*. His audio commentaries can be found on the Criterion DVD/Bluray editions of the films of Akira Kurosawa and other directors.

CINEMA STUDIES

from **(ᴓ) intellect**

CINEMA STUDIES

from 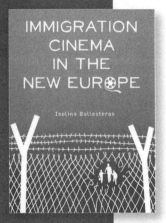 intellect

Immigration Cinema in the New Europe
Isolina Ballesteros

Examining a variety of films from the early 1990s, Ballesteros theorizes immigration cinema in relation to notions such as gender, hybridity, transculturation, border crossing, transnationalism, and translation.
Paper $40.00

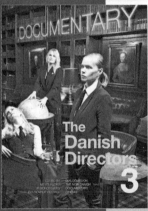

The Danish Directors 3
Dialogues on the New Danish Documentary Cinema
Edited by **Mette Hjort, Ib Bondebjerg,** and **Eva Novrup Redvall**

A comprehensive overview of new documentary cinema in Denmark, this volume of practitioner interviews focuses specifically on filmmakers born in the 1970s and their engagement with television and new digital media culture.
Paper $28.50

Australian Film Theory and Criticism
Volume 2: Interviews
Edited by **Noel King** and **Deane Williams**

This volume gathers interviews with national and international film theorists and critics to chart the development of different discourses in Australian film studies through the decades. It succeeds mightily in reasserting Australian film's place on the international scholarly agenda.
Paper $50.00

Distributed by the
UNIVERSITY OF CHICAGO PRESS
www.press.uchicago.edu

M | LSA SCREEN ARTS & CULTURES
UNIVERSITY OF MICHIGAN

UM Special Collections holds unique archival collections (i.e., scripts, correspondences, contracts, photographs) of key maverick directors, including Orson Welles, Robert Altman, and John Sayles (shown with Daryl Hannah on the set of *Silver City*).

Ph.D. PROGRAM IN SCREEN ARTS & CULTURES

Our doctoral program emphasizes the study of those forms of representation exhibited and consumed through a screen—whether a cinema screen, television screen, video monitor, computer display, or handheld device. We study the respective screen media in their social, cultural, national, transnational, and historical contexts through the methods of film studies, television studies, and digital media studies.

GRADUATE FACULTY

Giorgio Bertellini, Associate Professor, Silent Cinemas; Comparative Media Studies; Fascism; Italian Cinema and TV

Hugh Cohen, Professor, The Western; Film Criticism; Scandanavian Film

Caryl Flinn, Chair & Professor, Film Music & Musicals; Gender, Critical Theory & Cultural Studies

Colin Gunckel, Assistant Professor, American Film History; Chicano/Latino Film & Media; Latina American Cinema

Dan Herbert, Associate Professor, Media Industries; Media Geographies; Video Studies

Candace Moore, Assistant Professor, American Television; Queer Media; Production & Fan Cultures

Sheila Murphy, Associate Professor, Digital Media; Internet Studies; Video Game Studies; TV

Abé Mark Nornes, Professor, Asian Film; Documentary; Translation Theory

Yeidy Rivero, Associate Professor, International Media; Race & Ethnic Representations in Media

Matthew Solomon, Associate Professor & Director of Graduate Studies, French & US Film History and Theory; Authorship; Intermediality

Johannes von Moltke, Associate Professor, Film Theory & Critical Theory; Genre; Spectatorship; German Film History; Fascist Cinemas

Damon Young, Assistant Professor—Michigan Society of Fellows, French Film & Media; Gender & Queer Theory; Film & Media Theory; Cultural Studies

Professors Emeriti:
Richard Abel, Frank Beaver, Ira Konigsberg

Production Faculty:
Jim Burnstein, Dawn Hollison, Victor Fanucchi, Chris McNamara, Robert Rayher, Terri Sarris

Affiliated Faculty:
Susan Douglas, Amanda Lotz, Christian Sandvig, Herb Eagle, Lisa Nakamura, Aswin Punathambekar, Megan Sapnar Ankerson, Tung-Hui Hu, Geoff Eley, Daniel Herwitz

www.lsa.umich.edu/sac

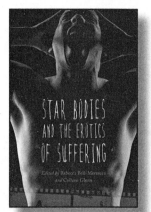
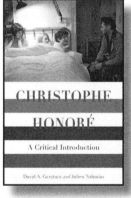

MOVING?

CINEMA JOURNAL

Please let us know in advance.
If you enclose your mailing label,
we can change your address quickly.
Place old address label here.

Please print your new address:

Name _____

Street _____

City _____ State _____ Zip _____

Country _____

Mail to: *Cinema Journal*, University of Texas Press, Journals
Division, PO Box 7819, Austin, TX 78713-7819

Forthcoming

- Diana Anselmo-Sequeira, "Gasps of Violet Ink": Excess and Agency in Popular Representations of Movie-Fan Girlhood Produced by American Film Fan Magazines during the 1910s

- Yomi Braester, The Spectral Return of Cinema: Globalization and Cinephilia in Contemporary Chinese Film

- Nick Jones, Variation within Stability: Digital 3-D and Film Style

- Anna Stenport and Garrett Traylor, The Eradication of Memory: Film Adaptations and Algorithms of the Digital

- Paul Young, Yours Sincerely, Lois Weber: Hypocrites and the Allegorical Mode of the Transitional Feature Film

- In Focus and Book Reviews: Gender identity and the superhero genre